PRO TOOLS® LE 7
I G N I T E !

The Visual Guide for
New Users

❆ ❆ ❆

Andrew Hagerman

THOMSON
───────✦───────™
COURSE TECHNOLOGY
Professional ■ Technical ■ Reference

ISBN: 1-59200-601-9

Library of Congress Catalog Card Number: 2005931883

Printed in the United States of America

06 07 08 09 10 PH 10 9 8 7 6 5 4 3 2 1

Publisher and General Manager, Thomson Course Technology PTR:
Stacy L. Hiquet

Associate Director of Marketing:
Sarah O'Donnell

Manager of Editorial Services:
Heather Talbot

Marketing Manager:
Mark Hughes

Senior Acquisitions Editor:
Todd Jensen

Marketing Coordinator:
Jordan Casey

Project Editor and Copyeditor:
Kim V. Benbow

Technical Reviewer:
Brent Heber

PTR Editorial Services Coordinator:
Elizabeth Furbish

Interior Layout Tech:
Shawn Morningstar

Cover Designers:
Mike Tanamachi
Nancy Goulet

Indexer:
Katherine Stimson

Proofreader:
Sean Medlock

THOMSON

COURSE TECHNOLOGY

Professional ■ Technical ■ Reference

Thomson Course Technology PTR, a division of Thomson Course Technology
25 Thomson Place ■ Boston, MA 02210 ■ www.courseptr.com

As always, For Junko Yoshida Hagerman

Junko-san my dove

Late-night spring rolls help me write

But your love saved me

Watashi wa anata o aishite imasu!

Acknowledgments

The creation of any book is a demanding task, and it is impossible to accomplish without the cooperation (and coordination) of people dedicated to excellence in their craft. The team at Course Technology is just such a community and has been truly outstanding. From Todd Jensen, who initiated this project and invited me to participate to Mark Garvey and Kim Benbow, for superb editing, this complex undertaking has been a real pleasure. Also, thanks to my friend and colleague Brent Heber for great tech editing!

Thanks also go out to the great folks at Digidesign, particularly Andy Cook, Mark Altin, Eric Kuehnl, and Claudia Curcio. Thanks also to Mari Matsuo and Greg Robles for your valuable assistance in helping me get this book quickly to press. I can say from firsthand experience that the skill, dedication, and downright passion of the Digidesign team are leading reasons for its success.

About the Author

Andrew Hagerman has been a professional musician for the vast majority of his 40 years, beginning with formal musical training as a classical tuba player (yes, tuba). During his four years at Northwestern University (working toward an eventual bachelor's degree), music technology began to take off in the form of MIDI, and Hagerman was immediately hooked. As the technology has advanced over the years, he does what he can to stay current and has been constantly amazed at the creative doorways that have been opened for all.

In addition to being a performing musician around the world (including at Disneyland, Walt Disney World, and Tokyo Disney Sea), Hagerman has channeled his study of music technology toward compositional pursuits. Especially active in the planetarium field, he has written original music for clients ranging from the American Museum of Natural History in New York to Caterpillar Tractors. He's also had the privilege of teaching others the art of digital audio in a number of ways, including lecturing at Full Sail, a media college in central Florida.

These days, Hagerman is busy working and playing in Tokyo, Japan. He works with musicians and educators throughout the growing Asia Pacific region, is an active composer with Singularity Arts, Inc. (www.singularityarts.com), and continues to create music for a variety of applications.

Contents

Contents ⸘

Contents 𝄐

❀ ❀ ❀

Contents }

Contents }

Introduction

First off, congratulations on becoming a Pro Tools user, and welcome! I guess that such sentiments are on page one of virtually every user's guide and manual, but when Digidesign says that their powerful digital audio workstation (DAW) is the industry standard (for good reason), you can believe it. Indeed, you'll find the full Pro Tools product line, from the Mbox all the way up to high-end HD systems, hard at work in every facet of audio and musical production. It's a serious, professional product, and your decision to buy it (and learn it) is a step in the right direction.

Speaking of steps, remember the old saying, "A journey of a thousand miles begins with a single step"? That's where this book comes in. Gaining a solid fundamental understanding of the basics will ensure that your journey starts off well prepared and heads in the right direction. In this book, you'll learn the basic techniques of creating, recording, editing, and mixing MIDI (*Musical Instrument Digital Interface*) and digital audio. You'll learn to harness the power of Pro Tools' impressive array of tools, from software effects to virtual instruments to mixes that are automated and edited with some of the best tools in the business.

This is my second book about Pro Tools LE, the first being about version 6 of the software. Even though the software was certainly a world leader then, version 7 has a real increase in features, especially for the musically creative. This DAW now encompasses MIDI and other musically powerful features, and the implications for creative individuals and smaller facilities are exciting, indeed. For those of you who are already familiar with version 6, you'll find the new tools of Pro Tools LE 7 described here.

If you're inspired to create and produce audio, Pro Tools is an obvious choice, and *Pro Tools LE 7 Ignite!* will be your companion during those critical first steps down the road to success and fun!

Who Should Read This Book?

This book is geared toward beginners with little or no experience in working with a DAW. You'll find that the book's highly graphic and plainly worded style makes it easy to follow. It will be a valuable reference later on as well. Nearly every step in the processes discussed is accompanied by clear illustrations, so you won't have to spend your time hunting around the screen for tools and menus. (What fun is *that*?)

Don't worry if you're not a formally trained musician or if you haven't really dealt with digital audio before. The beauty of Pro Tools (and computer music in general) is that even untrained (but creative) musicians can enjoy great success in this kind of environment. In fact, many of the new features in Pro Tools 7 make it even easier to be creative than with previous versions! Of course, any general music or audio knowledge you bring to the table is an added advantage, but certainly not a requirement for this book.

Pro Tools is a deep program, and even those of us who have been using it for years are still finding new tidbits now and then. For that reason, I can't dedicate the limited space I have in this book to covering basic computer operations. That means it's up to you to understand the most basic ins and outs of your particular platform (either a Mac running OS X or a PC running Windows XP). Don't worry too much, though—the general computer knowledge required to use Pro Tools is pretty basic; if you can locate, launch, and close programs already, you're in fine shape.

How to Use This Book

Music in general is a progressive process, and from creation to performance it's the result of many small steps taken in order. A solid mastery of Pro Tools works much the same way. The book is laid out to mirror the creative process, from setup through the recording process, editing, mixing, and the final touches. Additionally, the first sections of the book will also include a bit of information about the nature of DAWs in general so that you understand the logic of these devices and can work most efficiently. If you're just beginning with DAWs, you'll find this information valuable in the long run.

Since the book is arranged sequentially according to the production process, you'll be able to follow the book from the very start of a project through its completion.

If you're interested in some areas more than others, though (which is pretty common with more experienced users), feel free to read the chapters out of order—this book will work that way as well.

You'll find that most of this book is laid out in a tutorial-style format; there are even tutorial files you can download and use side by side with the book's examples. (Go to www.courseptr.com/downloads and click on the *Pro Tools LE 7 Ignite!* Web page.) Of course, you can also use this book as a point of reference using the clear, illustrated style of this format to your advantage as you locate specific functions.

Last but not least, you'll note that peppered throughout this book are a number of Notes and Tips. Take a look at these to find additional ways to increase your efficiency, additional information on key functions, and even warnings that point out common pitfalls and how to avoid them.

Finally, a Little History...

Pro Tools systems can be broken down into two families: HD and LE. HD systems have a hardware-based architecture, which means that there are dedicated PCI cards with chips dedicated to the tasks of running Pro Tools functions. This means two things: First, it is a reliable, scalable, powerful system—an obvious advantage for professional facilities. Second, it costs more (and it can be a *lot* more).

LE systems aren't hardware-based, they're host-based, which simply means that the host computer (meaning the computer that you're using to run the software) is charged with all the tasks of running Pro Tools, from recording and playback to effects and automation. This allows an LE system to be a good deal more economical than its HD counterpart. Of course, because your computer's CPU is doing *everything*, you won't get the same kind of power from an LE system, and there are a few features reserved for HD systems only.

The good news—and it's great news, really—is that the software environments in TDM and LE are nearly identical. This means you can take advantage of one of the most powerful and well-developed user interfaces on the market. What's more, if and when it becomes time for you to upgrade to HD, you'll already know the software.

Pro Tools has recently released its version 7 series (for PC and Mac), which incorporates some real advancements, especially for LE users. Among them are

* A cleaner user interface, and a well-designed reorganization of menus and tools.
* Additional editing power, including region looping and region groups.
* New MIDI features, such as dedicated instrument tracks, previewing options, and new MIDI editing tools.
* Free plug-ins, like Dynamics III and EQ III Band-Pass Filter.

Add this to powerful tools, like tempo controls and Beat Detective, that had been added to later versions of Pro Tools LE 6 (after my previous book went to press), and you'll see that there's much to learn and explore.

If a lot of this sounds like Greek right now, don't worry—we'll cover it in the chapters to come. Ready? Let's go!

1 Welcome to Pro Tools LE 7

Congratulations, and welcome to the world of Pro Tools! Through the over 20 years of Digidesign's history, Pro Tools has established itself at the forefront of the DAW (*Digital Audio Workstation*) community, and version 7 promises to provide a new level of power to the creative community. As a result, Pro Tools 7 will be found in virtually every level of the audio industry, from music production for CDs to surround sound for theatrical soundtracks. Now, armed with Pro Tools LE's powerful array of functions and features, you'll be able to tap into this world of digital audio for yourself to realize your own creative vision. Welcome to the party!

The first step in the process is to set up your system and master the basic functioning of Pro Tools. In this chapter, we'll discuss the structure, function, and most basic operations of Pro Tools LE 7, and you'll learn how to:

 ❋ Identify and assemble the hardware and software components of a Pro Tools LE system and understand their functions
 ❋ Organize sessions and data in Pro Tools
 ❋ Use Pro Tools' most basic functions
 ❋ Create, open, play, and close a session

What Makes Up a Pro Tools System?

Digidesign's Pro Tools systems fall into one of two families—LE or HD. Pro Tools LE, which we'll discuss in this book, is a *host-based* type of DAW, which means that the overall system completely relies upon the processing power of your computer's CPU (the *host*) for operations such as mixing and effects processing. HD systems, on the other hand, have dedicated PCI hardware cards added to the computer, which take care of those kinds of functions.

HD systems, because of their added processing horsepower and greater flexibility, tend to be more commonly found in professional recording studios, whereas LE systems have found their niche in the growing number of home and project studios worldwide. It bears mentioning that both types of systems are certainly pro-level in their own right, and the broad compatibility of Pro Tools allows projects to be begun in LE-based home studios, and then completed in more powerful HD-powered studios with ease!

Let's talk about your new Pro Tools LE system. LE systems, regardless of their specific configurations, all rely on a few key components.

The Heart of Your DAW—the Computer

The host computer is the cornerstone of your Pro Tools LE system. Your computer, particularly your computer's CPU (Central Processing Unit), will be called upon to do everything from mixing and automation to effects processing, so the more speed your CPU has, the more powerful your Pro Tools software will be. The host computer can be either a PC (running Windows XP) or a Mac (with OS X).

In addition to CPU speed, your computer's RAM (Random Access Memory) plays a role in how your digital audio workstation will perform. It probably comes as no surprise to hear that the more RAM your computer has, the better. Your RAM will allow your Pro Tools session to run more real-time effects, and make for an overall more powerful DAW.

Ideally, your DAW computer should be dedicated solely to music-related tasks. Other applications running on your system can steal from your computer's overall efficiency when running Pro Tools. The task of recording and playing digital audio can be very demanding on your computer's CPU, and other programs, interrupting the steady stream of data to and from your hard drive, can cause major problems. Of course, having such a dedicated computer can be impractical for many users; in that case, you should avoid resource-sapping applications (particularly games) and limit the number of programs active during your Pro Tools sessions.

Pro Tools Audio Interface

Your Pro Tools audio interface (which you purchased with your system) is the doorway for audio going to and coming from your computer. Generally speaking, your computer will connect directly to the audio interface, and your various audio devices (mixing boards, keyboards, and microphones) will connect to the interface's available audio inputs. To listen to your session, you should connect the audio outputs of your interface to an amplifier, and from there to monitor speakers. Following is a brief rundown of the audio interfaces available for Pro Tools LE systems and their key features.

Mbox 2

The Mbox 2 is a nifty little interface that delivers much for its modest price. Though it doesn't have the number of inputs and outputs of other Pro Tools interfaces, its portability is a very attractive feature for a lot of users. The core features of the Mbox 2 interface include the following:

* USB connection to the host computer, which powers the unit in addition to transferring audio information.
* Two analog inputs/outputs (Mic, Line, or DI instrument level), plus one stereo S/PDIF input/output, all of which can be used simultaneously
* Two microphone preamps with switchable phantom power for condenser mics
* Headphone outputs
* Supports up to 24-bit/48-kHz digital audio
* MIDI In and Out ports

NOTE

The Mbox 2, as you might guess from the name, is the next generation of the original Mbox (which has been an immensely popular LE interface). Do you have one of those original Mboxes? Not to worry—they will work just fine with Pro Tools LE 7!

Digi 002

The flagship of the LE hardware line is the Digi 002, which features not only expanded I/O, but a very cool mixer-style control surface. The core features of the Digi 002 interface include the following:

* IEEE 1394 (FireWire) connection to the host computer
* Eight analog inputs/outputs, one stereo S/PDIF digital input/output, and eight channels of ADAT optical input/output
* Built-in control surface, including eight touch-sensitive motorized faders
* MIDI I/O
* Four microphone preamps
* Headphone outputs
* Supports up to 24-bit/96-kHz digital audio

Digi 002R

The Digi 002 is available in two versions. In addition to the full-blown 002 shown earlier, there's the rackmount version, called the Digi 002 Rack, which is a two-rack space module sporting the same I/O complement as the 002, but without the control surface component.

TIP

If you want to learn more about the specifications of any Pro Tools hardware, the Digidesign Web site (www.digidesign.com) is a great place to start. From the Digidesign home page, click on the Products link (located in the upper-left corner) to view a list of the current Pro Tools products.

Hard Drive(s)

Just as traditional tape-based recording studios rely on magnetic tape as a recording and storage medium, Pro Tools relies on hard drives for the recording and playback of its digital audio. The drives can use SCSI, IDE/ATA, Serial ATA, or even FireWire connections.

It is important to remember two factors when choosing a hard drive for Pro Tools—size and speed. First, a larger-capacity drive will allow you to store more audio data. This can translate into more minutes of audio that you can store, higher-quality digital audio, or both. A fast drive will allow for more efficient transfer of data (also called *throughput*) when you are recording and/or playing back audio. A faster drive can also translate into higher track counts and more reliability when working with complex sessions.

Using a Second Hard Drive

Adding a second drive dedicated to the storage of your Pro Tools sessions will increase your Pro Tools system's performance greatly. You'll still install the Pro Tools application on your computer's system drive, but when you create your sessions, put them on your "audio" drive. That way, you'll have one hard drive occupied with the nominal tasks of your computer and another separate drive (with its own read/write head) dealing only with your Pro Tools session and audio.

 NOTE

Partitioning a single hard drive may give the outward appearance of creating a second drive, but in reality there is still only one hardware device. Although partitioning can be a convenient way of organizing your data, it doesn't add another physical drive with its own read/write head, so it won't help Pro Tools with the real-time tasks of recording and playing back digital audio.

A Great Resource:
Digidesign's Compatibility Documents

You might have noticed that though I've talked about desirable qualities of a powerful DAW system, I haven't mentioned many specific details about what kind of hardware you should be using (things like minimum CPU speed and RAM requirements, for example). Sorry for being so evasive, but the truth of the matter is that the ever-changing landscape of computer-based products changes and grows so rapidly that any specs that I quote here might well change over time. Don't despair though—Digidesign has provided the help you need in constructing a system that's completely up to date!

Digidesign keeps an up-to-date list of compatible hardware on its Web site. At www.digidesign.com/compato, you can find a list of Pro Tools systems along with their supported operating systems. Just click on the link for the operating system that matches your computer. This page (only a small part can be shown here) is comprehensive, and is constantly being updated to reflect the latest computers and peripherals available. All in all, it's a great resource for Pro Tools users at any level, and whenever you're in doubt about what might work with your system, this page will give you your answer!

Another way to access the compatibility docs is to visit www.digidesign.com and click on the Products link in the upper-left corner. On the Products page, select your audio interface (such as Mbox), and then choose [your interface] Compatibility Mac or [your interface] Compatibility Windows for a complete list of hardware-related information.

A Word about Installation

When it comes to installing your Pro Tools software, I've got good news and bad news. First the bad news: Because installation can vary from interface to interface and system to system, the installation procedure is tough to describe in a book like this. Not only are there many different configurations possible (with different audio interfaces, computers, and so on), but Digidesign is constantly upgrading and tweaking their products. Bottom line: The details of installation are constantly subject to change.

The good news is that, again, Digidesign has got you covered. The documentation you received with your Pro Tools LE software and hardware is the first place to look for information on installation. In the ever-changing world of computers, though, perhaps even that documentation could be slightly out of date. Once again, the Digidesign Web site is an invaluable resource for the latest software version updates and information on installation and troubleshooting.

From Digidesign's home page (www.digidesign.com), click on Support (in the upper menu of options). On the Support page, you will notice several options. Here are a few pages of interest:

❋ Tech Support. This page is a compilation of frequently asked questions, breaking information, and software downloads. From here you can search for an answer to your questions or contact Digidesign's tech support staff.

❋ Customer Service. This is similar to the Tech Support page, although it's a little more general in nature.

❋ Answerbase. On this page, you can type in keywords to see a list of useful links.

❋ Downloads. Check this page to find the latest version of Pro Tools LE for your system, in addition to a vast collection of drivers, utilities, and even legacy versions of Pro Tools.

❋ Compatibility. Again, this is an up-to-date listing of supported hardware and software.

The documentation that came with your Pro Tools hardware, combined with a little Net surfing (if needed), should allow you to successfully install and configure your Pro Tools LE system. Once that's done, you're ready to move on.

A Word about Pro Tools M-Powered

About a year ago, Avid Technology (Digidesign's parent company) acquired a company called M-Audio, which has been a leader in the home studio market. Since welcoming M-Audio to the family, Digidesign and M-Audio have been in close cooperation. This has culminated in a brand-new version of Pro Tools—Pro Tools M-Powered—which can run on M-Audio interfaces!

The list of supported M-Audio interfaces is impressive and growing all the time. To get a completely up-to-date list, take a look at their Web site (www.m-audio.com/products/en_us/ProToolsMPowered-main.html) to see all the different kinds of devices available. For many users, the different options (for example, a combined keyboard/MIDI interface/audio interface like the Ozonic) is quite attractive. But what about the software?

The good news is that the Pro Tools M-Powered software (which is *not* included with the interface—it must be purchased separately) is almost completely identical to Digidesign's Pro Tools LE. There are a few differences that do exist, however, that bear mentioning:

* Digidesign's high-end Ethernet control surfaces won't work with Pro Tools M-Powered.

* Avid video hardware doesn't work with Pro Tools M-Powered.

* Pro Tools M-Powered does not support DV Toolkit (a Digidesign bundle product for producing audio in sync with video material).

* Pro Tools M-Powered doesn't support DigiTranslator (which provides file interchange between ProTools and other media production applications like Avid systems, Logic Audio, and others).

As you can see, these differences between Pro Tools LE and Pro Tools M-Powered are really not great hardships for the beginning Pro Tools user. In fact, if you've got Pro Tools M-Powered, you'll be able to use the vast majority of this book as a production resource, with little concern about these small differences.

Understanding Sessions and Files

Now you've got your system set up, and Pro Tools is installed. Before you get any deeper into the world of Pro Tools, you should take a moment to understand the general principles behind this powerful digital audio workstation. An understanding of Pro Tools' functioning and how its different elements work together will serve you well as you continue to grow in this environment.

Pro Tools Is a Pointer-Based Application

It's common to refer to a cursor as a *pointer*, but when you're discussing a pointer-based application like Pro Tools, you're referring to the way the program deals with digital audio data. In Pro Tools' case, this pointer-based structure can be broken down to three interdependent elements—session files, folders, and audio files. In this situation the term "pointer" refers to the way your Pro Tools session file will access (or "point") to other files on your hard drive as your session plays.

A session folder is created when you create a new session; it contains the following items (as needed):

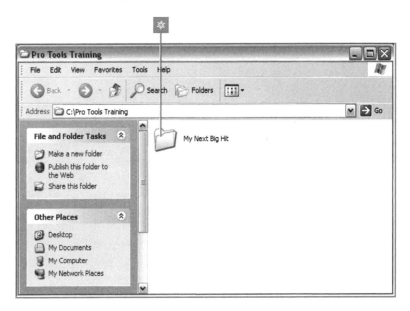

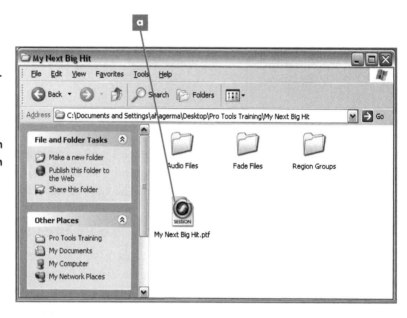

a Session file. The session file is at the top of the Pro Tools hierarchy. This is the file created by Pro Tools when you create a new session, and it's the file you open to return to a session you already created. Although this file is relatively small, it is the master of all your session elements. Session files have the .ptf suffix and contain the following elements of your session:

- The names, types, and arrangement of all tracks in your session
- All MIDI data
- Essential settings such as inputs and outputs
- All edits and automation data

❋ **NOTE**

It might sound like all you need is a session file, but that's not quite true. Although the session file contains all the important aspects of a project listed above, it doesn't in itself contain any audio. Instead, the session file refers (or points) to audio files located elsewhere on your hard drive.

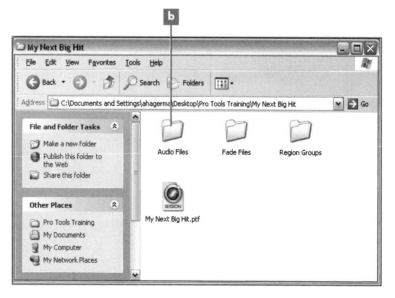

b Audio Files subfolder. As soon as audio is recorded, it is stored in an Audio Files subfolder in the session folder. Different takes are stored in this folder as individual audio files. When you play a session, Pro Tools calls upon, or points to, the audio files in this folder.

✺ **NOTE**

When you record audio in Pro Tools, the name of the file created follows the name of the track that it is recorded on. For example, if you record onto a mono (one-channel) audio track named Bass, the files created by Pro Tools in the Audio Files folder will be named Bass.01, Bass.02, and so on as you record takes on this track. In the case of stereo audio tracks, two mono files (one for the left side and one for the right) are created. If you record onto a stereo audio track named Stereo Piano, two files named Stereo Piano_01.l and Stereo Piano_01.r will be created.

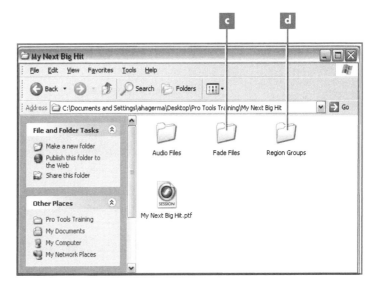

c Fade Files subfolder. When you start creating fades (including fade-ins, fade-outs, and crossfades), Pro Tools renders the created fades to files on your hard drive. Audio files are again created, but they're not stored in the Audio Files folder. Instead, they're stored in a folder named Fade Files. It's important to keep in mind that even though fades are audio files, they are significantly different in function from the audio files you record or import into your session (in ways that you'll learn about later). Thus they are stored separately.

d Region Groups. This is brand new in version 7. As the name suggests, Pro Tools now allows you to select multiple regions and link them together in a single region group. Digital audio and MIDI can be grouped together, and this new feature promises to really make editing much faster and easier. You'll learn more about region groups later, but for now just know that groups that you create are stored in this folder.

✺ ✺ ✺

If you start using video files and/or creating custom plug-in settings, Pro Tools will create additional subfolders as needed:

✻ Plug-In Settings subfolder. In Pro Tools you have the option of using plug-ins, which are programs designed to work within the Pro Tools environment and function as virtual effects. (You'll learn more about plug-ins in Chapter 8, " Mixing.") When you create specific plug-in presets, you can save them in this session subfolder.

✻ Video Files subfolder. When your session calls for a video track, you can save it in this session subfolder.

Don't worry about that too much yet—you'll be dealing with those situations later in this book.

Regions versus Files

Given the fact that Pro Tools records audio to individual files on your hard drive, how does the user access these files? When audio is recorded to an audio track (or even MIDI data to a MIDI track), Pro Tools creates an object or region in the Edit window. These regions refer (or *point*) to files on your hard drive, triggering them to sound as your session plays.

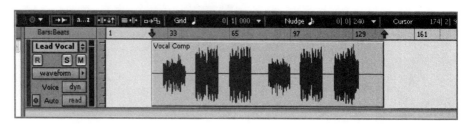

Here's a close-up of Pro Tools' Edit window. There's one audio track in this session, and only one region on that track. That region is referring to a file named Vocal Comp.

Working with regions has many advantages. One of the first that you'll discover is that you have the ability to move them earlier or later on the session's timeline, allowing you to precisely position the regions in time. An environment in which you have the ability to manipulate elements independently on the timeline is commonly known as *non-linear*. In addition to moving regions to different locations in time, you have the option of moving them to other similar tracks. (In other words, you can move a region on a mono audio track to another mono audio track, and so on.)

Non-Destructive Editing

Another great advantage of using regions is that you can non-destructively trim the audio that's being used in your session (meaning that no audio *data* is being lost, so you can always undo what you've done).

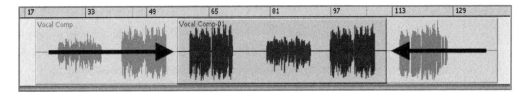

In this example, assume that the region named Vocal Comp is playing an audio file of the same name in the Audio Files subfolder. What if you don't want to use the whole song in your session? No problem—you can just adjust the start or end boundary of that region, effectively taking the unwanted bit of audio out of your session.

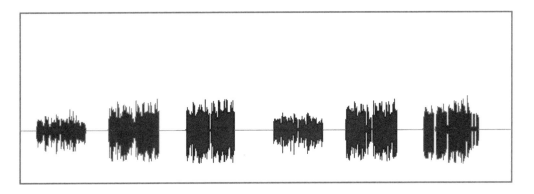

Does this mean that you've changed the file on your hard drive? No! You've changed only the region that is pointing to that file, so only a portion of that file will be heard in the session. Don't worry; because you haven't changed the audio file (only the region that is pointing to it), you can always drag the region boundaries back out if you change your mind later!

In addition to being able to trim data, there are other situations in which non-destructive editing can aid you in your production work, and you'll discover them as this book proceeds. The bottom line is that a non-linear pointer-based environment coupled with non-destructive recording and editing gives an educated Pro Tools user a huge amount of flexibility and power and the ability to undo changes and operations when needed.

Basic Pro Tools Operation

The end of the beginning: You've set up your system efficiently, taken some time to understand the way Pro Tools works, and now, based on that understanding, you're ready to start working. The last step before you dive deeper into Pro Tools is to open a pre-existing session:

> ❄ **NOTE**
>
> At this stage, you might not have a pre-existing Pro Tools session to work with, but that's not a problem. Go to the *Pro Tools LE 7 Ignite!* page at www.courseptr.com/downloads and download the file named Chapter 1 Session to your hard drive. This session already has some audio tracks with regions, so you'll have to download the session file and the Audio Files sub-folder.
>
> When you open your session, you may see a few message windows, including a Missing Files dialog box. It's not a big problem, but it is something you'll have to fix before moving on. Please take a look at the "Interoperability: Making Shared Sessions Work" section in Chapter 10, or refer to the "Setting up Your Downloaded Session" document on the download materials Web site.

Opening a Session When Pro Tools Is Running

Suppose you've already launched the Pro Tools application. Here's how to open a session:

1 Click on File. The File menu will appear.

2 Click on Open Session. The Open dialog box will open.

❋ **TIP**

As I mentioned earlier, Pro Tools includes shortcut keys that enable you to work more efficiently. The shortcuts for New Session and Open Session (Ctrl+N and Ctrl+O, respectively, in Windows, and ⌘+N and ⌘+O, respectively, on a Mac) are very useful—and easy to remember as well!

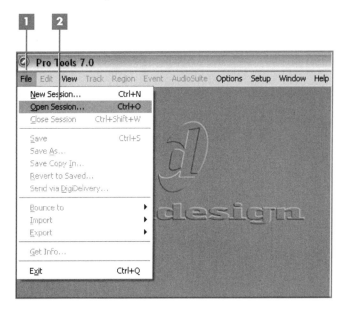

3 Navigate to the desired drive (the one that holds your session).

4 Select the drive that contains the audio session. The drive will be selected and the folders on that drive will appear.

5 Click on the folder that contains the session folder. The folder will be selected, and the scroll bar will automatically move to display the contents of that folder.

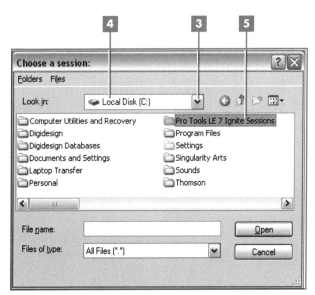

6 Click on the subfolder that contains the session file. The contents of the subfolder will be displayed.

7 Click on the desired session file. The file will be selected.

8 Click on Open. The session will be loaded into Pro Tools.

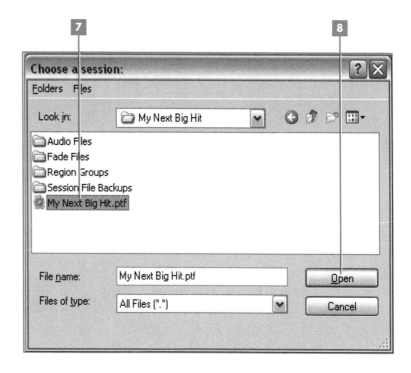

Opening a Session When Pro Tools Is Not Yet Launched

In this case, suppose Pro Tools is not yet launched. To open a session, follow these steps:

1 Select the hard drive that contains your session. On a PC, this will involve using My Computer or Windows Explorer. On a Mac, you can use the Finder or simply click on the hard drive icon on your desktop.

2 Open any folders that contain your session folder. The contents of the folder will be displayed.

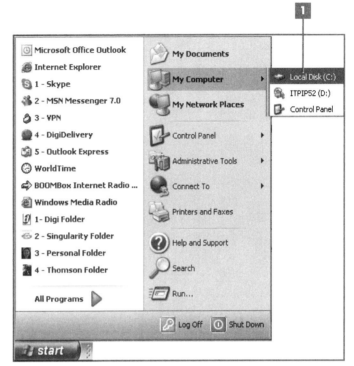

3 Open the folder that contains the session file.

The contents of the folder will be displayed.

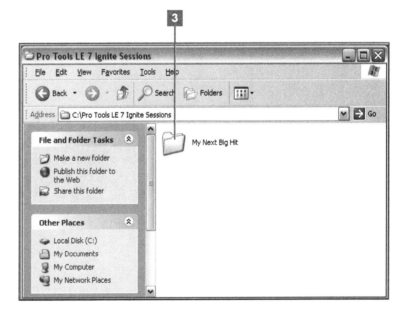

4 Double-click on the desired session file (in this case My Next Big Hit). Pro Tools will be launched automatically, and the session will be loaded.

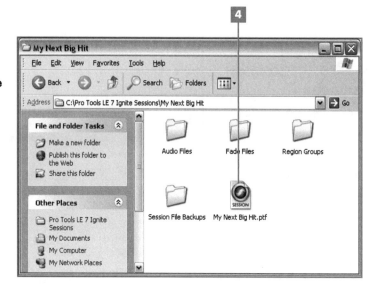

Creating a New Session

Now that you've got your system put together and everything's installed, you can create a new session. The earlier discussion of how Pro Tools works will come in handy here. In addition to the previous concepts, you'll have to start thinking about how you can best set up your new session and maximize your computer's resources.

Starting the Process

After you've launched Pro Tools, you'll see the program's basic array of drop-down menus. Here's where the important process of creating a session begins!

1 Click on File. The File menu will appear, containing a list of Pro Tools' basic functions. Because there is no session open at this time, only the New Session and Open Session options will be available; the rest will be grayed out.

2 Click on New Session. The new session window will appear.

❄ **TIP**

As you explore Pro Tools further, you'll notice that there are many functions that have shortcut keys associated with them. These shortcut key combinations are displayed to the right of the commands. Although there are far too many shortcuts to learn all at once, learning the combinations for popular functions, such as opening or creating a session, can help you work more efficiently.

For a complete list of Pro Tools shortcuts for PC or Mac, see Appendix B, "Keyboard Shortcuts."

Choosing the Name and Place

Two of the most important skills you can learn as a DAW user are file management and documentation. Though this is a fairly simple and straightforward task, you shouldn't underestimate its importance. The last thing you want is to misplace a session and waste valuable time trying to find it—or worse, inadvertently delete a session because it was in the wrong place!

Knowing where your sessions reside and what kinds of resources they use is critical, especially when you start working on multiple projects at once!

1 The first thing you have to choose is the name of your session. Type the name in the File Name text box.

❋ **NOTE**

According to this screen, this new session will be created in the My Documents folder. This means that the session will be created on your system hard drive. As I mentioned earlier, this is not the best place to keep your session. Choose a location on your audio hard drive instead.

2 Click on the arrow button to reveal the Navigation window.

3 According to your operating system, navigate to the desired drive. (If you've got a hard drive devoted to digital audio, go to that drive).

4 Next, you might want to create a new folder for your session. Create a new folder according to the normal conventions of your operating system.

5 Type a name for your new folder, and then enter that folder according to the conventions of your operating system. Your screen should look something like this.

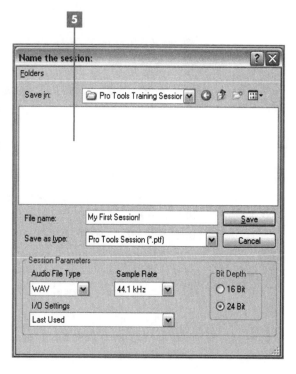

❋ ❋ ❋

Choosing Session Parameters

You've named your new session and assigned it to a specific location on a hard drive. Now that you've done this, your next task will be to choose your session parameters, which will determine other important aspects of your session.

1 Click on the Audio File Type arrow button. A drop-down menu will appear. Choose a file type from the following options:

a WAV. A WAV file is a Windows standard file. This is a good format choice for session files that will be used in Windows XP systems.

b AIFF. This is the standard audio file format for Macs.

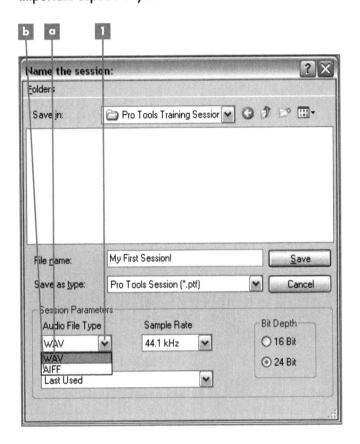

❋ **TIP**
Pro Tools' default file format is BWF (.WAV) or Broadcast Wave, and this generally works for most applications. If you are planning to share files between Mac and Windows systems, this is the preferred file format.

2 Click on the Sample Rate arrow button. A list will appear, determined by the sample rates supported by your audio interface.

3 Select a sample rate for your session.

4 Select either 16 bit or 24 bit audio as the bit depth for your session. The bit depth will be selected.

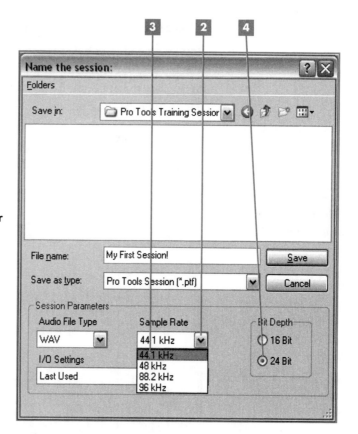

NOTE

Once selected, the sample rate and bit depth will become the overall sample rate and bit depth for all audio in this session. This means that any audio you import into the session (a process I'll go through in Chapter 3, "Getting Started with Audio") will either have to match these specs or be converted to match the session.

5 Click on the I/O Settings arrow button. The I/O Settings drop-down menu will appear.

6 Select your I/O (Input/Output) settings for this session. For now, choose Stereo Mix. The option will be selected.

7 You've made all the choices you need to make to create a new session! Click on Save. Pro Tools will begin to build your session.

❋ **NOTE**

Your I/O settings determine the assignments and names of inputs, outputs, inserts, and buses. Don't worry if this doesn't make a lot of sense now—you'll learn more about how to make the most of your I/O settings later.

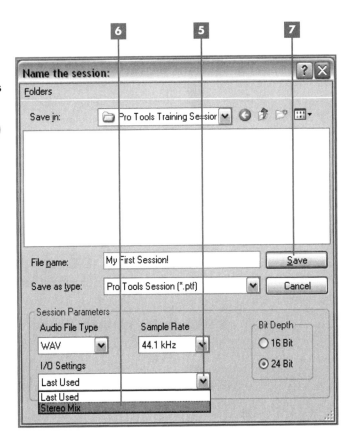

Playing a Session

Let's assume that you've got Pro Tools running, and you've opened up a pre-existing session (for example, the online session that I referred to earlier). How to play it? No problem!

A recent addition to Pro Tools is a transport section in the upper-right area of a window that Pro Tools calls the Edit window (which you'll learn more about in the next chapters). It looks very much like the same controls you would find on almost any media player—let's take a look at the basic ones:

> ❄ **NOTE**
>
> If you're not seeing any transport-style controls at the top of your Pro Tools window, that means that you've opened your session into another window (called the Mix window). Getting to the Edit window is very easy—just go to the Window drop-down menu at the top of the Pro Tools window, and choose the Edit menu item.

a   The Play button will play back your session from the current position.

b   The Stop button—you guessed it—stops playback.

c   The Return to Zero button takes you directly to the beginning of your session.

d   Rewind quickly moves your playback point earlier in your session.

e   Fast Forward quickly moves your playback point later in your session.

f   The Go to End button takes you directly to the end of your session

Finishing Up

Now that you've got the very basics down, now is the time to think about winding things up. This is a crucial stage, and it's important to do the job correctly.

Saving Your Work

There are a number of ways to save your work, each with its own specific advantages.

Save

This is a pretty standard feature, and as straightforward as they come.

1 Click on File. The File menu will appear.

2 Click on Save. Your work will be saved, and you'll remain in the saved session.

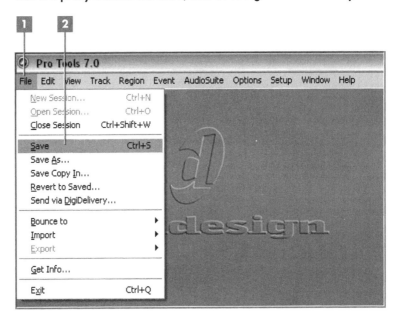

Save As

If you use the Save command, the previous version of the session will be overwritten with the new one. What if you don't want to overwrite the old session? That's where Save As comes into play.

1 Click on File. The File menu will appear.

2 Click Save As. The Save dialog box will appear.

3 Type a different name for your session in the File Name text box to avoid overwriting the original session.

❄ **NOTE**

It's important to note that both the original session file and the new version of the file can reside in the same session folder and can access the same source audio files.

4 Click on Save. The new version of the session will be saved with the name you specified in Step 3.

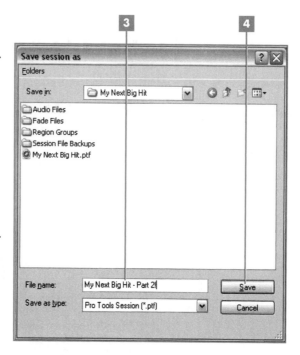

Save Copy In

If you want to save your session with a different name *and* create a new folder, complete with all the dependent audio files, the Save Copy In feature is for you! This is commonly a part of the final archiving process when a project is complete (which you'll learn more about later).

1 Click on File. The File menu will appear.

2 Click on Save Copy In. The Save dialog box will open.

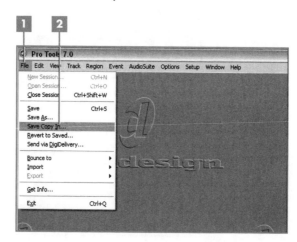

3 In the File Name text box, type a descriptive session name that is different from the original session name.

4 Select a location for your session. This section is identical to the related sections in the dialog boxes when you choose Save or Save As. This time a new folder will be created for your new session, though.

5 If you want to create your session folder *within* another folder, click on the New Folder button.

27
✳ ✳ ✳

Save Copy In also gives you the option to resave all of the elements of your session (audio files, fade files, and so on), which gives you a whole new dimension of flexibility. Here are some things to consider:

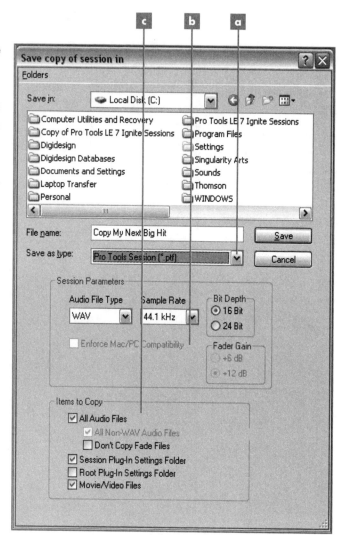

a Save As Type menu. This drop-down menu contains options for previous versions of Pro Tools. You might select one of these other formats if you intend to open this session in an older version of Pro Tools.

b Session Parameters section. These are the same options you saw when you initially created your session. You can select different file types, sample rates, and/or bit depths for your session. Pro Tools will automatically convert audio files as needed in your new session's Audio Files folder.

c Items to Copy section. You can choose the elements of your original session that you want to copy over to your new session folder. Click to select the boxes that represent aspects of your old session that you want to create in your new session folder.

TIP

Backing up (or *archiving*) your work is a tremendously important part of production. It might not be terribly exciting, but you'll be glad you established good file-saving habits if something unexpected happens!

Save Copy In is particularly suited to archiving because it makes copies of your original session in a separate (and hopefully safe) place. Additionally, this process intelligently gathers all the elements your session needs (assuming you selected them in the Items to Copy section) and saves them in one central location. Bottom line: When you're backing up your session (for example, making a CD-ROM of your work for long-term storage), Save Copy In is a very smart way to go!

Closing Your Session

The last basic procedure you have to complete is to close down your session.

1 Click on File. The File menu will appear.

2 Click on Close Session. Pro Tools will shut down the current session and make itself ready for the next step.

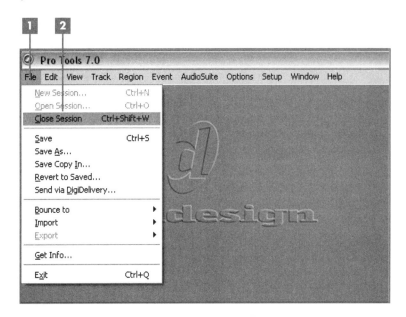

> ❊ **NOTE**
>
> Before your session closes completely, a window might prompt you to save your changes. This window appears when you make *any* changes to your session and then try to quit Pro Tools before saving those changes. You can choose Save or Don't Save and move on.

Quitting Pro Tools

The actual quitting of Pro Tools varies slightly depending upon the operating system you use:

❊ If you're using Pro Tools on a PC, closing the software is exactly the same as the process in virtually every other program you've used in Windows. Simply click on the File menu and select Exit.

❊ For Mac users, again quitting Pro Tools is just like quitting any other program. Click on the Pro Tools menu, and select Quit Pro Tools.

That's it!

2 Getting Around in Pro Tools

You've taken the time to install and set up your Pro Tools system. You've gone the extra mile and learned how Pro Tools thinks about sessions and files. You've even reached the point of creating, opening, and playing session files. Now, before you go to the next level of using Pro Tools, it's time to get better acquainted with the layout of the Pro Tools desktop.

Think of this chapter as a brief vocabulary lesson in the Pro Tools way of getting the job done. Based upon the general architecture discussed in this chapter, you'll be able to more efficiently navigate through the operations and features we'll go through later.

For some more experienced computer-based producers, you'll immediately see similarities between Pro Tools LE and other well-designed DAWs, but it will be a good use of your time to learn the proper names and layouts of these new workspaces. There are a number of windows in Pro Tools, many with specific functions, and you'll find that getting acquainted with the most common ones will really pay off later. In this chapter, you'll learn how to:

* Recognize the main sections of the Edit window and how to customize them
* Recognize the basic layout and functions of the Mix window
* Access other useful windows such as the Big Counter, System Usage windows, and Workspace Browser

Pro Tools' Primary Windows: Edit and Mix

When you open a session, it will display any number of window configurations. These configurations will reflect the windows that were displayed the last time you saved that session. Generally speaking, one of Pro Tools' two main windows, the Edit window or the Mix window, will be shown. It's important to know what each of these two windows does and how to navigate between them. There's one more window that's crucial for Pro Tools operation, called the Transport window (you used a smaller version of that window when you played a session in Chapter 1). Let's take a quick look at the general layout of these important windows.

Working with the Edit Window

If there's a primary window in Pro Tools, it's the Edit window. This workspace is packed with useful tools and information about your Pro Tools session!

The Track Area

The screens in this section should look familiar—they're from the same session that you opened and played in Chapter 1. As it happens, this is a good representation of a garden-variety Edit window. To follow along, just open the session named Chapter 1 Session.

When you begin a new session from scratch, the Track area will be an empty white field. Any kind of track you create (audio, aux, MIDI, or master fader) will appear in this area as horizontal rows. Here, for example, there are five audio tracks, four stereo and one mono (the bass track). As discussed in Chapter 1, the colored blocks are called *regions*.

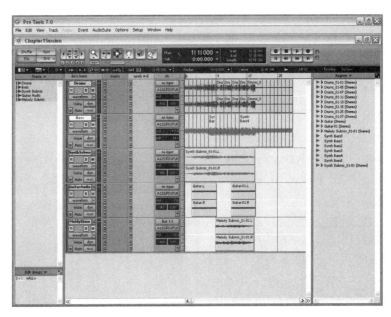

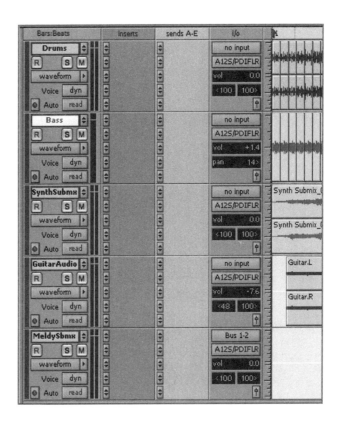

For each track there is a specific track name. When you need to select a track, you can do so by clicking on the track name button. Tracks that are selected will be highlighted (in this case, the bass track is selected). Each track strip shows a lot of information besides regions and track names; you'll get into that in Chapter 3.

The Track Show/Hide and Edit Groups Areas

Immediately to the left of the Track area, you'll notice two vertical cells—the Show/Hide Tracks area and the Edit Groups area. The Show/Hide Tracks area can be divided into two main parts.

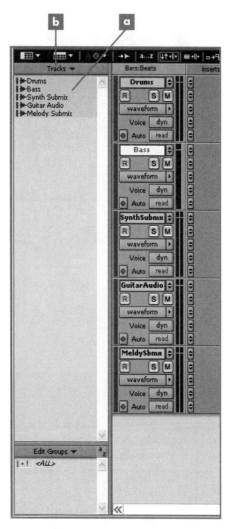

a Tracks list. All the tracks in your session, whether visible or hidden, are listed in this area. Shown tracks are high-lighted in this list.

b Tracks List button. In addition to being a heading for this list, you can click on this button to view a list of options related to displaying and hiding each of the tracks in your session.

❋ NOTE

All active and unmuted tracks, whether they are shown or hidden, will sound during playback. The ability to hide or show tracks is simply a feature to help you manage your editing and mixing desktop. (But it's a feature for which you'll be grateful when your tracks start adding up!)

An edit group is a user-definable selection of tracks that can be edited as one. As with the Tracks area, the Edit Groups area can also be divided into two main parts.

❊ Edit Groups list. As you create edit groups, they'll show up here. As with the Tracks list, active groups will be highlighted.

❊ Edit Groups button. Like the Tracks List button, you'll see a list of group-related functions when you click on the button at the top of the Edit Groups list.

❊ **NOTE**

You'll notice that there's already a group (named All) shown in this list, even though you didn't create it. The All group is created automatically when a session is created. Clicking on the word All will toggle between selecting and deselecting all the tracks in your session. (We'll cover the creation and use of additional Edit Groups in Chapter 6.)

The Regions Lists

Just to the right of the Tracks area, you'll find another vertical area. This is the storage area for regions that are or will be used in your session.

❊ **NOTE**

If you are familiar with previous versions of Pro Tools, note that this area is just a little bit different. Earlier versions of Pro Tools had a dedicated Audio Regions list and MIDI Regions list. With version 7, the two lists have merged into a more powerful and manageable single list.

a Regions list. This is a complete collection of all the regions (audio and MIDI) in your session, whether or not they're being used actively in a track. From here you can drag and drop regions onto the appropriate tracks.

b Regions List button. At the top of the Regions list, you'll find the Regions List button. In addition to serving as a heading for this area, it will display a drop-down menu of region-related functions when you click on it.

✳ **NOTE**

We'll go into MIDI and how to use it in Pro Tools in Chapter 7, "Using MIDI."

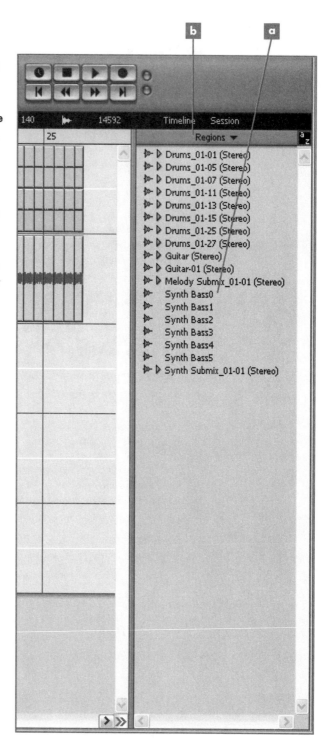

The Ruler and Tools Areas

The Ruler area allows you to view the passage of time in your session in a number of different ways. Different scales, such as minutes and seconds or bars and beats, will be useful to you depending upon the kind of work you are doing in Pro Tools. Any combination of the following ruler types can be shown:

❋ Timeline ruler types (Bars:Beats, Min:Secs, or Samples)

❋ Conductor ruler types (Tempo, Meter, or Markers)

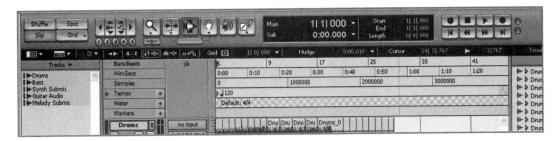

The Timeline itself can be displayed simultaneously in many time scales, with each visible ruler's type displayed to the left of the Timeline.

The Edit Tools area can be broken down into a number of functional areas:

a Edit modes

b Zoom tools

c Basic Edit tools

❋❋❋

Last but certainly not least, the location and selection displays can give you location information.

d The Main and Sub time scales will tell you exactly where you are in your session.

e The selection area will tell you the beginning, end, and duration of your selection.

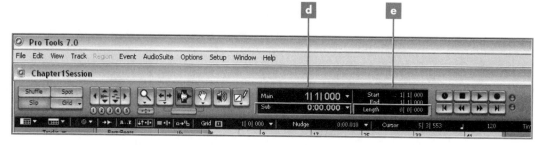

Customizing the Edit Window

Now that you've identified the overall layout of the Edit window, here are a few ways of setting up the window to make working easier in any given circumstance:

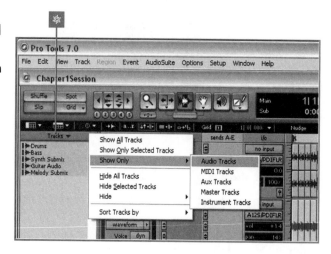

Viewing Menus

As you learned earlier, the tops of each of the four Edit window lists serve not only as identifiers, but also as buttons that will reveal drop-down menus of operations specific to that area if you click on them. For example, here's how you can show the Tracks list's drop-down menu:

❋ Click on the Tracks List button. The Track Show/Hide pop-up menu will appear. The menu will allow you to control which tracks will be shown and which will be hidden. You'll find that the menu is very easy to navigate and understand, and has a degree of flexibility as well (as shown in the Show Only submenu).

❋ Here's what you'll get when you click on the Edit Groups List button...

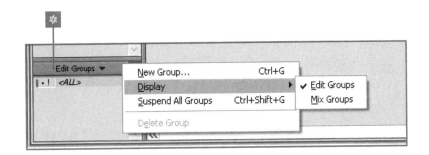

❋ And the Regions List button...

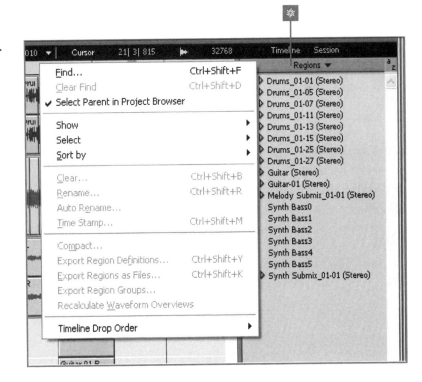

Adjusting List Size

You can customize your desktop in other ways as well. For example, if your session calls for more groups than tracks, you might want to give a little more room to the Edit Groups list on your desktop.

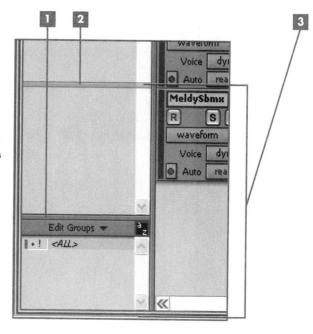

1 Move your cursor to the boundary between the Edit Groups list and the Tracks list. The cursor will change from the usual arrow into a double arrow cursor (which you've no doubt seen when resizing areas in other programs as well).

2 Click and drag the boundary up or down as needed. As you drag, you'll see a light gray line marking the movement of the boundary.

3 Release the mouse button. The boundary will be "dropped," and the lists will be reorganized.

❋ NOTE

You can adjust any of the boundaries (horizontal or vertical) for the Tracks list, Edit Groups list, and Regions list. Adjusting the vertical edges of these areas can affect how much area you have on your screen for tracks.

Hiding Lists

In addition to adjusting the sizes of these lists, you can hide them entirely when you're not using them.

1 Click on the arrows at the inner corners of either (or both) vertical sections. The columns will be hidden immediately, and more of your Edit window will be usable by your Track area.

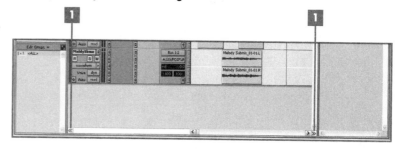

2 Not seeing your lists? Click again on the arrows in the lower corner(s) of the Edit window. The sections will reappear immediately.

❋ **NOTE**

Remember, the window arrangements that appear when you open a session are the same as they were in the session when you last saved it. It can be a bit surprising to open a session and see no region areas in your Edit window. Don't worry, though—you can always follow the aforementioned steps to display the lists.

Displaying Track Columns

There are a number of columns in the Edit window's Track area that provide track-specific information on things such as inputs, outputs, inserts, sends, and comments.

1 Click on View. The View menu will appear.

2 Click on Edit Window. A submenu of the available columns that can be shown in the Track area will appear. Checked columns are currently displayed.

3 Click on any column to check or uncheck it.

4 To quickly get to the Edit Window View menu, you can also click the Edit Window View Selector icon.

41
❋ ❋ ❋

❋ **NOTE**

The view lists are *nearly* identical, whether you use the View menu or the Edit Window View Selector icon, with the following exception: The View menu's list includes the ability to show or hide the transport controls in the upper-right area of the Edit window.

❋ **TIP**

In addition to selecting columns individually, you can select All or None to show or hide all columns, respectively.

Displaying Time Scales

You can also choose which time scales (rulers) are shown.

1. Click on View. The View menu will appear.

2. Click on Rulers. A list of the available time scales you can show in the Rulers area will appear. Checked scales are currently displayed.

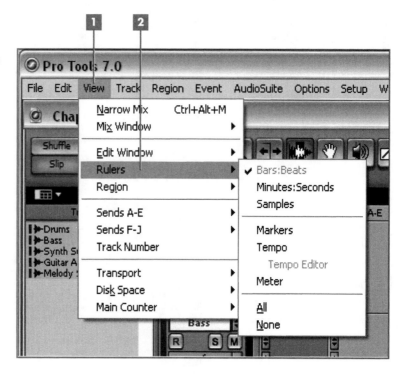

3 There's another way to get to the same list: Click here to show the Ruler View Shows submenu.

Adjusting Track Heights

In Pro Tools, you have the ability to change individually the height of each track. This can come in handy, particularly when you have many tracks in your session and you want to see them all, or when you really want to do some microsurgery on one track in particular. Here's how:

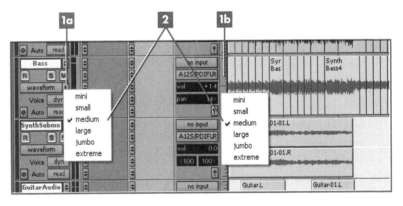

1a Click **the** Track Height Selector button **on the desired track. The Track Height drop-down menu will appear.**

OR

1b Between each track's columns (I/O, Inserts, Sends, Comments) and the region area is a small vertical area showing the amplitude scale. Click in this area. The Track Height drop-down menu will appear.

2 Select **the desired** track height. **The track will change immediately to match your height choice.**

❋ **NOTE**

You can change the height of any Pro Tools track (including MIDI and aux tracks, which you'll explore in later chapters). However, the thin vertical area for other types of tracks looks a little different than the amplitude scale of an audio track. MIDI tracks, for example, show a keyboard-like display. In any case, clicking in this area will bring up the same Track Height menu.

TIP

Here's a useful shortcut: Hold the Option key (Mac) or the Alt key (PC) while you change the height of any one track, and the heights of all shown tracks will change at once.

New: Custom Colors

This isn't exactly a new feature to version 7, as it was added to later versions of Pro Tools LE 6. Like other Edit window customizations, this won't change the *sound* of your music, but it can really help you control how it looks. Users of all levels will find this sort of control a powerful ally in organizing your tracks, regions, and more!

1a From the Window menu, choose Color Palette. The Color Palette window will appear.

OR

1b Double-click **the** colored area at the leftmost edge of the track you want to change. The Color Palette window will appear.

2 Click **the** desired color box, and the selected track(s) will immediately change color coding to match.

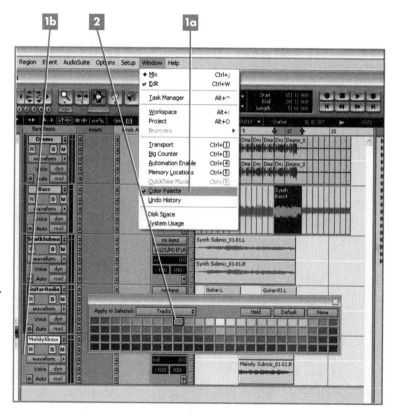

But wait, there's more!

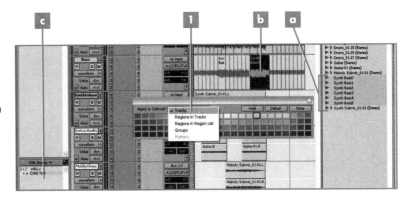

1 Click the Apply to Selected drop-down button (which will display "Tracks" when the window first appears). A menu will appear, as shown here.

a Regions in Tracks. This will change the color of regions that have been selected in the track area of the Edit window. In this case, the Synth Bass 4 region will be recolored.

b Regions in Region List. Selecting this menu item will allow you to change selected regions in the Regions List area. In this case, Synth Bass 0 through Synth Bass 5 will be recolored.

c Groups. This will allow you to recolor the color coding of selected groups. In this case, Edit Groups Color Test will be changed.

d Markers. Markers may also be color coded, which you'll learn more about in Chapter 6.

Working with the Mix Window

After the Edit window, the other primary window you'll use in Pro Tools is the Mix window. Although there's a good bit of common ground between the Mix and Edit windows, the layout and function of the Mix window is geared toward the mixing and automation phases of your production.

※ **TIP**

You'll be making the switch often between the Mix and Edit windows, so doing this as quickly as possible will be very useful. The shortcut to toggle between the Mix and Edit windows is Ctrl+= (equals key) for Windows or ⌘+= for the Mac. You'll move between these windows a lot, and this shortcut will help you do it quicker!

Understanding the Mix Window Layout

Most of the general layout of the Mix window is similar to the Edit window.

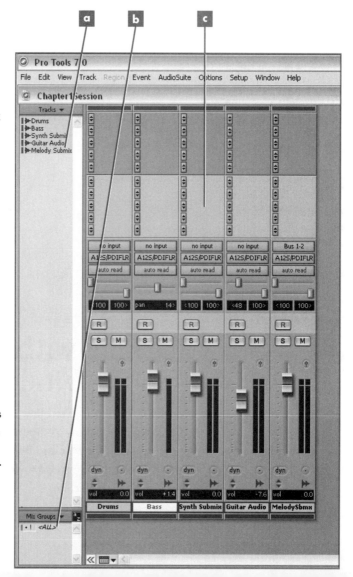

a Tracks list. This area functions similarly in both the Edit and Mix windows. In the Mix window, as you toggle each track in your session, channel strips to the right will appear and disappear.

b Mix Groups area. As you create mix groups, they will show up in this area.

c Channel Strips area. When you create any kind of track (audio, aux, master fader, MIDI, or Instrument), it will appear as a vertical strip.

※ **NOTE**

Tracks that appear at the top of the Edit window will appear on the left side of the Mix window. As tracks descend in the Edit window, they move from left to right in the Mix window's Channel Strips area.

NOTE

There is a one-to-one correspondence between the tracks that are shown (or hidden) in the Edit and Mix windows. Also remember that whether or not a track is shown does not affect that track's audibility.

Customizing the Mix Window

Tailoring your Mix window for maximum ease and efficiency will make mixing much easier. This section presents some of the most common customizations for the Mix window.

❈ **TIP**

As in the Edit window, clicking on the double arrows in the corner of the Mix Groups area will hide both the Tracks list and Mix Groups sections. This will give you more space on your desktop for channel strips.

As with the Edit window, you can control the aspects of your mixer that are displayed.

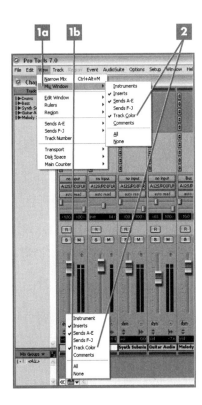

1a Click the View menu, then choose Mix Window. The Mix view submenu will appear.

OR

1b Click the Mix Window View Selector icon. The Mix view menu will appear.

2 Click on any element (Comments, Inserts, Sends, Track Color, or Instruments) to check or uncheck it.

❈ **TIP**

In addition to selecting columns individually, you can select All or None to select all the columns or none of them, respectively.

❄ **NOTE**

Sends and inserts are particularly useful in the mixing process, and the ability to show and hide them will be helpful as you tweak your mix. You'll learn more about mixing techniques in Chapter 8.

Suppose you have a lot of tracks in your session, and you'd like to see as many of them as possible in the Mix window. Here's how to squeeze more tracks onto your limited desktop.

1 Click on View. The View menu will appear.

2 Select Narrow Mix. Technically, the Mix window itself won't narrow, but the individual channel strips will, allowing you to fit more tracks within a given space.

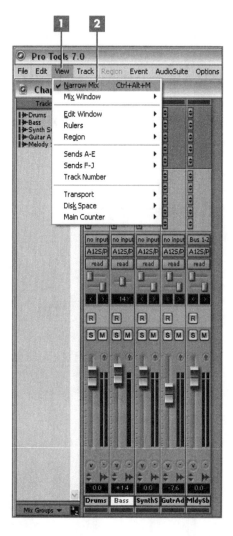

Last but not least, you might be wondering if you can use track color coding in the Mix window as well as the Edit window. Absolutely you can, and you'll find that the colored areas (shown at the top and bottom of every track) will aid you greatly in organizing more complex mixes.

a Double-click on either of the color code areas of a given track to open the Color Palette window. From there, you can change the color coding of selected tracks just as you do in the Edit window.

b You can also use the Window drop-down menu to access the Color Palette window (again, just as we discussed earlier with the Edit window).

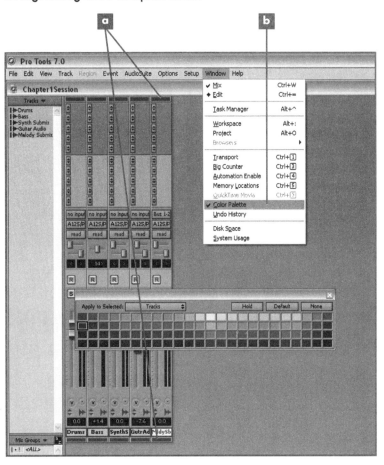

❊ **NOTE**

Since the Mix window doesn't deal with specific regions, you will probably want to limit your color coding to tracks and groups in this window. Color changes made in this window will be applied to the Edit window as well.

The Transport Window

Yet another window, the Transport window, will be useful in playing your session.

1 Click on Window. The Window menu will appear.

2 Click on Transport. The Transport window will appear. Like the Edit and Mix windows, the Transport window has a number of functions, but for now we'll focus on just the basic Transport controls:

a Go to Beginning

b Rewind

c Stop

d Play

e Fast Forward

f Go to End

g Record

h Main Time Scale

i Sub Time Scale

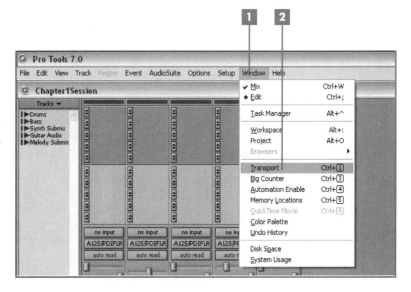

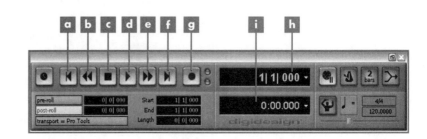

3 Click on the Go to Beginning button to make sure you're at the beginning of your session.

4 Click on the Play button. Your audio will begin playing, as shown in this illustration. You'll notice that a long vertical line travels from left to right in the track area of the Edit window. This is called the timeline insertion, and you'll notice that as it intersects with different regions, different audio will sound.

5 Click on the Stop button when you're finished. The playback will stop.

Customizing the Transport Window

It bears discussing the Transport window and how to customize it as well. This window is especially useful when working in the Mix window, as this window has no built-in transport controls.

1 Click on View. The View menu will appear.

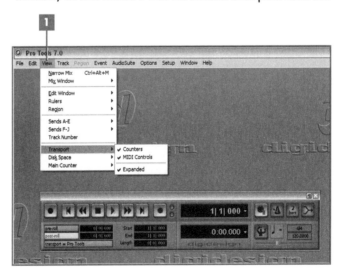

2 Click on Transport. The Transport View submenu will appear with the following options:

❋ Counters. This option will add the main counter to the Transport window.

❋ MIDI Controls. This option adds basic MIDI controls to the Transport window (which will be discussed in detail in Chapter 7).

❋ Expanded. This option will add additional transport controls to the bottom half of the Transport window. In addition to functions like pre-roll and post-roll, this option adds the sub-location indicator below the main one and adds secondary MIDI controls below the primary ones.

❋ Clicking on this icon will also show (or hide) the expanded features of the Transport window.

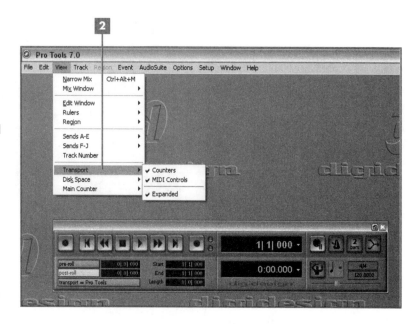

Other Useful Windows

Even though you'll spend the majority of your Pro Tools life working in the Edit and Mix windows, there are a number of other windows that serve specific purposes. These windows usually operate in conjunction with either the Edit or Mix window (whichever one you're using). You can access these secondary windows through the Windows menu, like so:

1 Click on Window. The Window menu will appear, displaying an assortment of choices.

2 Click on the window you want to display. The following list details some of the available windows.

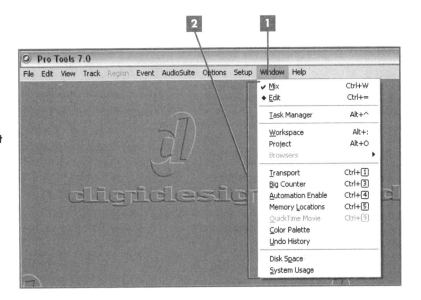

❅ **NOTE**

You've already worked with the Transport window. (Remember, the shortcut is Ctrl+1 on the PC and ⌘+1 on the Mac.) Like the Transport window, the windows discussed here will open on top of either the Edit or Mix window.

Big Counter

❅ Big Counter. The Big Counter window is simply a larger display of your main counter, but it really comes in handy when you want to watch your session's progress from across a room! The shortcut for the Big Counter window is Ctrl+3 on a PC and ⌘+3 on a Mac.

Automation Enable

❋ Automation Enable. **Automating Pro Tools is a topic you'll work with later in this book. Simply put, it's a way for you to make your mixes and effects more dynamic as your session plays. The Automation Enable window shown here allows you to enable or disable various aspects of your session for automation. The shortcut for the Automation Enable window is Ctrl+4 on a PC and ⌘+4 on a Mac.**

Memory Locations

❋ Memory Locations. **As you become more advanced, your sessions will naturally become more complex, that's for sure. You'll find that navigating around your intricate session will start taking more and more time and effort. Wouldn't it be great if there was a way to immediately jump to a specific location, or even a specific region of your session? That's exactly what memory locations are. As you'll learn later, memory locations are a powerful and flexible way to get from place to place instantly! For those of you who will use this feature frequently, you can open it by pressing Ctrl+5 on a PC and ⌘+5 on a Mac**

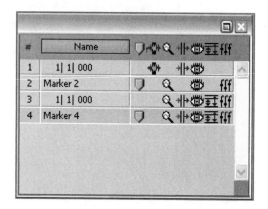

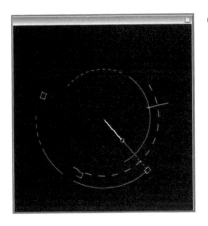

QuickTime Movie

❋ QuickTime Movie. Though Pro Tools is an audio application, that doesn't mean that you can't work with video. Though your video editing options are limited to be sure, importing video files into your session is easy, and viewing your movie as your session plays is as simple as choosing QuickTime Movie from the Window drop-down menu. You can also get to this window quickly by pressing Ctrl+9 on a PC or ⌘+9 on a Mac.

Session Setup

❋ If you are experienced with previous versions of Pro Tools, you might think that the Session Setup window, which was in the Window drop-down list, has been removed! Not to worry, it just moved to another drop-down menu. Here's how to open the window:

1 Click on Setup. The Setup menu will appear, displaying an assortment of window choices.

2 Click on Session. The Session Setup window will appear:

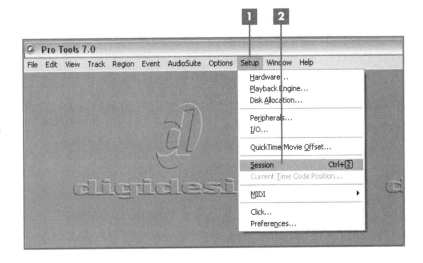

❋ **Session Setup.** The Session Setup window displays useful information about your session's configurations. The shortcut for the Session Setup window is Ctrl+2 on a PC and ⌘+2 on a Mac.

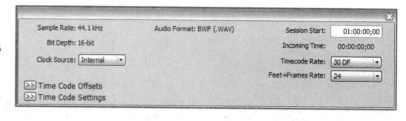

System Usage and Disk Space

Last but not least, these two windows will give you important information about how your system is doing. There are no shortcut keys for these windows (you'll have to open them from the Window drop-down menu), but they're critical windows nonetheless!

a System Usage. As you learn more about how to efficiently use Pro Tools, you'll want to refer to the System Usage window from time to time to check on how your computer is dealing with the tasks associated with Pro Tools. This window gives a simple and efficient view of the workload for your system.

b Disk Space. The size of a hard drive in a DAW is like the amount of tape in an analog recording studio—the more you have, the more you can record. The Disk Space window will let you know how much free space you have for recording audio and how much time you have left to record (at a given sample rate and bit depth) on each of your computer's hard drives.

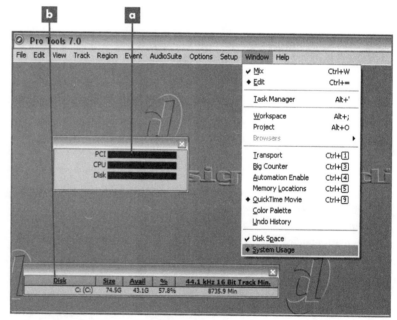

Congratulations! You now have a fundamental understanding of what Pro Tools is and how it functions, which will help you be a more intelligent user as you delve deeper into this powerful environment. Now you're ready to begin actively using Pro Tools LE and making music!

3 } Getting Started with Audio

Now that you have a solid basic understanding of what Pro Tools is and what it can do, it's time to start making things happen. The first step down this road to Pro Tools proficiency is to set up your session and start using audio. In this chapter, you'll learn how to:

- ✳ Set up and customize your inputs, outputs, inserts, and buses
- ✳ Create audio, aux input, and master fader tracks
- ✳ Import audio into your session
- ✳ Play your session in different ways

Setup

Before you can move to the next step, you'll have to call upon knowledge that you gained in the first chapter and create a session on which you can work.

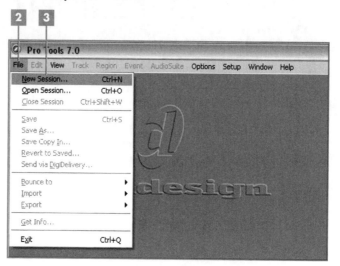

1 Launch Pro Tools.

2 Click on File. The File menu will appear.

3 Click on New Session. The Name the Session dialog box will open.

4 Type Chapter 3 Session in the File Name text box.

5 Select WAV from the Audio File Type menu. The option will be selected.

6 Select 44.1 kHz from the Sample Rate menu. The option will be selected.

7 Select the 24 Bit radio button in the Bit Depth area. The option will be selected.

8 Select Stereo Mix from the I/O Settings menu. The option will be selected.

9 Click on Save. Your session will be created and opened automatically.

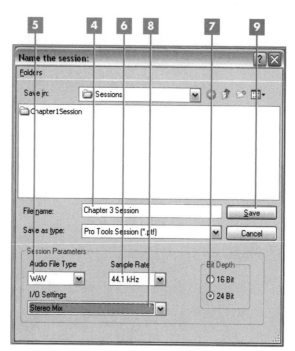

Customizing Your Session: I/O Setup

An understanding of Pro Tools' signal flow is critical to using this powerful DAW, and at the heart of signal flow is the I/O (Input/Output) Setup dialog box. Take a look.

Setting Up Inputs

When you created this session you chose Stereo Mix as your I/O (Input/Output) setting. This I/O setting is Pro Tools' generic setup for stereo work, and although it works fine as is, you can customize it to match your own studio's setup and boost your productivity right from the start! You can start by taking a closer look at the input setup for your studio—in other words, the connections going into your audio interface, and from there to the Pro Tools software environment.

1 Click on Setup. The Setup menu will appear.

2 Click on I/O. The I/O Setup dialog box will open.

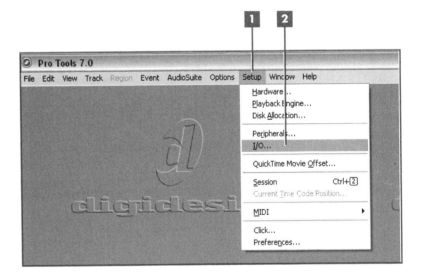

3 Click **on the** Input tab**. The tab will move to the front.**

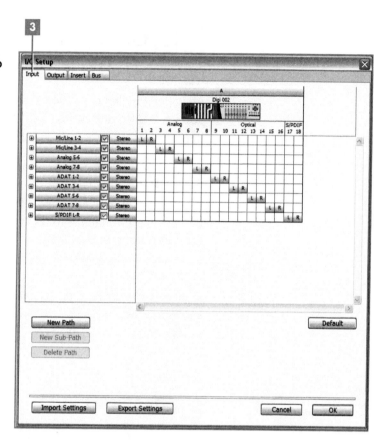

The examples in this chapter show the windows you'll see if you have a Digi 002 system. If you have any other kind of interface, the window will look a little different (although the function will be the same). At the top of the window, you'll see your audio interface (Mbox, Mbox 2, Digi 002, or Digi 002R). Directly below the interface, you'll see a listing of all the available inputs for that interface.

Customizing Your Inputs

The grid area and the labels to the left represent paths, which allow you to assign inputs in the Pro Tools software to the physical inputs of your Pro Tools hardware. The dialog box currently displays a default input setup. You'll want to customize your inputs, and the easiest way to do that is to delete these paths and start from scratch. Here's how:

1 Click on the top path name. The name will be highlighted.

2 Press the Shift key and click on the remaining path names until all the paths are highlighted.

3 Click on Delete Path. All the input paths will disappear.

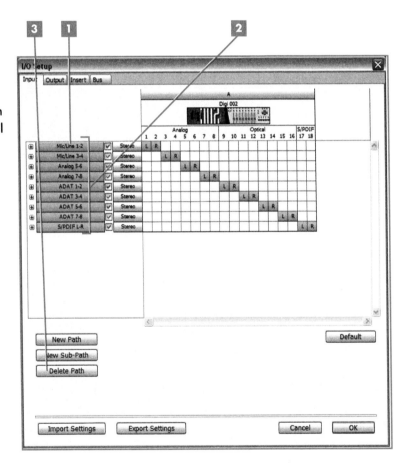

4 Click on New Path. A single new path will appear with the default name of Path 1.

5 Click on New Path 11 more times. Additional paths will be created, again with default names.

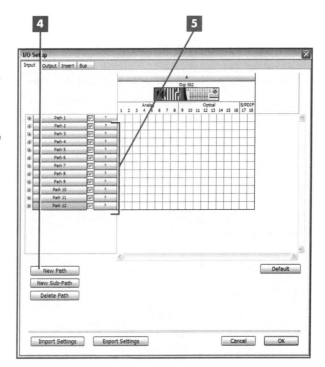

6 Although you've created input paths, they haven't been configured or assigned to physical inputs on your interface yet. That's your next job. Double-click on the top path name. The path name will be highlighted.

7 Type a descriptive name for this path.

8 Repeat Steps 6 and 7 for the other applicable default paths, naming each input descriptively.

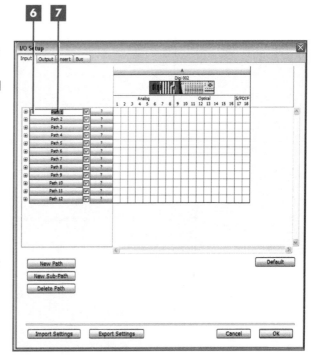

Configuring a Path as Stereo or Mono

Now you need to configure each path as either stereo or mono.

1 Click on the question mark (?) to the right of a path name. A path type pop-up menu will appear.

2 Choose a type for each path (stereo or mono). The type will be selected.

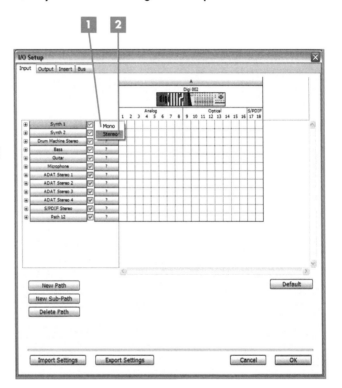

Assigning Your Path

Now it's time to assign your path (in this case, Front Inputs) to specific inputs of your audio interface (in this case, Synth 1).

1. Move your cursor to the grid area in the top row. Your cursor will change from an arrow to a pencil.

2. Click in the square that matches the input you desire. Because this happens to be a stereo path, two blocks will appear, marked L and R (for left and right).

3. Repeat Step 2 for all your paths.

✳ **NOTE**

In the case of a stereo path, click on the square that is assigned to the left channel.

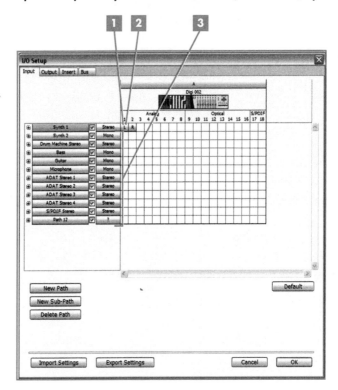

Setting Up Sub-Paths

You've set up your paths, and now it's time to think about sub-paths. *Sub-paths* are individual assignments within a path. For example, take a look at the first ADAT path—ADAT Stereo 1. If you have a stereo signal going into those two inputs, you're all set; however, if you want to use each input separately, you should consider setting up a couple of sub-paths within that stereo path.

1 Click on the desired stereo path name. The name will be highlighted.

2 Click twice on New Sub-Path. Two sub-paths will be created below the first path, with default names (Path 1 and Path 2).

3 Double-click on each sub-path and name it, just like you did with the paths.

4 As you did with the paths, you need to assign a physical output to each sub-path. Click on the desired grid square. A block with an M (for mono) will appear.

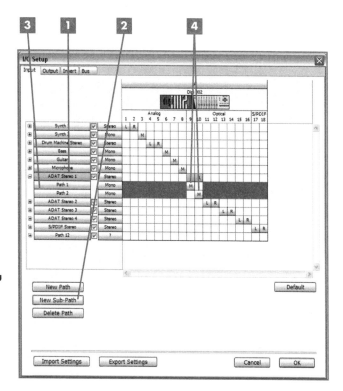

Changing a Path's Input Assignment

Once you've created a path (or sub-path) and assigned a physical interface input to that path, you're all set. But what if you want to change the input of a specific path? For example, let's assume that the bass in my studio is actually plugged into input 7 and the guitar is actually plugged into input 6. Changing the inputs is extremely easy, and one of the real beauties of the I/O Setup dialog box:

1 Click and hold the block you want to change.

2 Drag the block until it is directly beneath the desired input. A hollow box will show where your input path will be redeposited.

3 Release the mouse button. The path's input block will be moved to the selected interface input.

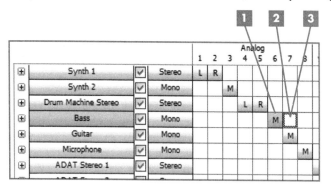

Setting Up Outputs

You've set up your system to deal with incoming audio—good job! The next step is to customize how audio exits your audio interface. For the examples shown below, we'll once again create a basic setup that happens to work in my studio—your setup will reflect your personal needs and I/O capabilities. The good news is that the Output tab of the I/O Setup dialog box is laid out similarly to the Input tab, so this should go a lot quicker!

1 Click on the Output tab in the I/O Setup dialog box. The tab will move to the front.

2 Double-click on the first output path name and type Main Output. (This is the same method you used to name input paths.) The path will be renamed.

3 Repeat Step 2 for the next three output paths (if your interface has them) and rename the paths as follows:

❀ Drum Cue Mix

❀ Bass Cue Mix

❀ Guitar Cue Mix

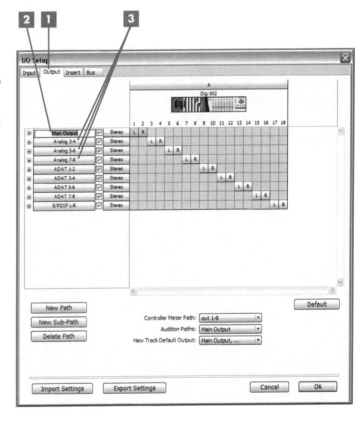

❀ **NOTE**

This kind of a setup is pretty common for stereo projects. In this case, you would typically use Main Output for your studio monitors. Use the Cue Mix outputs for individual headphone mixes for your recording musicians. Remember, though, that these are all line-level signals and they will need amplification before they go to speakers. Keep in mind also that different interfaces have different numbers (and types) of outputs, so it's a good idea to check your interface's documentation for specific information.

4 Click on the plus sign (+) to the left of each path to show any existing sub-paths it contains. Because you simply renamed the paths that existed in the first place, each stereo path should have a couple of sub-paths, which will be automatically renamed as well.

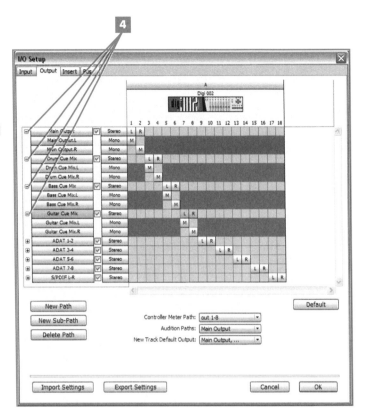

> ❋ **NOTE**
>
> Here again, the prime directive of inputs is applicable to outputs: Paths cannot overlap. (In other words, two active paths cannot both use the same physical output.) Sub-paths, on the other hand, *can* overlap.

Setting Up Inserts

In the world of DAWs, you'll be able to use software effects (reverbs, delays, and so on) called *plug-ins*. Does that mean you won't be able to use the rackmount effects you've got in your studio? Not at all—you can bring them into the Pro Tools environment through a configuration of your inputs and outputs called hardware or I/O inserts. You'll learn more about inserts and how to use them in Chapter 8, "Basic Mixing."

One thing you need to know about hardware inserts now, though, is how to connect your gear. The rule is simple: Use the same number inputs for the insert that you used for the outputs. For example, if you have a rackmount stereo reverb unit that you want to use with Pro Tools, you have to use a pair of outputs (for example, #17 and #18) to send signal to the unit, and you have to use the same numbers (#17 and #18) on the input side to get audio from the reverb back to Pro Tools.

As we did when we configured our Inputs, let's start by deleting everything, then building things up from scratch. Technically this isn't necessary, but it will make it easier to work with in the long run.

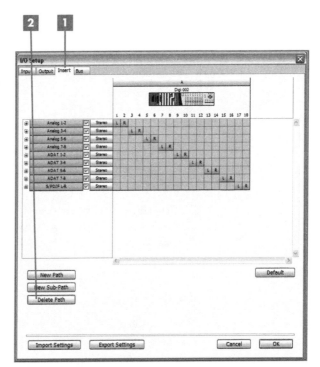

1. Click on the Insert tab in the I/O Setup dialog box. The tab will move to the front.

2. Click on every path name to select them, then click on Delete Path, just like you did with the inputs. The paths will be deleted.

3 Click on New Path to create a new path for each of your effects units (to the extent that your audio interface has the available physical inputs and outputs to connect effects units) and name each path the same way you did on the Input and Output tabs (and configure it as either stereo or mono).

4 Again, using the same method you used for setting up your inputs and outputs, assign each path to the inputs/outputs to which your effect is connected. In this case, my EQ is connected to I/O #17 and #18. As mentioned before, you are setting an input and output pair, with signal leaving your computer through an interface output and returning to the Pro Tools environment through the same numbered inputs.

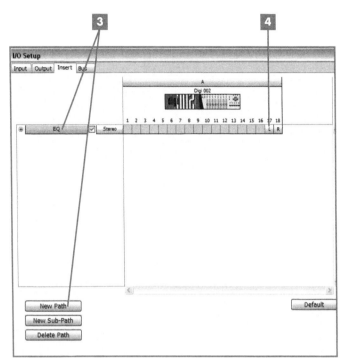

Setting Up Buses

Last but not least is the Bus tab. Buses are like virtual audio cables that you can use within the Pro Tools mixing environment. You'll use them for internal routing in Pro Tools, such as sending "dry" audio from an audio track to a reverb on an aux track. Don't worry if that sounds like Greek—you'll be doing this sort of thing in Chapter 8, using Pro Tools' trusty buses.

❋ **NOTE**

For those of you who've used buses in previous versions of Pro Tools, you're in for a pleasant surprise. Pro Tools has *doubled* the number of available buses, from 16 to 32!

Often the default naming of the buses will suffice, and their generic names will suit their multipurpose functions. Sometimes, though, you might decide to name your buses more descriptively. Here's how:

1 Click on the Bus tab. The tab will move to the front.

2 Because buses are so multi-functional, you really don't need to name them all. In this case, just name the last pair so you know to reserve it to use later for your vocals. Double-click on the last path name and type Vocal Verb. The path will be renamed.

3 Click on OK. The dialog box will close. You're finished!

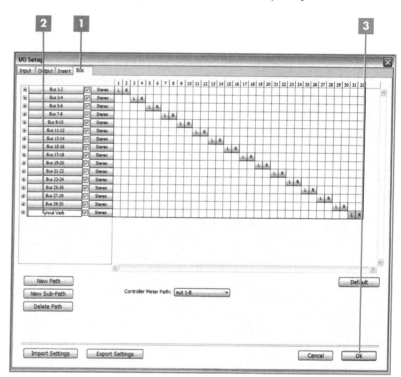

> **NOTE**
>
> Notice how this tab is different from the others. There aren't any references to your interface's physical inputs or outputs at the top of the window. That's because your buses are entirely a part of your Pro Tools software and not physical in any way!
>
> Another thing you might have noticed about this tab is that it has been resized (just as you would resize any window in your operating system). This is a new feature in Pro Tools 7.

Tracks

Whether you're looking at the Edit window or the Mix window, you'll notice that your new session opened without any tracks in it. It's up to you to create the tracks you'll need in your session.

Making Tracks

No matter what kind of track you want to create, you'll start by following the same first few steps.

1 Click on Track. The Track menu will appear.

2 Click on New. The New Tracks dialog box will open.

❊ **TIP**

Because you'll be making many tracks as you work more and more in Pro Tools, you might want to learn the shortcuts. Shift+Ctrl+N (PC) or Shift+⌘+N (Mac) will call up the New Tracks dialog box.

3 The dialog box is set up right now to create one mono audio track. For this example, you want to create four tracks instead. Double-click in the Create field to highlight it (if it isn't already highlighted), and then type 4 for the number of tracks you want to create.

4 Click on Create. The New Tracks dialog box will close, and the tracks will be created in your session.

❊❊❊

> ❄ **NOTE**
>
> The first drop-down menu allows you to specify whether your track will be stereo or mono. The second drop-down menu allows you to select the kind of track you will create. You'll learn more about the different types of tracks available in Pro Tools (such as audio, aux, MIDI, and master fader) and how to use them later.

Now you can create a couple of stereo audio tracks.

1 Open **the** New Tracks dialog box **as you did in the previous section.**

2 Type 2 **in the Create field to create two tracks.**

3 Click **on the** Track Format drop-down menu. **The menu will appear.**

4 Click **on** Stereo. **The option will be selected.**

5 Click **on** Create. **Two stereo audio tracks will be created, just as you specified.**

Creating an Auxiliary Input Track

An Auxiliary Input track (also commonly called an Aux Input or simply an Aux track) is similar to an audio track in many respects, except it doesn't use any audio regions. Its main function is to serve as a means of routing audio from a source to a destination or as a place to process one or more audio signals with plug-in effects.

You'll learn how to use aux tracks in Chapters 7 and 8, and you'll find that knowledge very handy, particularly when you get down to the business of mixing. To begin, let's start with the process of creating a couple of stereo aux tracks, which is almost identical to creating audio tracks.

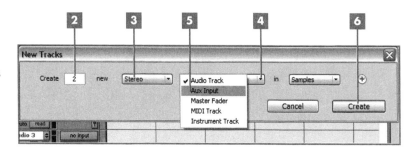

1. Open the New Tracks dialog box as you did in the previous sections.

2. Type 2 in the Create field to create two tracks.

3. Click on Stereo in the first drop-down menu to make these aux tracks stereo. The option will be selected.

4. Click on the second drop-down menu. A list of all the different types of tracks that you can create in Pro Tools will appear.

5. Click on Aux Input. The option will be selected.

6. Click on Create. Two stereo aux tracks will be created, just as you specified.

Master Faders, MIDI, and Instrument Tracks

As you probably noticed, there are three other types of tracks listed in the track type drop-down menu—Master Fader, MIDI, and Instrument tracks. Although you might not use these kinds of tracks in every session you create, they will be very useful when you need them.

If you've ever worked with a traditional mixing board, you know what master faders can do. These are the faders that control the overall volume of your entire mix after you have blended all the individual tracks. A master fader in Pro Tools does pretty much the same thing. Simply put, it is a fader that controls the overall volume of a given output path. It will also allow you to add plug-in effects to the entire mix at once.

MIDI is not audio. Rather, it is a digital language that allows different musical devices to communicate, somewhat like a network. You can record (and then edit) MIDI data on a MIDI track in Pro Tools. When combined with Pro Tools' powerful set of audio features, this will open new creative doors! Related to MIDI, Pro Tools 7 has added a new kind of track, called an Instrument track, which will allow you to use MIDI and virtual instruments together in one convenient track.

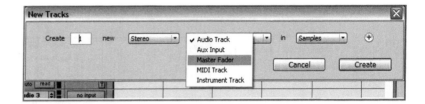

The method of creating a Master Fader, MIDI, or Instrument track is almost identical to creating any other kind of track. The only difference is that you'll choose your type of track accordingly. Just for practice, try creating one new stereo master fader, using the steps outlined earlier.

> **NOTE**
> When you choose to create a MIDI track, you'll notice that there is no stereo or mono option available. Don't worry, it's not a malfunction of Pro Tools—it's because MIDI isn't audio, so the terms *stereo* and *mono* don't really apply in this case.

Managing Your Tracks

There are a few techniques you can use to make the creation of tracks even easier, and set them up for efficient use after they've been created.

Creating Multiple Tracks

In the previous sections of this chapter, you created different kinds of tracks one type at a time (mono audio tracks, then stereo audio, aux tracks, and so on). This was the way the job got done in earlier versions of Pro Tools, but in the last versions of Pro Tools, a neat little time-saver was added. Take a look:

1 If you've opened up the New Tracks dialog box, and want to create more than one type of track in one path, simply click the plus (+) sign at the right end of the dialog. A second row of track parameters will appear.

2 You can continue creating different kinds of tracks by continuing to click the plus sign, as shown here.

3 Did you go one step too far, and do you now want to remove one of the rows? It's easy—just click the minus (–) sign to the left of the row you wish to delete.

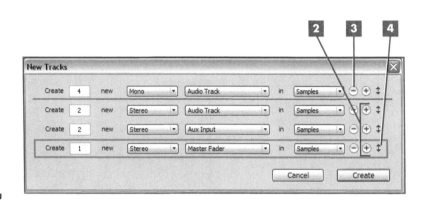

4 The tracks shown here will be created in your session from top to bottom, just as shown in this dialog box. If you want to re-order the arrangement of tracks, just click and hold the double-arrow icon at the far right of the row that you wish to move. A blue box will appear around that row, indicating that it's ready to be moved (the Master Fader in this case). Still holding your mouse button down, drag the row up or down. A dashed line will appear, displaying where the track will be deposited when the mouse is released.

Naming Your Tracks

One of the most important (maybe *the* most important, depending on who you talk to) aspects of working in a DAW is documentation. Keeping track of your sessions, files, tracks, patches, and so on is absolutely critical, especially as your sessions become more complex.

When Pro Tools creates a new track, it assigns a generic name (such as Audio 1) as a default. Descriptively naming your tracks is a big part of session documentation—and the good news is, it's easy!

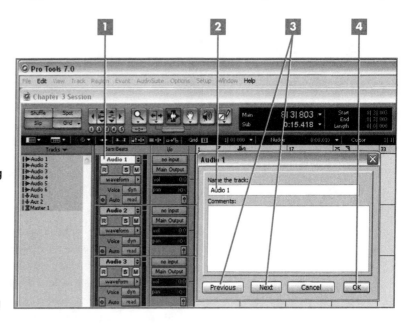

1 Double-click on the name of the track you want to rename. A dialog box will open.

2 Type a name for the track in the Name the Track field.

3 If you want to continue naming tracks, click on Previous to name the track above the current track, or click on Next to name the track below the current track.

4 When you're finished naming tracks, click on OK. The dialog box will close.

❄ **NOTE**

If you've been following along with this chapter's examples, you should have four mono audio tracks, two stereo audio tracks, two stereo aux tracks, and one stereo master fader. To keep the ball rolling, name each of the tracks as follows: Bass, Guitar, Vocal, Sax, Drums, Synth, Vocal Reverb Aux, Drum Reverb, and Master Volume.

Moving Tracks

After you've assigned names to all your tracks, you might want to reorganize them so that related tracks are near each other. Although moving tracks around in the Edit or Mix window won't change how they play back in any way, a logical arrangement of tracks can make the entire production process much easier. There aren't any hard-and-fast rules on how to arrange your tracks—each session is unique, and you have to decide how to arrange your tracks so they make sense to you.

In this example, I want to move my Drums track to the top of my Edit window:

1 Click and hold on a track name in the Edit area of the Edit window. The track will be selected.

2 Drag the track up or down to the desired location. As you drag the track, a thin line will appear, indicating the position the track will assume when it is dropped in its new location.

3 Release the mouse button when you have the track at the desired location. The tracks in your session will be reorganized.

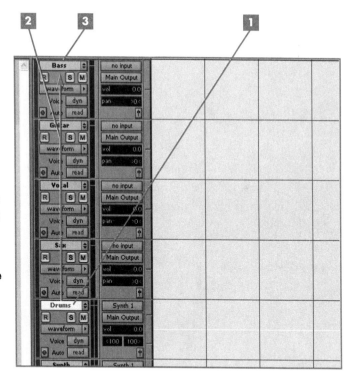

❄ **TIP**

Here's another way to do it: Click and hold on the track name in the Track Show/Hide list. A thin line will appear below the track name you have selected, indicating that it's ready to be moved. Drag the track up or down to the desired position. (The thin line will move, indicating where the track will be moved.) When you release the mouse button, your tracks will be reordered.

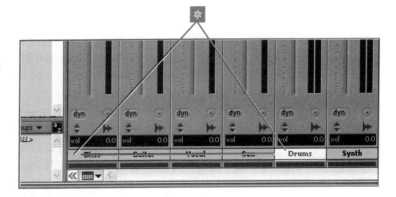

❄ In the Mix window, you click and hold to drag any track to a new location. Of course, instead of dragging up or down, you drag left or right.

❄ **NOTE**

The Mix window reflects any rearrangement of tracks you make in the Edit window. Tracks are listed in the Edit window from top to bottom; in the Mix window, they're displayed from left to right.

Duplicating Tracks

From time to time, you'll want to do a little more than create a new blank track—you'll want to "clone" your track. Here's how it's done:

1 Select the track(s) you want to duplicate by clicking the track name.

2 Click on Track. The Track menu will appear.

3 Click on Duplicate. The Duplicate Tracks dialog box will open.

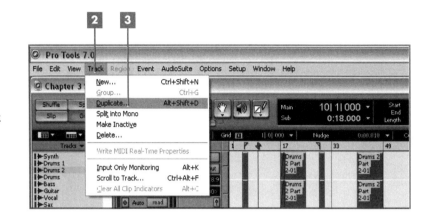

4 Type the number of duplicates you wish to make.

5 Choose the aspects of the track that you wish to copy. At this point, these terms might have little meaning, though we'll explore them in later chapters. To make a complete duplication of the selected track(s), check all boxes in the Data to Duplicate section.

6 Check the Insert After Last Selected Track box to have your new tracks created directly adjacent to your selected tracks. With the box unchecked, your new tracks will be created at the bottom of your Tracks list.

7 When you're done, click OK. The duplicate track(s) will be created.

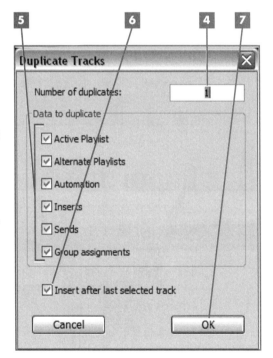

Deleting Tracks

Also from time to time, you'll want to delete tracks that you've created but are not using for one reason or another. Let's say you've created a duplicate track (as you have just done), then decide it was a bad idea! No worries—it's even easier than creating tracks.

1. Select the track(s) you want to delete by clicking the track name.

2. Click on Track. The Track menu will appear.

3. Click on Delete. The track will be deleted.

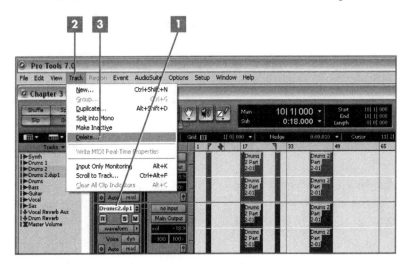

Importing Audio

While you can certainly record live audio in Pro Tools (it wouldn't be much of an audio workstation if you couldn't!), that's not the only way to get sounds into Pro Tools. Indeed, one of the great advantages of a computer-based DAW is that you can import digital audio files into a preexisting project, bypassing the recording process entirely!

Importing digital audio into Pro Tools is a fast and easy way to get a project started, and as with so many of Pro Tools' operations, there are a number of ways to do it.

Importing into the Regions List

First, try importing an audio file to the Regions list. Once you've imported to the Regions list, you will be able to use the audio in any suitable audio track.

 NOTE

The examples shown in the remainder of this chapter are using the Chapter 3 online materials. In particular, you'll be using sessions and audio in the Import Materials folder, which you should now download to a specific location on your computer's hard drive.

Choosing Where to Import Audio From

The first thing you need to do is locate the file you want to import into Pro Tools.

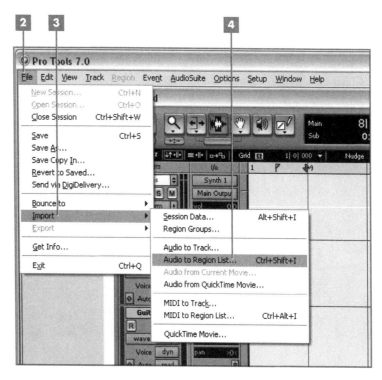

1 If you're looking at the Mix window in Pro Tools, you'll want to switch to the Edit window. From the Window menu choose Edit, and the Edit window will appear.

2 Click on the File drop-down menu.

3 Choose Import. A second drop-down menu will appear.

4 Choose Audio to Region List. The Import Audio dialog box will open.

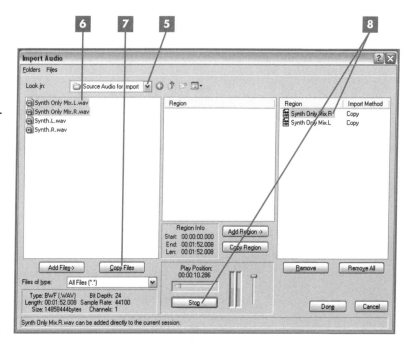

5 Now it's time to choose an audio file to import into your session. According to the conventions of your operating system, navigate to the folder that contains the audio you wish to import (if you downloaded the Import Materials folder, navigate to the Source Audio for Import subfolder).

6 Click on the audio file(s) you want to import into your Pro Tools session. The file(s) will be selected. If you're working with the online materials set up for this book, select the two Synth Only Mix files.

7 The box on the left shows audio in folders, but that audio has not actually been incorporated into your session as of yet. To do that, you'll need to add those files to the box on the right. Click the Copy Files button. The files will be added to the right box, as shown here.

8 To audition any single file before importing, select the desired audio file, then click on the Play button to preview your selected file. The file will begin to play.

❄ **NOTE**

The Import Audio dialog box gives you relevant information regarding the file you select in the lower corner of the window.

❄ **NOTE**

You'll notice that there's an Add Files and a Copy Files button at the bottom of the leftmost box. Clicking Add Files will simply add the file to the Pro Tools session, and Pro Tools will play the audio file from its original location on your hard drive (which in this case is in the Source Audio for Input folder). Clicking Copy Files instead will actually make a copy of those files and place the copies in the session's own Audio Files folder.

When importing audio files with different sample rates or bit-depths from your Pro Tools session, those files must be copied (and converted).

❄ **TIP**

If you don't hear your selection, you might want to check the Audition setting in the I/O Setup dialog box. Review the "Customizing Your Session: I/O Setup" section earlier in this chapter for more information.

Before you proceed, you should notice a couple things:

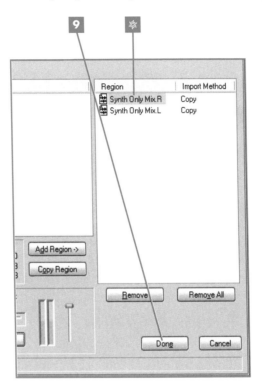

❋ This file has .L listed before the file extension (in this case, it's a .wav file). This indicates that the file is the left half of a stereo track. The Synth Only Mix.R.wav file is listed right below this file. These two files together are elements of a stereo audio track.

9 Click on Done when you're finished. The audio will be immediately incorporated into your session.

Choosing Where to Import Audio

When simply adding the audio to your session, the process is as simple as the steps I've just described. *If you choose to copy the files, you'll import in the following manner:*

a After selecting your file(s), click the Copy Files button. Again, the files will be shown in the rightmost box.

b When you're finished selecting your files, click Done, as you did before. This time though, the audio won't be immediately shown in your session. Instead, you'll have to choose where copies of these files will be created.

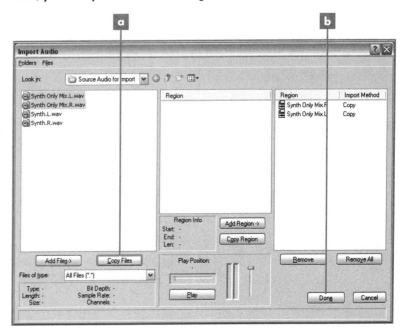

1 By default, Pro Tools will choose to copy the audio files to your session's Audio Files folder, as shown here, but you can choose to place that copy in any location on your hard drive. If you wish to change the location of the copies, simply navigate to the desired location according to the conventions of your specific operating system.

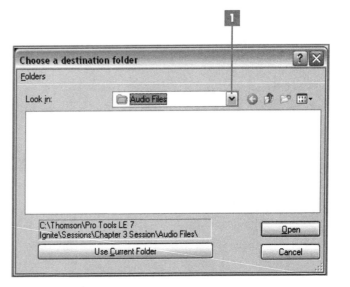

The bottom-left corner of the Choose a Destination Folder dialog box will always show you where your copied files will be placed.

2a Click on Use Current Folder. The audio file will be copied to the folder, and imported into your session.

OR

2b If you have subfolders shown in the window that you want to use for your copied audio, select the desired folder and click the Open button. Once inside the desired folder, click Use Current Folder, and your audio will be copied and imported.

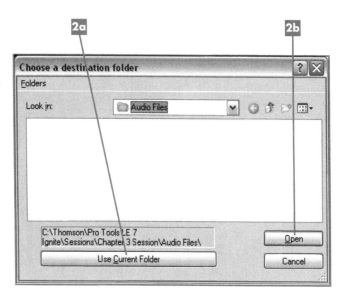

Users regularly fall into a little trap during this last phase of importing. Often, they are tempted to open the folder, and then try to save the file in it. In this particular case, you just choose the folder itself, simply by highlighting it. The file will automatically be saved inside it.

You'll notice that although the audio file is imported into the Regions list, there is no audio region visible on any of the tracks that you created. Don't worry—that's the way this method of importing is supposed to function. Later, you'll drag this audio file onto an audio track and use it as a sounding element for your session.

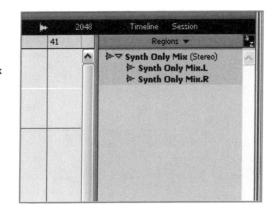

TIP

For every stereo region in your Regions list, you'll see a triangle by the region name. You can click on the triangle to reveal a list of the component mono audio files that make up that stereo audio region.

Importing Audio to a Track

Sometimes, instead of importing an audio file into the Regions list and using it later, you'll want to import audio directly into a track. Pro Tools makes this very convenient by creating a new audio track just for the audio you are importing.

Just as you did when you imported audio into the Regions list, the first step here is to locate the audio that you want to bring into your session.

1 Click on File.

2 Choose Import. A second drop-down menu will appear.

3 Choose Audio to Track. The Import Audio dialog box will open.

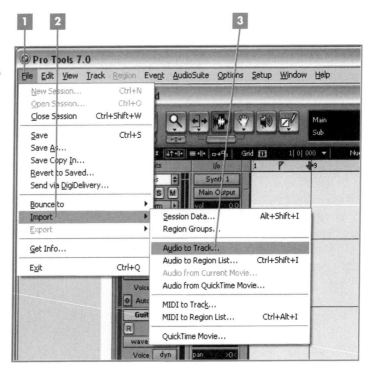

4 Select the audio file(s) to import into your session. If you're following the example shown here, you'll want to choose Synth.L and Synth.R.

5 Click the Add Files button (or the Copy Files button, if you prefer), then Click on Done when you're finished making your choices. Again, the procedure for this exercise is the same as what you did in the previous section. You can still preview the file using the Play button in the lower-left part of the dialog box. The Choose a Destination Folder dialog box will automatically open if you are copying audio files.

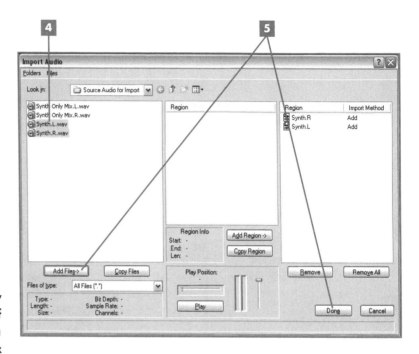

You'll notice that Pro Tools has done multiple operations with the click of a single button:

a Pro Tools has imported the desired region (in this case Synth) into the Regions lists. This means that the region is completely accessible in the session.

b Pro Tools has *also* created a brand-new track, named Synth (named for the audio file being imported). Since the files being imported had an "L" and "R" after them, Pro Tools recognized them as being left and right channels, and so incorporated them into a single stereo audio track. Pretty cool, don't you think?

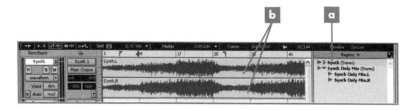

Importing Tracks

Importing audio into a track is certainly an easy way to get going with audio, but there is a limitation. The region that you import will be placed at the beginning of your session's Timeline, with no specific editing or mixing. But what if you want to import a tweaked-out track you created in another session? No problem—Pro Tools can import tracks from a previous session, preserving all edits, volume, panning, and so on, for you to use in your current session!

1 Click on File.

2 Choose Import. A second drop-down menu will appear.

3 Choose Session Data. The Choose a File to Import Session Data From dialog box will open.

4 Navigate to the session from which you want to import a track. Remember, you're not importing just audio anymore, but rather an entire track. That track exists in the session file, which is why you're selecting a session file, not an audio file. If you're following the example shown here, you'll find a folder named Source Session for Import within the Import Materials folder. Select the session named Source Session for Import.

5 Click on Open. The Import Session Data dialog box will open.

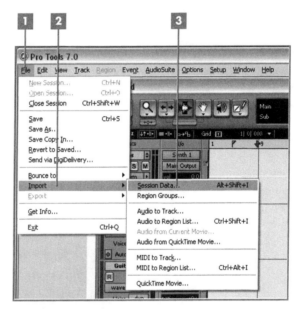

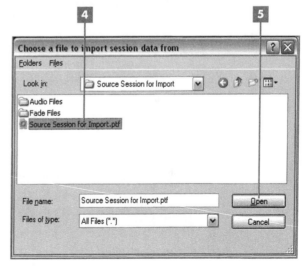

The Source Properties section of the Import Session Data dialog box provides a wealth of specific information regarding the session from which you'll be importing tracks. Of particular note are the Name, Audio Bit Depth, Audio Sample Rate, and Audio File Type(s) fields shown in the upper-left corner. The bottom of the dialog box contains a list of all tracks in this session.

6 Click on the Drums 1 (Stereo audio) button. The import menu will appear.

7 Choose New Track. The option will be selected.

8 It's possible to import more than one track at a time. Click on the Drums 2 (Stereo audio) button and select Import As New Track. The option will be selected.

9 Before you leave this window, you should choose whether to simply add any audio files to your session, or copy that audio to your audio files folder. Click the Audio Media Options button. A drop-down menu will appear.

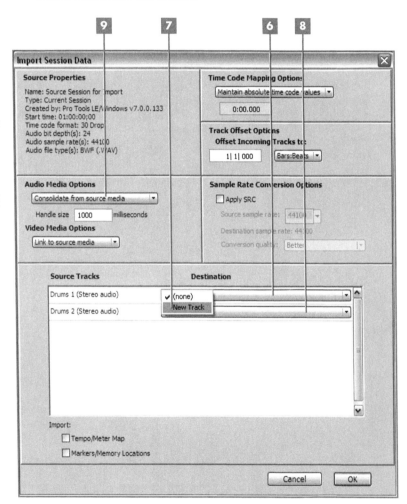

89
❋ ❋ ❋

10 For our purposes, the Link to Source Media and Copy from Source Media options are the most commonly used. Linking to source media will not make a copy, but rather will direct the session to refer to audio files in the original session. Copying from source media will copy the audio media to the session's Audio Files folder. In this case, let's choose Copy from Source Media.

11 When you're done, click OK.

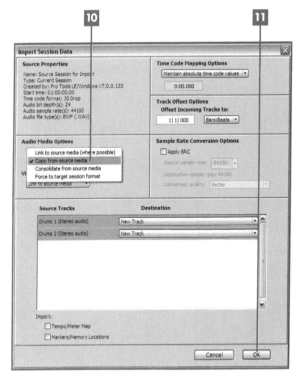

Again, you'll see that Pro Tools as done a number of operations with one user command:

a Two new tracks will be created in your session. The interesting thing you'll notice about both tracks is that you've imported a number of audio regions, and they are already arranged at specific times in your session.

b Note also that each separate region in each of the tracks is listed individually in the Regions list.

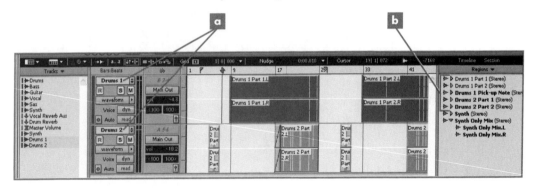

The Workspace

A nifty new feature was added to Pro Tools in version 6, called the Workspace window. This window provides you with yet another way to import audio into your session, and it offers a few other useful tools as well.

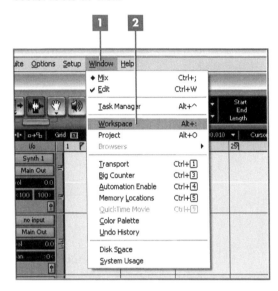

1 Click on Window. The Window menu will appear.

2 Click on Workspace. The Workspace window will appear.

Searching for Audio Using the Workspace

You can easily search for audio using the Workspace window.

1 Click on the magnifying glass button. The Find section will appear.

2 Click on the check boxes to select the drives you want to search. The drives will be selected.

3 Type the name of the file (or keyword) you want to find in the Find text box.

4 Click on Search. Matching results will appear in the bottom section of the Workspace window.

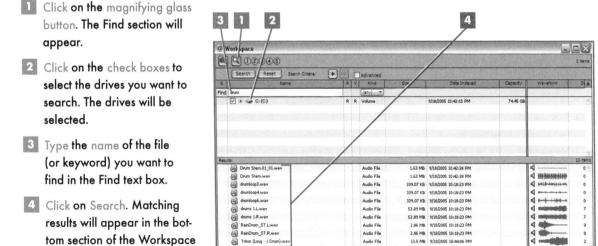

You can also navigate this window in a more traditional way, if you know where to look for a specific file. For this example, import audio yet again from the Chapter 1 session.

1 In the Find section, double-click on the hard drive where your audio file resides.

2 Navigate through the folders and subfolders of your drive until you find the desired file.

3 Double-click on the Audio Files folder. The audio files in the folder will appear.

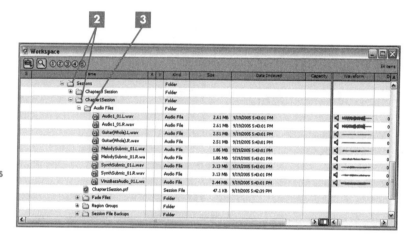

This window provides a few interesting features.

a The secondary window will give you additional information about each of the files (such as sample rate, bit depth, date created, and comments). Use the scroll bar at the bottom of this section to view different aspects of each file.

b You can audition each audio file by clicking the speaker icon to the right of each file name. The waveform display to the right of the speaker icon will give an indication of the file's characteristics. To stop playback, simply click on the speaker icon again.

❋ **CAUTION**

Do *not* click on the session file. You're not importing a track this time; clicking on a session file will only cause Pro Tools to close the present session and open that session file. Don't worry too much, though—Pro Tools will double-check before doing this, and you can always choose to cancel the operation if you clicked on the session by mistake.

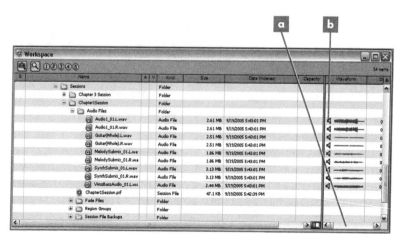

TIP

You can make this section of the Workspace window a bit more functional by arranging the columns to suit your needs. Just drag and drop each column heading!

TIP

If you're auditioning a particularly lengthy audio file, you can click at any point within the blue audio waveform to begin playback from that point.

4 Here's the cool part. Click and hold the file you want to import into your session. For our purposes, choose the Audio 1_01.L.wav and Audio 1_01.R.wav files.

5 Drag the audio file onto the Edit window. An outline of the region will appear in the Tracks area.

6 Release the mouse button to drop the file at the desired location. For this example, please deposit the regions on the Drums track. The region will be deposited on the desired track at the desired point on your timeline.

7 Again, you'll notice that adding a region to a track will automatically add an audio region to your Regions list.

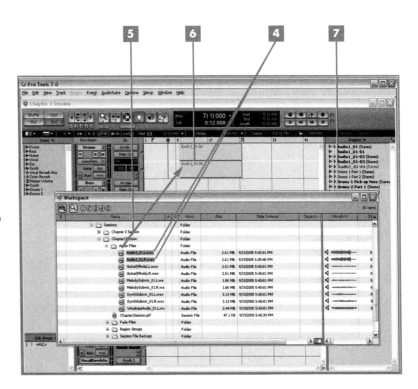

CAUTION

Is there any way to tell what the regions Audio 1_01.L.wav and Audio 1_01.R.wav sound like, just by looking at the names? Nope! This is an intentional example of what *not* to let happen, and what *will* happen if you record audio without naming your tracks first!

> **TIP**
>
> There are other ways to drag and drop from the Workspace window. For example, you can drag and drop from the Workspace window directly to the Regions list (no region will be automatically deposited on any tracks). Also, if you happen to drag files to an empty part of the Edit window, the appropriate track will be created, and the audio deposited at the point that you release the mouse!

> ❄ **NOTE**
>
> Did you notice that you didn't have to do any sample rate or bit-depth conversion? Pro Tools automatically converts the file if it's necessary! While the conversion process is happening, these buttons will change from green to red, indicating that there is background processing at work.

Making Selections and Playing Audio

Now that you've learned how to import audio into your session, you ready to move to the next level of playback. Being able to play your session in a few different ways (in addition to being able to play it from the beginning of the session) will allow you to concentrate on specific parts of your project.

First, start with a basic playback scenario.

1 Click on the Selector button. The Selector tool will be selected.

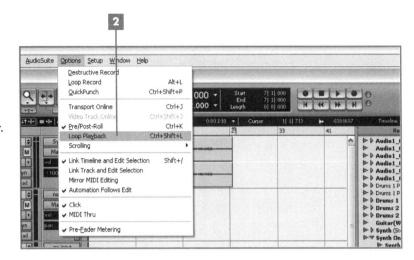

2 If there is a circular arrow in the Play button, deselect the Loop Playback option in the Options menu. The arrow in the Play button will disappear.

Selecting and Deleting Tracks

Do you need to move a number of tracks? Want to get rid of the tracks you're not using? It's very easy—let's start by moving our newly created tracks to the top of the Edit window:

1 Holding the Shift key, click the track names of the track(s) you wish to move. In this case, I've selected the Synth, Drums 1, and Drums 2 tracks.

2 Just as you did when you moved a single track, click and drag the group of tracks to the desired location in your Edit window. If you drag the tracks to the top of the window, your Edit window should look something like this:

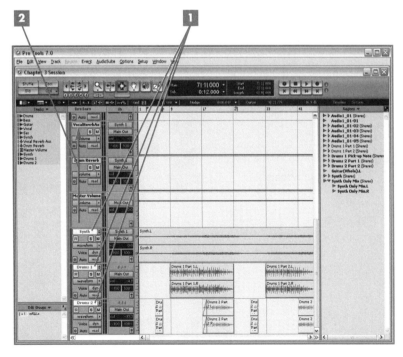

If you've been following the exercise throughout this chapter, you'll notice that we have two tracks named "synth." Let's delete the empty track, to avoid any confusion in the future:

1 Click the name of the track that you wish to delete (in this case, the empty Synth track).

2 Click on Track.

3 Click Delete. The track will be removed permanently.

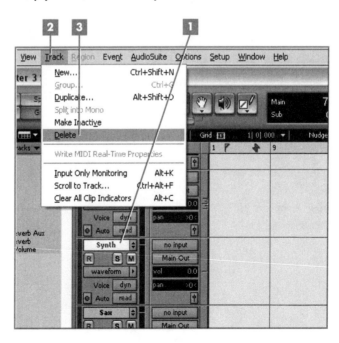

Muting and Soloing Tracks

Many readers probably know what these terms mean already, but here are some definitions for those who don't know what exactly Mute and Solo mean:

- ✳ Mute. Tracks that are muted will be inaudible.
- ✳ Solo. Tracks that are soloed will be heard, and any non-soloed tracks will be inaudible.

Muting a Track

1 Click on the M button to silence a given track. In this case, the Drums track will be removed from the mix.

2 Click on the Go to Start button, then click the Play button. Playback will begin from the beginning of the session. You should hear all un-muted tracks (in this case, the Drums track).

Soloing a Track

1 Click on the S button to listen to a single track in your session. In this case, you will hear a bass part only. All other tracks will be shown as muted.

2 Click on the S button again to un-solo the track.

✳ **TIP**

Clicking the S button on multiple tracks will allow you to solo more than one track at a time.

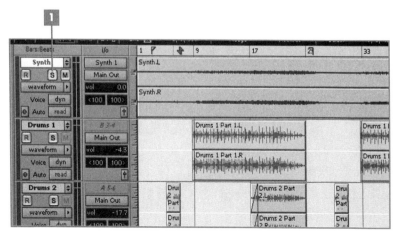

✳✳✳

Playing a Selection

Playing a selection may just be the easiest process of them all!

1 With the Selector tool selected, click and drag over a section of any region in your session. The area you select will appear dark.

❄ **NOTE**

Note that the selection you make is also shown in the Timeline.

2 Click on the Play button to play the selection one time.

❄ **TIP**

Here's a useful shortcut: You can press the spacebar instead of clicking on the Play button to play the selection.

Here's another way to play a selection:

1 Click on Options. The Options menu will appear.

2 Select Loop Playback. The option will be set.

3 Click on the Play button (or press the spacebar) to begin loop playback of your selection. The selection will repeat until you press the Stop button (or until you press the spacebar again).

Good work! Next—recording!

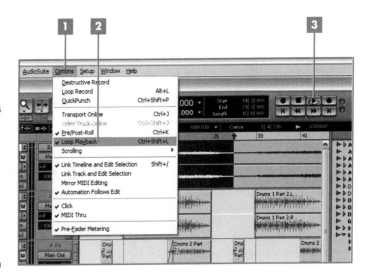

❄ **TIP**

Here's a useful shortcut to activate loop playback: In the Transport window, right-click on the Play button (PC), or hold the Control key and click on the Play button (Mac).

4 } Recording Audio

Everything we've talked about up to this point is crucial to being an informed Pro Tools user. Sooner or later, though, you'll want to move beyond simply importing audio and actually *record* an audio performance! No problem—this is another area where Pro Tools shines, and the flexibility this software affords has helped it earn its place as a leader in the field. In this chapter, you'll learn how to:

* Set up a click track
* Make your first recording
* Use punch-in/punch-out recording and other recording options
* Make the most of your monitoring options

Getting Started:
Signal Flow 101

You took a good first look at the Edit window in Chapters 1 and 2. Now it's time to take a closer look. First, though, you'll need to create a new session. (See Chapter 1 for a complete rundown of this process.)

If you don't have any musicians on hand to record, don't worry, we've got you covered. Included in the online content you've used before, you'll find audio files for use in Chapter 4. Just download the files and burn them to an audio CD, MP3 Player, or other external playback device. Once that's done, play back the audio from the external device and route it into one of the inputs of your Digidesign audio interface to simulate an actual recording situation.

1 After you launch the Pro Tools application, click on File. The File menu will appear.

2 Click on New Session. The Name the Session dialog box will open.

3 Choose **your new session's** name, location, **and** settings, **and then** click on Save. **Your new session will be created by Pro Tools.**

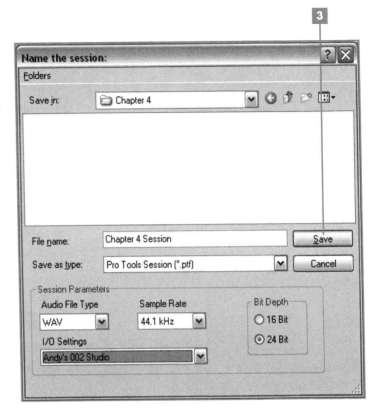

✻ **NOTE**

Take special note of the I/O settings. By default, Pro Tools' Name the Session dialog box opens with Last Used as an I/O setting. These are the settings that were last used by Pro Tools on this system. Of course, you might not know what settings you'll get, especially in a multi-user facility. Generally speaking, you'll want to specify an I/O setting of your own (like the I/O settings you created in Chapter 3).

If you're going to record audio, you need to create an audio track on which to record.

1 Click on Track and New. The New Tracks dialog box will open.

2 Click on Create. A single mono audio track will be created.

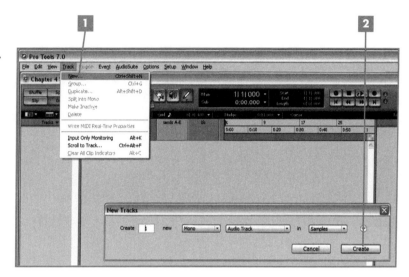

3 Double-click on the track name, and type a descriptive name for the track in the Name the Track text box.

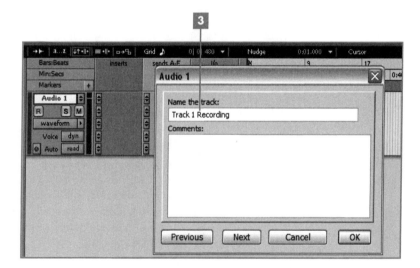

How I/O Settings Affect Your Session

It's time for the work you put into your I/O settings to start paying off. The configuration of the I/O Setup window (and any customizations you've made) will determine how your tracks receive and output audio.

Setting Up the Output

There is an output assignment button in the I/O column of each track. By default, each track will be assigned according to the Default Output setting in the I/O Setup dialog box. In a typical studio setup, this output will be connected to your studio monitors. If you want to change the output assignments, however, changing the output is easy—just follow these steps.

1 Click **on the** Output button for any track. An output drop-down menu will appear.

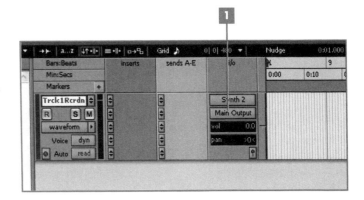

2 Click **on** Interface. A submenu will appear from which you can select any output path or sub-path you created earlier in your I/O setup.

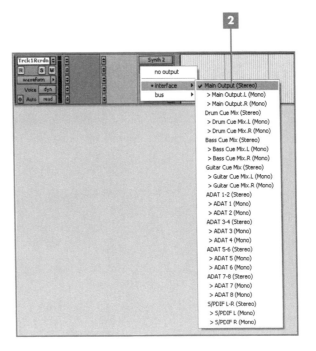

Setting Up the Input

The top button in the I/O column of each track shows the input of the track. You can click on the button to select an input.

1 Click on the Input button. A drop-down menu will appear.

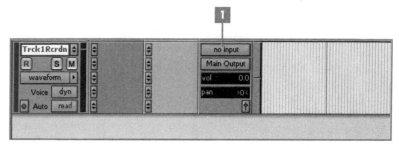

2 Click on the physical input or bus that your audio will be coming from (as specified in your I/O settings). The input will be selected.

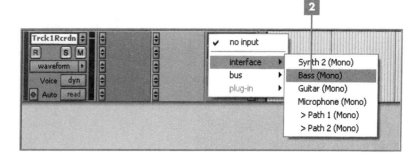

❋ **NOTE**

Since the track in this example is a mono track, only the mono input paths (and sub-paths) you created will be displayed.

Setting the Output Volume

The third field shows the volume of the track's output. You can adjust the volume by clicking in this field.

1 Click in the Volume field. A volume fader will appear.

2 Click and drag the fader to the volume level you desire, and then release the mouse button. The volume will be adjusted.

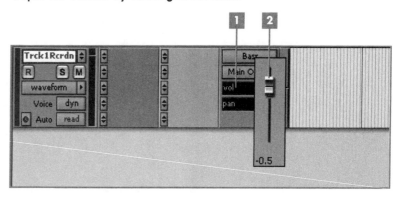

Setting the Output Pan

The fourth field shows the pan (placement of the audio between the left and right speakers) of the track's output. You can adjust this setting by clicking in the field.

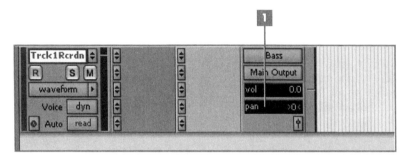

1 Click in the Pan field. A small slider will appear.

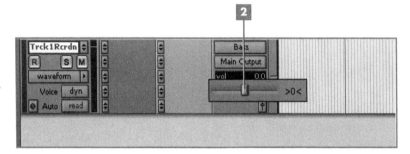

2 Click and drag the slider bar to the pan you desire, and then release the mouse button. The output pan will be set.

❊ **NOTE**

The output volume and output pan control the track's output only, not the input level. This means that to avoid clipping when recording, you'll want to bring down the level of your sound source (instrument, microphone, and so on) rather than the volume fader on the track.

Using an Output Window

There's another way to view and manipulate this essential track-related data. An Output Window (also commonly called a "tear-away strip") allows you to adjust many of your track's parameters within a single mixer-like format:

1. Click on the icon beneath the output pan display. (The icon looks like a tiny fader.)

   A track tear-away strip will appear. Note that much of the track-related data you've set up on the track is shown here as well:

   a Track name

   b Input button

   c Output button

   d Pan knob

   e Volume fader, with a volume meter to its right

   f Mute button

   g Solo button

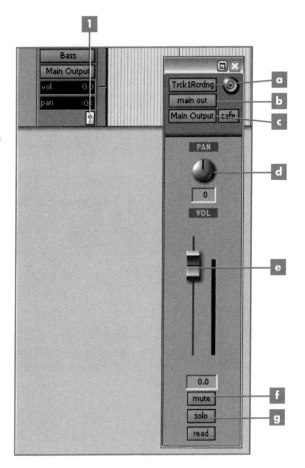

You can click on the input or output buttons and assign those in the same way you did in the track itself, or you can use the pan knob or volume fader to change position or volume.

Setting Up a Click Track

You might be wondering just what a click track is. Fair question—even though it's is a fairly common term, it's surprising how many musicians don't know what a click track is or what it's used for. The answer: A click track is an audible track in a multitrack environment that indicates the tempo of a song through a series of short tones (usually click sounds, hence the name). This is much the same way that a metronome helps a musician keep tempo in the practice room. This feature is not specific to Pro Tools—indeed, click tracks have been used for decades, dating back to the earliest analog recording studios, when multiple musicians would all listen to the same click track on their headphones as they played, in order to stay in time with each other.

Although you certainly won't need a click track every time you work with Pro Tools, you'll find that click tracks are a convenient way to keep everything in sync as you add track upon track to a complex session. Especially suited to music-oriented work, click tracks are very common in studios worldwide, and the ability to work with them is considered an essential skill.

More Signal Flow:
Audio Tracks versus Aux Tracks

Your click track will be an aux track. Why? Go ahead and create an aux track, and you'll see what makes it different from an audio track.

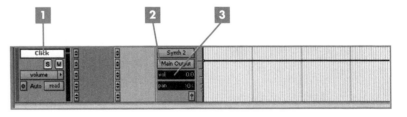

1 Create a mono aux track named Click. (See Chapter 3 if you need a quick review of how to create a mono aux track.)

2 Assign the outputs so you can hear the track through your monitor speakers.

3 Set the output volume to unity (0.0).

Notice that the aux track is virtually identical to the audio track above it. In fact, audio tracks and aux tracks are closely related. However, even though an aux track is an *audible* track, it certainly isn't an audio track. The main difference between the two is that an audio track can play back regions in your session (as you've already seen), whereas an aux track cannot. To play back audio regions, an audio track uses voices. (A *voice* is loosely defined as a channel of audio going to or coming from your hard drive.) Mono audio tracks use one voice and stereo audio tracks use two, up to a maximum of 32 active voices in a Pro Tools LE system.

The most significant difference between an audio track and an aux track is that an aux track doesn't use a voice, which means you can't use audio regions on an aux track. However, because an aux track doesn't eat up one of your session's 32 voices, using an aux track whenever possible (like, for example, for a click track) will conserve resources so you can get the maximum performance out of your system.

You can start by using your newly created aux track for a click track.

Using the Click Plug-In

Plug-ins are programs that run within your Pro Tools system. They can be anything from virtual effects, such as reverbs and equalization, to virtual instruments, such as the click plug-in, which plays click sounds. In this case, the plug-in will create a click for your session. You'll learn more about plug-ins in Chapter 8.

1 You will need to use an insert to launch your plug-in. Click on one of the five available insert selector buttons on your aux track. An insert menu will appear.

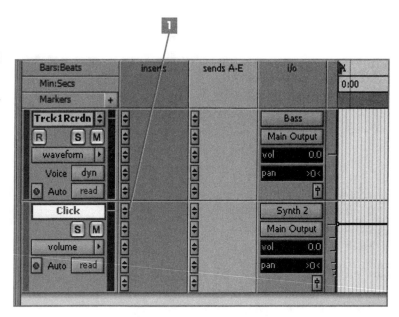

Setting Up a Click Track

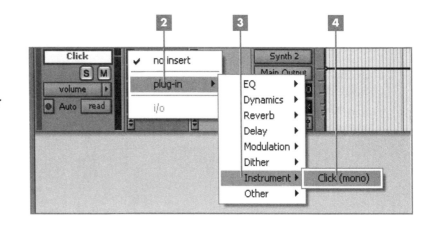

2 Choose Plug-in. **A submenu will appear.**

3 Choose Instrument. **Another submenu will appear.**

4 Click **on** Click (mono). **The Click plug-in window will appear.**

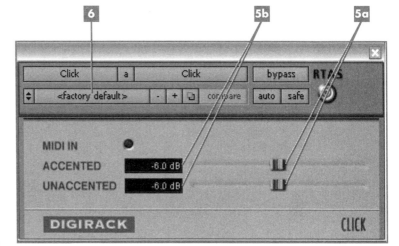

5a Adjust **the** Accented **(for each measure's beat 1) and** Unaccented **(for the other beats)** sliders **to get the best overall volume. You can change these values at any time in your session.**

OR

5b Type **a** value **in the Accented or Unaccented field to adjust the values manually.** Press **the** Enter key **when you're finished to confirm you entry.**

6 Click **on the** plug-in preset name. **A preset drop-down menu will appear, from which you can choose a tone for your click.**

7 Choose a tone for your click track. The tone will be selected. Again, you can change this choice at any time in your session.

8 When you're finished, click on the Close button. The Click plug-in window will close.

9 If you want to change your settings as you work, click on the Insert button to reopen the Click plug-in window.

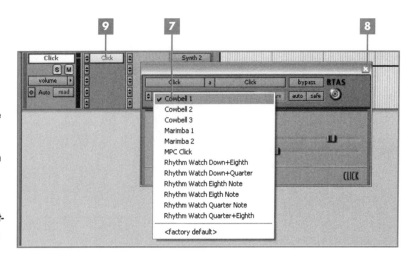

Setting Click and Tempo Options

The final thing you need to do is set up how your click track will behave.

1 Click on Setup. The Setup menu will appear.

2 Choose Click. The Click/Countoff Options dialog box will open. This dialog box controls when the click will play.

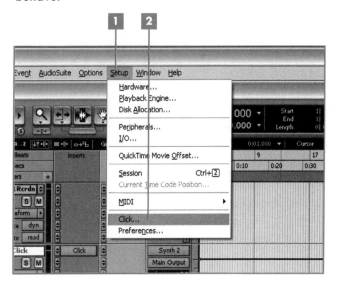

❄ **TIP**

Another way to access the Click/Countoff Options dialog box is to double-click on the Metronome icon in the Transport window.

3 You'll see that the Only During Record radio button is selected by default. This means that you'll hear the click when you're recording audio, but when you're playing back the click won't be heard. Generally, this is a common way to use a click, so we'll leave this mode selected.

4 You have the option of sending click information to a MIDI synthesizer (which we'll discuss more in Chapter 7, "Using MIDI"). In the case of using a MIDI synth for a click, you'll want to enter specific notes, velocities, and durations for the Accented and Unaccented fields according to the layout of your specific MIDI device. Since the click plug-in isn't a MIDI synthesizer per se, you won't need to make any changes in this case.

5 Again, if you're using a MIDI synthesizer for your click source, you'll need to click on the Output menu and select a MIDI output port for your click information. The option will be selected.

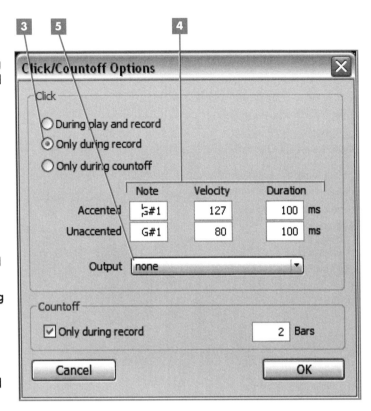

❊ **TIP**

If you're using the click plug-in, you don't need to worry about assigning a MIDI output.

6 Select the Only During Record check box to ensure that your countoff will only be heard before recording. During regular playback, you won't be bothered with the countoff.

7 Enter the number of bars you want for your countoff in the Bars field. Two measures is a common setting.

8 Click on OK. The Click/Countoff Options dialog box will close.

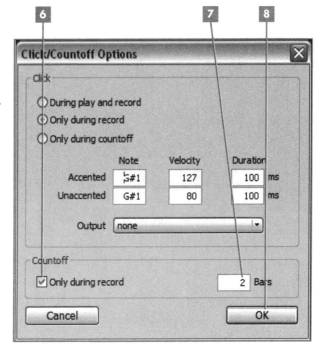

Now that the parameters of the click have been set up, you'll want to make sure that the click is actually enabled. To do this, you'll need to open the Transport window (you can launch it from the Window drop-down menu).

9 Click on the Metronome icon in the Transport window to activate the click, if it isn't already selected. The icon will be highlighted.

10 Click on the Countoff icon in the Transport window, if it isn't already selected. The icon will be highlighted. (Remember, you can disable the countoff at any time by deselecting this icon.)

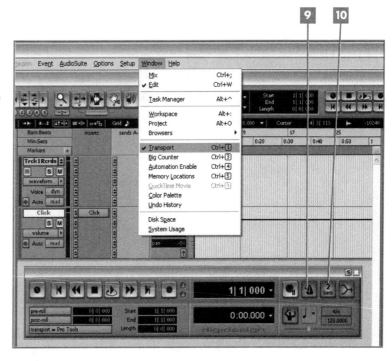

11 Deselect the Conductor icon. The tempo slider will appear solid now.

12a Use the tempo slider to set the desired tempo. The tempo value (shown in green in the lower-right corner) will change accordingly.

OR

12b Click the tempo value area, and type a tempo in the numeric tempo value field.

❄ **TIP**

Here's another way to enter a tempo: You can click the tempo numeric display, and then press the T key on your computer keyboard in tempo. The numeric display will change to reflect the tempo of your clicks. You can cycle through the beats as many times as you want until you settle upon the tempo you want to use.

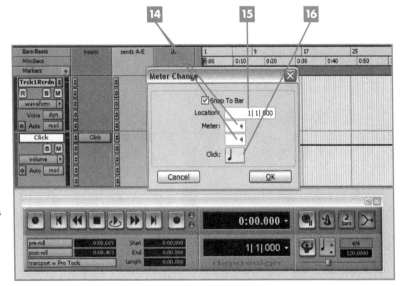

13 Double-click on the meter display to change the meter. The Meter Change dialog box will open.

14 Type a value in the Meter field to select the meter you want to use.

15 Type a location value in the Location field to change meters throughout your music. The value in this field is displayed in bars|beats|ticks.

16 Now let's determine which kind of note will be the resolution of your click track. Click on the Note icon. The Note menu will appear.

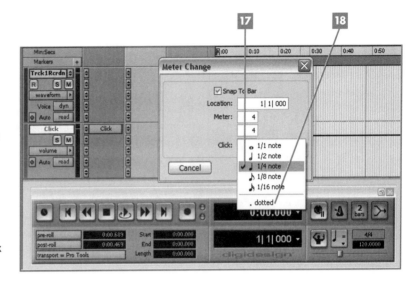

17 Click on the note value that matches the desired value of your click. The value will be selected.

18 Click on dotted if you want to use a dotted-note value for your click. The option will be selected.

19 Click on OK. Your meter changes will be applied, and the Meter Change dialog box will close.

Basic Recording

You're all set—let's go! Now you're ready to record some audio from the outside world into the Pro Tools environment.

 NOTE

Here's where your downloaded audio files can help out. You can burn them to an audio CD or MP3 player, or even play them from your computer's sound card. After you start recording, just start playing the files, and you can record them into an available input on your Mbox or 002 (just make sure that you're familiar with the input assignments in your I/O settings window).

1 Click on the R button to arm the desired track for recording. The track will be armed.

2 Click on the Record button in the Transport window (or the Edit window's transport section). The Record button will begin to flash.

3 Click on the Play button. Recording will begin. As you record, Pro Tools will display the incoming waveform.

❋ **TIP**

The shortcut for record/play is Ctrl+spacebar (PC) or ⌘+spacebar (Mac).

4 Click on the Stop button when you want to stop your recording. An audio region will be created in your track.

5 A new region will be shown in the track, and also will be listed in the Regions list.

6 Before you listen to your track, click the R button, and make sure the Record button is not highlighted and the track is not armed.

7 Click on the Play button. You will hear your newly created track.

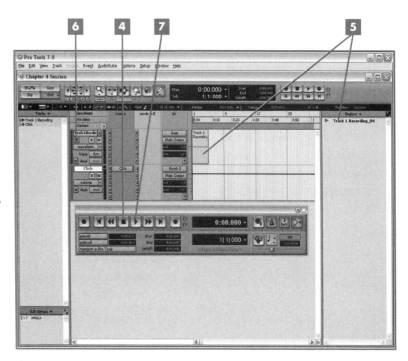

Other Recording Options

Congratulations! You've taken another important step down the road of Pro Tools use. Now I want to explore some different ways to record audio that can come in useful when you need to accomplish specific goals.

Punching In and Punching Out

Suppose you recorded a perfect tape, except for that one measure! Not a problem when you're working with Pro Tools; you can specify a segment of your audio and replace it. Remember, too, that Pro Tools operates non-destructively, so you don't have to worry about losing your original take!

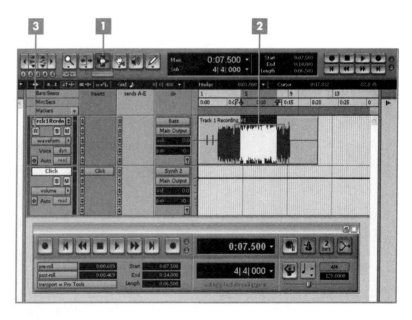

1 Click on the Selector tool. The tool will be highlighted.

2 Mark the area of audio upon which you want to re-record by clicking and dragging.

3 Click on the R button on the audio track you want to re-record. The track will be armed for recording. You'll note that the selection in the Rulers area, which is usually bordered by blue arrows, is now bordered by red arrows.

※ **TIP**

There is another way to make your selection. While you're playing back your track, press the down arrow key to begin your selection and the up arrow key to end your selection.

4 If you want to hear a little bit of your original track before or after your punch in/out, you'll want to set up a pre-roll and/or a post-roll. Click on pre-roll. The option will be enabled.

5 Click inside the text box to the right of the pre-roll button and type the length of your pre-roll value.

6 Press Enter to confirm your entry. Bear in mind that the scale of this value follows the Main Counter display. A small green flag in the Rulers area will represent your enabled pre-roll.

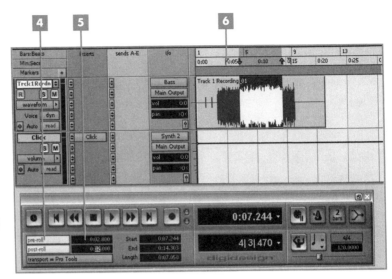

7 Click on post-roll. The option will be enabled.

8 Click inside the text box to the right of the post-roll button and type the length of your post-roll value.

9 Press Enter to confirm your entry. Bear in mind that the scale of this value follows the Main Counter display. A small green flag in the Rulers area will represent your enabled post-roll.

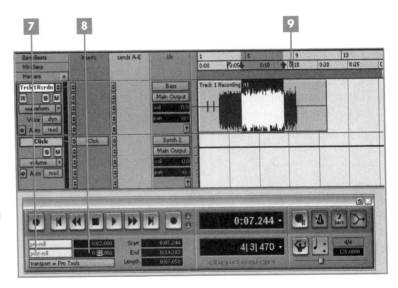

10 Click on the Record button.

11 Click on the Play button. Play will begin at the pre-roll location because you selected a pre-roll.

12 When the timeline insertion reaches the selected area, Pro Tools will begin recording and will continue recording until the end of the selection. Pro Tools will then exit recording mode and continue playing for the post-roll duration. When the playline reaches the end of the post-roll duration, it will stop playing.

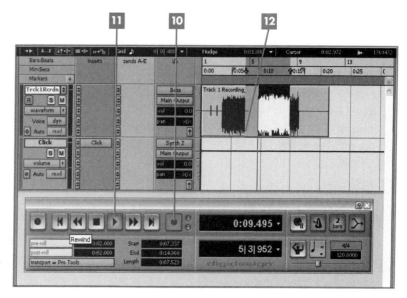

Here's what you'll end up with:

a Your original region has been split into two other regions.

b Both regions now appear in the Regions list. However, these regions are not shown in bold text because they are only incomplete parts of a whole file.

c Your punch has been recorded as a new region. For this example, I've recorded silence for visual effect.

d Your punch region appears in bold text because it is a whole file region, which means that it represents an entire file in your Audio Files folder.

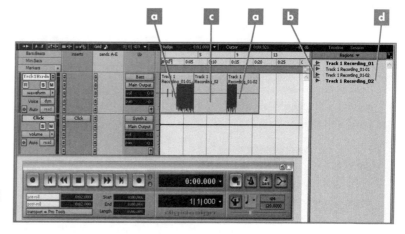

QuickPunch Recording

The main limitation of basic punch-in and punch-out is that it's a one-shot thing. So what if you want to make a single pass, but you want to punch in and out more than once? QuickPunch is for you! There are a couple ways to get into QuickPunch mode.

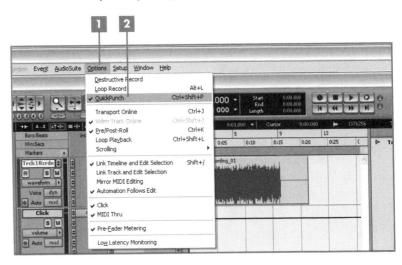

1. Click on Options. The Options menu will appear.

2. Click on QuickPunch. The QuickPunch feature will be enabled, indicated by a letter P displayed on the Record button.

3. Click on the R button on the audio track you want to re-record.

4. Click on the Play button at a point prior to when you want to record new audio (in this case, I'm starting from the beginning of the session). Your session will play as normal.

5. Click on the Record button when you want to begin recording. Recording will start.

6. Click on the Record button again when you want to stop recording. Recording will stop. To toggle recording, simply click the Record button.

❋ TIP

Here's another way to access QuickPunch mode: Right-click on the Record button (PC) or hold the Ctrl key while clicking on the Record button (Mac) to scroll through various recording modes. QuickPunch mode is indicated by a P on the red Record button.

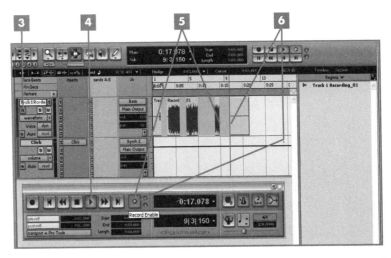

> ❋ **TIP**
>
> Here's another way to punch in and punch out in QuickPunch mode: During playback, press Ctrl+spacebar (PC) or ⌘+spacebar (Mac).

Here's what you'll end up with:

a New regions will be created in your track to reflect each time you engaged and disengaged recording.

b As you might expect, new regions will also be added to the Regions list. The regions created in the track are not whole file regions. They are regions of a larger file.

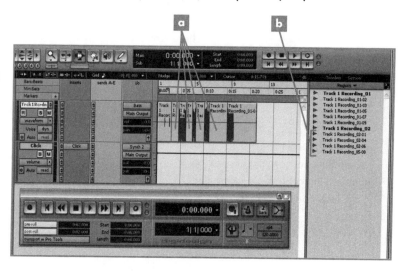

Loop Recording

Suppose you want to record several passes of a certain section (a guitar solo, for example), and then pick the best one. You'll want to use Pro Tools' Loop Record function.

1 Click on Options. The Options menu will appear.

2 Click on Loop Record. The Loop Record feature will be enabled.

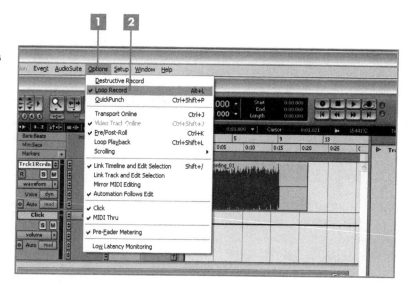

❋ ❋ ❋

3 Use the Selector tool to select the section you want to loop. The area will be selected.

4 Click on the R button on the audio track you want to re-record.

5 Click on the Record button.

6 Click on the Play button.

Playback will begin at the pre-roll position (if pre-roll is enabled). When the selection is reached, Pro Tools will begin recording audio. At the end of the selection, recording will begin again from the beginning of the selection (even if pre-roll is enabled).

7 When you've got enough takes, click on the Stop button. The latest take will appear in the selected area.

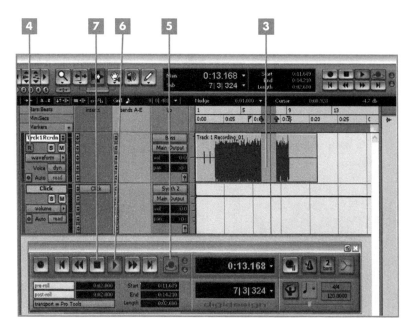

❊ **NOTE**

In the Audio Regions list, notice that there is a whole file region (in bold text) that contains all the takes in sequence. Although it is not specifically used in the track, it represents the parent file in which all the individual takes reside. Below the whole file region are individual takes numbered sequentially in the order in which they were recorded.

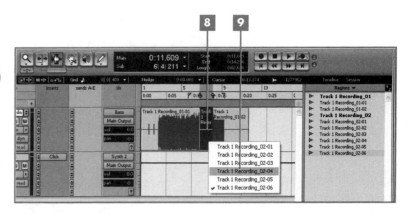

8 With the Selector tool chosen, Ctrl-click **(PC)** or ⌘-click **(Mac)** inside the region to reveal a drop-down menu that displays all the regions that have the same start time as the current region—in this case, all of your takes.

9 Click on the take you want to use. The take will be selected, and the region replaced. This is a great way to audition different takes to find just the right one!

For the Brave: Destructive Recording

Thus far, you've only seen non-destructive recording, meaning that you never actually erase any audio in the process of punching in, punching out, or looping, and you can always undo your recording with no loss. This is a huge advantage over working with tape, and was one of the initial attractions to DAWs in general. You can, however, record directly into an audio file that you created earlier. Be careful, though; there's no way to undo what you've done if you make a mistake!

1 Click on Options. The Options menu will appear.

2 Click on Destructive Record. The Destructive Record feature will be enabled.

3 Use the Selector tool to select the section of the audio track that you want to overwrite. The area will be selected.

4 Click on the R button on the audio track you want to re-record.

5 Click on the Record button.

6 Click on the Play button.

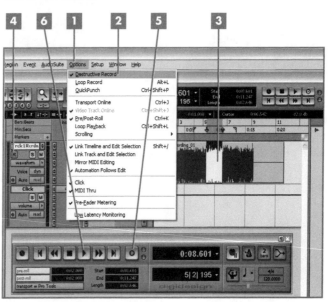

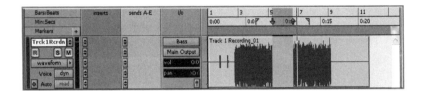

At this point, the process works exactly the same as basic punching in and punching out. Your session will begin playing at the pre-roll position (if you've enabled pre-roll), and then it will automatically begin recording at your selected area. It will stop recording at the end of your selection and play for the post-roll amount (if enabled). The real difference between destructive recording and the other modes becomes apparent when the dust has settled.

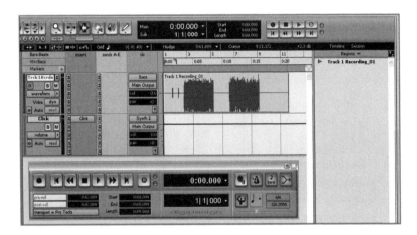

The important distinction between destructive recording and other modes is that no new regions have been created—in the track itself or in the Regions list. What you've done is permanently change the file you originally recorded!

Tips, Tricks, and Troubleshooting

Fantastic! You're on your way to running a great tracking session! This section includes a few final thoughts to call on when you need them.

Naming Tracks and Files

One very important thing to remember when it comes to good file management practices: The names of the regions that you record will follow the names of the tracks on which you're recording them. That means a track named Drums, for example, would yield recording passes named Drums_01, Drums_02, and so on.

That being said, the rule of thumb is to name your tracks *before* you record audio to them. However, if you ever forget to do this or if you ever want to change the name of a region after that region has been created, it's easy to do.

1. Double-click on the region you want to rename (either in the Regions list or in the track with the grabber tool selected). The Name dialog box will open.

2. Type the new name for the region in the Name the Region text box.

3. If the region is a whole file region, you have the option of naming the region in the session only or changing the name of the region *and* the file name as it appears on your hard drive. Click on Name Region Only (which will leave the audio file name unchanged) or Name Region and Disk File radio button to select an option, if available.

4. Click on OK. The Name dialog box will close and the region will be renamed.

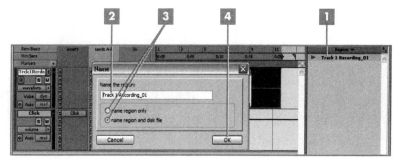

124

Understanding the Monitor Modes

In addition to all the different modes of recording that you've learned about, there are two monitor modes that affect how you hear your audio during the recording process. The two modes, called Auto Input Monitoring and Input Only Monitoring, will be useful in different situations.

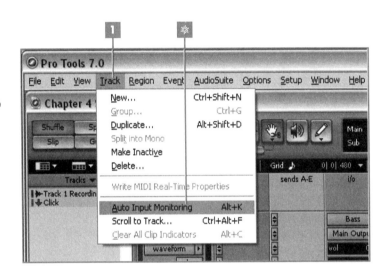

1 Click on Track. The Track menu will appear.

❀ The monitor mode that you're *not* in will be shown as an option in this menu.

2a Select Auto Input Monitoring if you want to hear what you previously recorded right up to your punch-in point. Pro Tools will behave as if it is in playback mode during pre-roll and post-roll periods, and will automatically switch over to monitoring your input only during the selected overdub area.

❀ A green light to the right of the transport controls (in the Edit window or the Transport window) will not be illuminated when you're in Auto Input Monitoring mode.

OR

2b Select Input Only Monitoring if you don't want to hear what you've already recorded during a punch-in/punch-out situation. Pro Tools will still only record during the selected area, but for the pre-roll and post-roll durations, you'll hear the live input rather than the previously recorded audio on the track.

❋ A green light to the right of the transport controls (in the Edit window or the Transport window) will illuminate to signal that you're in this mode.

Low Latency Monitoring—and a Trick!

When you are recording, you might notice a bit of delay (called *latency*) between the time a note is played and the time it is heard through monitors or headphones. The bad news is that this is the normal functioning of host-based DAWs in general, a by-product of the conversion of analog and digital audio. The good news is that there's a solution to this problem in Pro Tools, called *low latency monitoring*. This monitoring mode minimizes the process of running audio through the host computer's CPU, reducing the delay you hear.

1 Click on Options. The Options menu will appear.

2 Click on Low Latency Monitoring. The good news is that your latency problem just got a lot better.

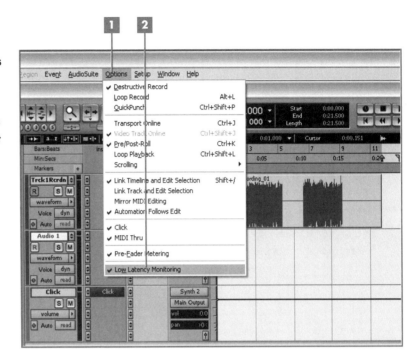

The bad news (you knew there'd be some, right?) is that the click plug-in has turned dark, indicating that the plug-in has become inactive. This is the price of low latency monitoring—plug-ins become inactive. Does that mean you have lost the use of your click? Yes and no—read on!

Because the click plug-in won't work in this mode, you need to figure out another way to hear it. The solution to this problem is to bounce—in other words, record—from one track to another. Because this bounce is internal (entirely within the Pro Tools environment), you can use a bus to make this transfer. I'll go deeper into the application of such concepts in Chapter 8, but for now let's just solve the problem!

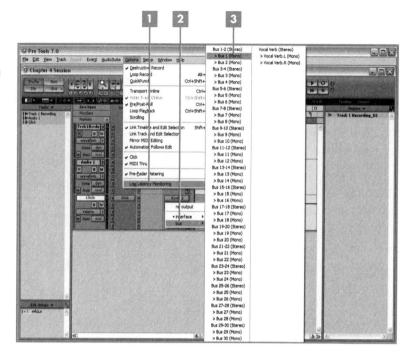

1 First, make sure that you're not in Low Latency Monitoring mode, as shown here (indicated with no check by the menu item).

2 Click on the click track's output. A pop-up menu will appear.

3 Choose an unused mono bus. In a session, already used buses appear in bold text.

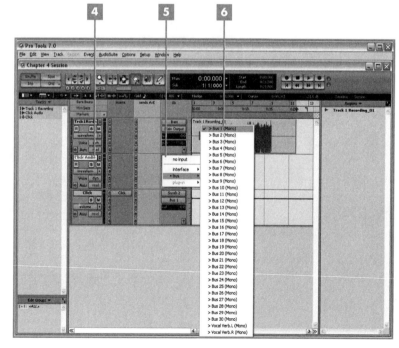

4 Create a mono audio track and name it descriptively.

5 Now you need to set the input so you can record from the click track. Click on the track's Input button. A pop-up menu will appear.

6 Choose the same bus you selected for the click track's output. The bus will be selected.

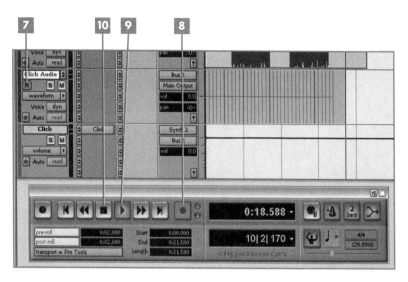

7 Click on the R button. The track will be armed for recording.

8 Click on the Record button.

9 Click on the Play button. Recording will begin on the audio track. Whereas the click plug-in creates the click in real time, the click track will be recorded as audio on the audio track.

10 Click on the Stop button when you've recorded enough of the click. The recording will stop.

❋ **TIP**

Make sure you deselect the R button on any other armed tracks in your session, or you'll be recording on them as well!

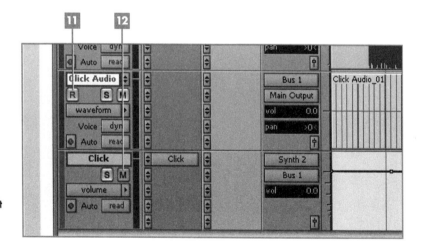

11 Click on the R button again. The click audio track will be disarmed.

12 Mute the click aux track. The track will be muted.

❋ **NOTE**

Alternatively, you can delete the click aux track entirely. You don't need it anymore!

You will now hear your click even when you're in low latency mode!

Mbox and Mbox 2 No Latency Operation

If you're working with an Mbox audio interface, you'll notice that Pro Tools doesn't give you a low latency monitoring option. Does that mean you're out of luck? No way! The solution lies in the Mbox's Mix knob, which is second from the bottom on the front of your Mbox, or the third knob from the headphone output of the Mbox 2. When the knob is all the way to the input side, you'll monitor signal coming directly into the interface only, and you won't hear the Pro Tools software at all. When the Mix knob is set all the way to playback, you'll only hear audio coming from Pro Tools. Here's how to eliminate the latency problem using the Mbox's mix knob:

1 Set the mix knob to twelve o'clock as a starting point, giving you an even balance between input and playback.

2 Record arm the audio track on which you want to record. Now if you play, you should hear a doubled signal. (The earlier signal is from the input side of the mix; the latent (delayed) signal is coming from the Pro Tools software, routed through the playback side of the mix.)

3 Mute the track on which you want to record on. You can still record onto the track, but you won't hear that annoying delayed signal.

4 Adjust the Mix knob to get the desired balance between your live input and the Pro Tools software playback.

5 Record as normal.

6 When you're finished recording, you can change your mix to playback so you won't be distracted by any audio going into your Mbox or Mbox 2.

NOTE
This is an elegantly simple solution to a significant problem with DAWs. You'll even be able to use your click plug-in!

NOTE
Included with this chapter's download materials are a number of audio files that together can be played back as a complete mix. If you record all these files into your session (from a burned CD, MP3 player, or from your computer's sound card's output), you'll be able to use it in Chapter 8, when you learn about mixing.

Next step—editing!

5 } Editing

Production can be broken down into a number of phases—tracking (recording), editing, mixing, and mastering, to name but a few. Because it's a computer-based workstation, Pro Tools perhaps shines brightest in the editing phase. In its non-linear environment, you can accomplish in seconds what used to take minutes or hours with a tape-based system. And of course, there is always the Undo function if you make a mistake. Even better news, Pro Tools 7 has introduced a number of impressive new editing features that will make your work even more fun! In this chapter, you'll learn how to:

❋ Take full advantage of the functions of the Edit window

❋ Use Pro Tools' edit modes to their greatest advantage

❋ Work with Pro Tools' basic editing features

❋ Use processes such as cut, copy, and paste to create your own arrangements

Understanding the Edit Window

You took a good first look at the Edit window in the previous chapters, and now it's time for a closer examination of this powerful window. For the purposes of this chapter, I'll be reconstructing a song from rough elements, so if you want to follow the screen shots, please download the Chapter 5 Session data from the *Pro Tools LE 7 Ignite!* Web site at www.courseptr.com/downloads.

Using the Tools of the Trade

Some of Pro Tools' most useful tools are located in the top row of the Edit window.

* In the upper-left corner are the four edit modes—Shuffle, Spot, Slip, and Grid. The mode you choose will determine the manner in which regions can be moved in time in your session. You'll learn more about these modes in the section "Moving Regions on the Timeline: The Edit Modes" later in this chapter.

* Moving to the right, you'll see the zoom tools. These will allow you to zero in on a very brief section of your session (useful for fine editing) or zoom out to view longer sections in your project. You can also zoom in or out using other methods, which will enable you to view your regions in different ways. I'll discuss this more in the next section of this chapter.

❋ These are the most popular editing tools in the Pro Tools arsenal. From left to right, the tools are Zoom, Trim, Selector, Grabber, Scrub, and Pencil. These tools operate directly on specific regions within your session.

❋ Last but not least are the location displays. To the left you'll see a Main and a Sub display. Both of these displays show you exactly where you are in your session. To the right are the Start, End, and Length displays, which show you the beginning, end, and duration of your selections.

Navigating

Before you can do anything else, you need to know the basics of how to get around. You'll find that the Selector tool is best suited to this task. Along with this tool, you need to use the location displays so you know where you are.

1 Click on the Selector tool. The tool will be selected.

2 Click on the arrow to the right of the Main time display. A drop-down menu will appear.

3 Choose the desired scale with which you wish to navigate through your session. For the purposes of this example, choose Bars:Beats. The time scale of the Main display will change to reflect your selection.

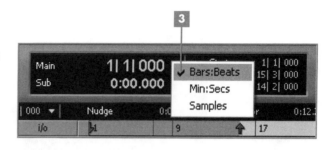

✻ NOTE

The scale of the selection display (to the right of the Main and Sub location displays) will change to match the Main display's scale. For example, if you change the scale to Bars:Beats, the Main time display will count your session as it plays in bars and beats. When you make a selection, that selection will also be shown in bars and beats.

4 Click on the arrow to the right of the Sub time display. A drop-down menu will appear.

5 Choose any time scale for this display. You can choose a different scale than the one in the Main display; that way, you can view your session in two different ways simultaneously.

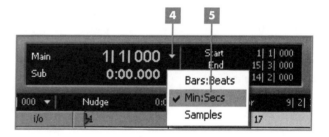

6 Click anywhere in the session's Edit area. A small line (called a *timeline insertion*) will appear where you clicked. Also, a small blue figure will appear at this location in your Rulers area.

In the Main and Sub time displays, your timeline insertion's location is precisely displayed.

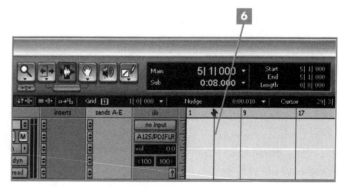

Also, the selection display will show the timeline insertion location. Because you've selected only a single location, the Start and End values are identical and the Length value is zero.

Now, try to make a different kind of selection.

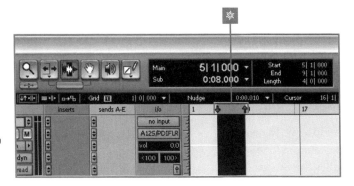

❄ Click and drag in the Track area to make a selection with a length greater than zero. The wider your selection, the more time you've selected.

In addition to the selection you make in the Track area, a selection is made in the Rulers area. This time, however, the blue figure has split apart into a down arrow (indicating the beginning of the selection) and an up arrow (indicating the end).

The Main and Sub time displays will show the start of your selection.

The selection display will show the start, end, and length of your selection.

Here are a couple more ways to get around, this time using the Tab key.

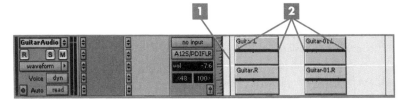

1 Still using the Selector tool, click on a track with a number of regions, before any (or all) regions. A timeline insertion will appear where you click.

2 Press the Tab key. The timeline insertion will move to the next region boundary (the start or end of a region).

Each time you press the Tab key, the timeline insertion will move to the next region boundary.

❄ **TIP**
Here's a twist on using the Tab key: Hold the Alt key (PC) or the Option key (Mac) while you press the Tab key to move the timeline insertion to the previous region boundary.

Here's another way to use the Tab key.

1. Click on the Tab to Transients button. The option will be selected.

2. Click once on a region with audio to move the timeline insertion. The timeline insertion will be moved.

3. Press the Tab key. This time, instead of moving to region boundaries, the timeline insertion will jump from transient to transient.

❋ TIP

Again, the Alt key (PC) or the Option key (Mac) will move the timeline insertion backward in time.

❋ NOTE

So what the heck *is* a transient anyway? Simply put, a transient is the initial high-energy peak at the beginning of a waveform, such as one caused by the percussive action of a pick or hammer hitting a string. Different types of instruments have different kinds of transients, but they tend to be good visual cues when editing, indicating the beginnings of notes (or words, in the case of a spoken track).

When you're using the Tab to Transient button, you might want to get a closer look at the audio. That's where zooming comes in!

Zooming

Sometimes when you're editing, you'll want to get a close look at your audio. When you're finished, you might want to get an overview of your entire session. To do this, you need to know how to use the zoom tools.

1 Click on the left zoom arrow to zoom out. Each time you click on this button, your view will encompass a greater span of time.

2 Click on the right zoom arrow to zoom in. Each time you click on this button, you will gain a finer view of your session.

❊ **TIP**

You might use these shortcuts more than any others covered in this book: On PCs, it's Ctrl+] (right bracket) to zoom in and Ctrl+[(left bracket) to zoom out. On Macs, ⌘+] will zoom in and ⌘+[will zoom out.

Here's another way to zoom in on a specific section.

1 Click on the Zoom tool. The tool will be selected.

2 Click and drag on a track to select an area. The area will be selected.

3 Release the mouse button. The view will zoom in on the selected area.

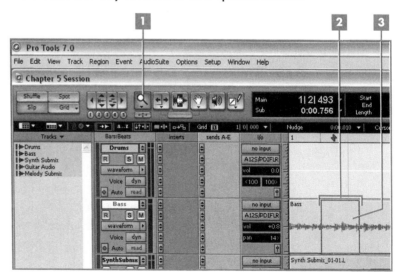

Moving Regions on the Timeline: The Edit Modes

Pro Tools has four edit modes that determine how regions behave in your session. Each mode is unique, and soon you will get a feeling for which mode is best suited to a given task. For the purposes of illustration, we'll work with the drum track of this session.

Using Slip Mode

When you need it, Slip mode gives you the most freedom of motion with your regions.

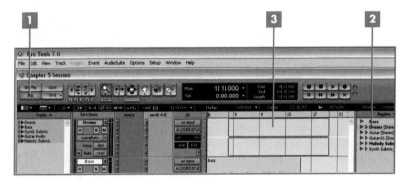

1 Click on the Slip mode button. The mode will be selected.

2 Click and hold a region in the Regions list. The region will be selected.

3 Drag the region onto a track. You will see an outline of the region, indicating where it will be placed when you release the mouse button.

NOTE

It is important to remember that when you're working with mono regions, you can only drop them onto mono tracks. On the other hand, when you drag stereo regions onto the Timeline, they can occupy a single stereo track or two mono tracks.

Using Grid Mode

Sometimes it is convenient to have your regions snap to predetermined increments or grids. This can be particularly useful when you're working on a music-based project, when it's important to have your regions align themselves to bars and beats.

First (if you haven't done so already), you should set up your Main location display and Grid value so you can maximize the effectiveness of this mode.

❄ **NOTE**

If you're following the chapter, you should have a selected region on your drum track that you deposited while using Slip mode. Let's get that region out of there before we move on. Since the region is selected, all you have to do is press the Delete key to remove it (note that the region is still present in the Regions list, so you're not losing anything).

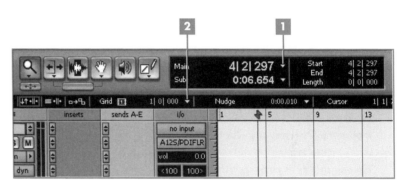

1 Click on the Main down arrow and change the Main location display to Bars:Beats. The scale will be shown in Bars | Beats | Ticks. Note that the selection display will also change scale.

2 Click on the Grid Value arrow. The Grid menu will appear.

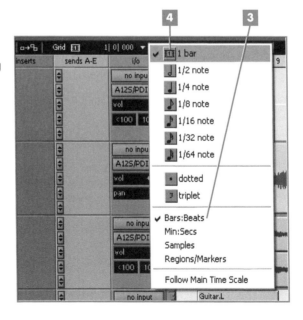

3 Select the desired scale of your grid. Since we're working with music, Bars:Beats is the one for this example. The option will be selected.

4 Choose the desired resolution for your grid. For our purposes here, 1 bar will do the trick. The option will be selected.

❄ **NOTE**

Because this scale is musical, you will see grid resolutions such as bars, half notes, quarter notes, and so on.

❄ **NOTE**

Notice that the Grid indicator to the left of the drop-down menu will change to match your choice.

5 Click on Grid. The mode will be selected.

6 Drag a region from the Regions list onto the Track area. The region will snap from bar to bar as you drag it.

7 As you drag the region, you'll notice that the selection display will reflect the beginning, end, and duration of the region. Because you're in Grid mode and your grid resolution is 1 bar, the start value will always change in one-measure increments.

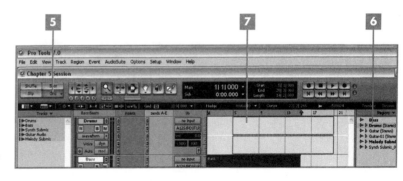

Using Shuffle Mode

Shuffle mode operates in a much different way than either Slip or Grid mode. In this mode, regions move end to end with each other. When you see how this mode works, you'll see how it can be useful for stitching together verses, choruses, and so on, into a seamless final product!

1 Click on Shuffle. The mode will be selected.

2 One by one, drag and drop various regions from the Regions list onto a single track. For the purposes of this demonstration, try dragging Guitar first, then Melody Submix, and finally Synth Submix. Wherever you drop these regions, they will snap end to end with the previous region, starting with the first region, which automatically snaps to the beginning of your track.

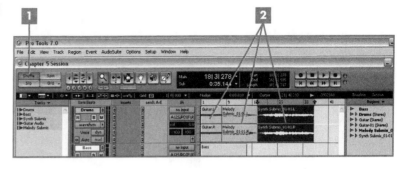

※ **NOTE**

Again, you should go ahead and delete the region that you've dragged onto the drum track while you worked with Grid mode—just hit the Delete key (assuming that the region is still selected). Also, you might want to zoom out a bit to see this mode in its best light.

3 Now you can actually "shuffle" the regions a bit. Click on the Grabber tool. The tool will be selected.

4 Click and hold on a region. The region will be selected.

5 Drag the region over another region on the track.

6 When a dark line appears at the beginning of the preceding region, release the mouse button to drop the region. The regions will be reorganized.

Note that all regions remain end to end, despite the fact that they have been moved. Of course, you can move more than one region at a time. In fact, you can shuffle regions forward and backward at will and create new arrangements of these regions, while keeping all the regions snugly end to end.

❉❉❉

Using Spot Mode

You can use Spot mode when you want to assign a region to a specific numeric value. This is of particular use when you're assigning audio to sync with video (also known as *spotting*). Although this mode lacks the freedom of motion of the other modes (by design), it is a quick way to place a region at a specific location.

❄ **TIP**

Once more, you'll want to clear the drum track for this section. This time, though, you'll have to clear all your regions, and here's a quick way to do it. With the Selector tool, triple-click anywhere in the track you wish to clear. All the regions in that track will be selected, and you can now remove them by pressing the Delete key.

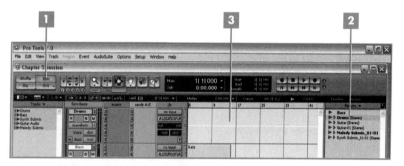

1. Click on the Spot button.

2. Select a region and drag it onto an appropriate track.

3. Release the mouse button to drop the region on the track. The Spot dialog box will open.

4. Click on the Time Scale button and select the timescale you want to use to position your region (you can choose Bars:Beats, Min:Secs, or Samples). The timescale will be selected.

5. Typically, you're most concerned about the start of the region. Type exactly where you want your region to start in the Start field.

6. Click on OK. The region will be placed on the track at the specified location.

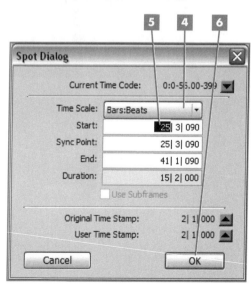

Basic Tool Functions

The three major edit tools you'll use are the Trim, Selector, and Grabber tools. We touched on some of these functions earlier, but lets go just a little deeper before you start putting them into action. I'll take them one at a time, from left to right.

Understanding the Trim Tool

The first tool in line is the Trim tool.

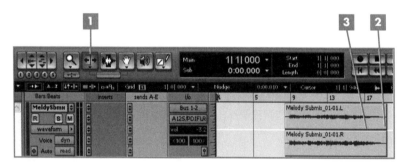

1 Click **on the** Trim tool. **The tool will be selected.**

2 Position **your** cursor **at the beginning or end of a region. The cursor will take on the appearance of a bracket, indicating that you're using the Trim tool.**

3 Click and drag **the region's edge. The region boundary will change.**

❄ **NOTE**

There are a few things to keep in mind when you're using the Trim tool.

- Trimming a region is non-destructive. The fact that you're trimming the region only changes the part of the audio file you are choosing to use in your session.

- Every time you use the Trim tool, a new region is created in the Regions list.

- When you're in Grid mode, your trimming will snap to the current grid values.

Understanding the Selector Tool

You already used the Selector tool to select a segment of your session to play. Now you're going to use it to clean up your session over a number of tracks.

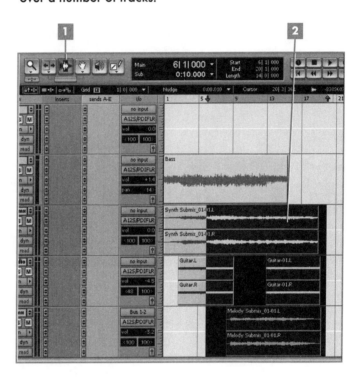

1 Click on the Selector tool. The tool will be selected.

2 Starting in one corner, click and drag a square area that includes regions you want to remove from your session. The regions will be selected.

3 Press the Delete key. The regions will be removed from your tracks.

> ❉ **NOTE**
>
> Remember that you're working in a non-destructive environment. The regions you clear from your tracks won't be removed from the Regions list or your hard drive. *Non-destructive* also means that you can easily undo what you've done (choose Undo from the Edit menu), which you should do right now!

Understanding the Grabber Tool

Finally you get to the Grabber tool. You've used it before, but this section will show you how to move more than one region at a time.

1 Click **on the** Grabber tool. **The tool will be selected.**

2 Click **on a** single region. **The region will be highlighted.**

3 Press and hold **the** Shift key **and** click **on** additional regions. **The regions will be highlighted.**

4 Drag and drop **the** regions **you selected. Take care, though—all regions that fall within your selection area will be moved as a group!**

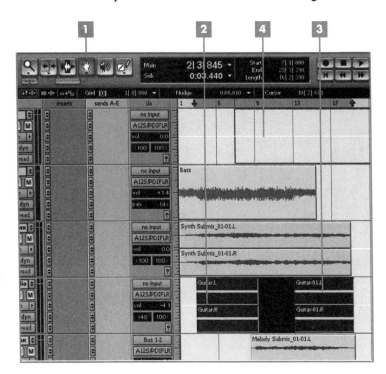

❉ **NOTE**

As you grab additional regions using the Grabber tool, a shaded area will appear. This area will include not only all the regions you directly selected, but also all regions that fall within that area.

❉ **NOTE**

Once more, please undo any changes you've made before progressing to the next section.

Basic Editing Operations

Now you're going to combine a number of tools you've already learned to use with a few new tricks to recreate the bass line from the Chapter 1 session. In addition to tools from this chapter, you'll be drawing on some knowledge you picked up in earlier chapters. Put it all together, and you'll have a good idea of how to put together tracks of your own!

Capturing a Selection

Here's the situation: In this example, you have a reference track named Bass, which simply contains a single region. Your task is to reconstruct the bass track from this single region.

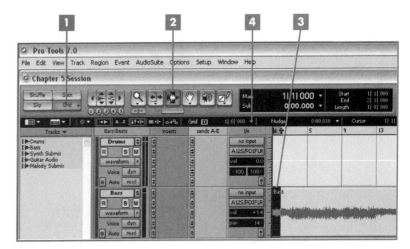

1 Click on Grid. The Grid mode will be selected.

2 Click on the Selector tool. The tool will be selected.

3 Double-check the grid resolution to make sure it is 1 bar.

4 Select the first measure on the Virus Bass Audio track. The measure will be selected.

5 Click on Region. The Region menu will appear.

6 Click on Capture. The Name dialog box will open.

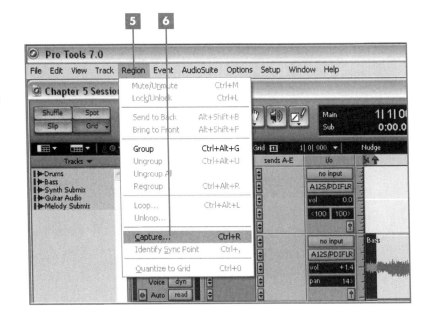

7 Type a descriptive name for the region you want to capture in the Name the Region text box.

8 Click on OK. The Name dialog box will close, and the new region and file that is a copy (or capture) of the area you selected will be created. You can see your newly created region in the Regions list.

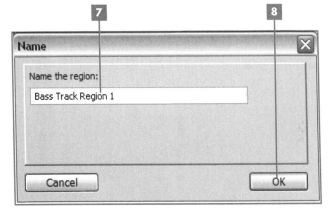

Separating a Region

Here's another way to create a region. This time, instead of capturing a selection, you're simply going to start chopping up your big region into smaller, more manageable regions. Visually, these two methods might appear quite similar, but by separating a region, you won't be creating any new files on your hard drive. (When you capture a selection, Pro Tools renders a new audio file in your Audio Files subfolder.)

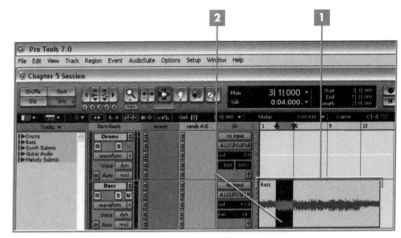

1 If you're working with the Chapter 5 session, double-click on the region named Bass to highlight it. Listen to the region alone to get an idea of how it sounds. You'll want to solo the track to hear it by itself. (See Chapter 3 for a refresher on how to solo a track.)

2 Select measures 3 through 5 on the Bass track. It's easy when you're in Grid mode with a whole measure grid!

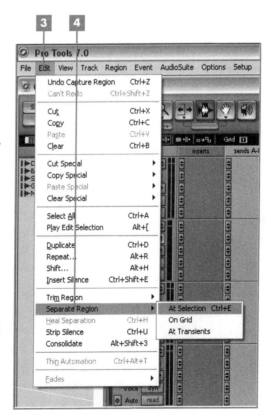

3 Click on Edit. The Edit menu will appear.

4 Click on Separate Region. Another menu will appear.

5 Choose the At Selection option. A new region will be created.

❋ **TIP**

What if Pro Tools might or might not ask you to name your new region? You can disable or enable the Auto-Name feature by selecting the Setup menu, choosing Preferences, and then clicking on the Editing tab. You can select or deselect the Auto-Name Separated Regions field to enable or disable this feature, respectively.

Your original region will be cut into three smaller regions. The region that matches your selection will be in the middle.

❋ **NOTE**

If you're working with the Chapter 5 session and you're following the steps in this chapter, then you're well on your way to building the bass part from scratch. Good for you! Now you're ready to do some work on your own.

To get to the next step, you need to use either the Capture Region or Separate Region function to create the next three regions. To do so, follow these steps:

1. Import the Reference Bass track from the Reference Bass Track Session (in the Session 5 Import Materials subfolder). This will be your guide in rebuilding the bass track.

2. Listen to the region beginning at measure 9 on the Reference Bass track. Find the section on the Bass track that matches it, and then capture or separate a region. Name this region Bass Part Reassembly 3 (if prompted for a name).

3. Repeat the same steps to create a new region that sounds like the one beginning at measure 12 of the reference track, and name it Bass Part Reassembly 4 (if prompted for a name).

4. Finally, create a region that matches the region on the reference track that starts at measure 15 and ends at measure 20. (Keep in mind that this section is five measures long.) Name this region Bass Part Reassembly 5 (again, if prompted).

One last thing to keep in mind: Although capturing or separating will do the job as far as the session goes, there are differences in the way each function works. Capture will leave the original region intact on the Timeline and will create a new file in your Audio Files folder. Separating a region will alter the region in your track, and it won't create any new files in your session's Audio Files folder.

There are two different ways you can create the final region you need to build the Bass track—trim or crop.

Trimming a Region

There are two ways to trim a region. Because you're in Grid mode, trimming with the Trim tool is easy to do.

1 Click on the Trim tool. The tool will be selected.

2 Click and hold on the region border you want to change and drag the boundary to the desired location. As you drag, Pro Tools will indicate where the boundary is moving.

3 Release the mouse button. A new region will be created (but not a new audio file) with the new region boundary.

4 If necessary, repeat Steps 1–3 for the other end of the region.

Here's another way to get the job done:

 NOTE

Before you can re-edit this region to get the same results, you need to undo the trimming you just did. You can access the Undo function from the Edit menu, or you can use the shortcut keys (Ctrl+Z on a PC and ⌘+Z on a Mac).

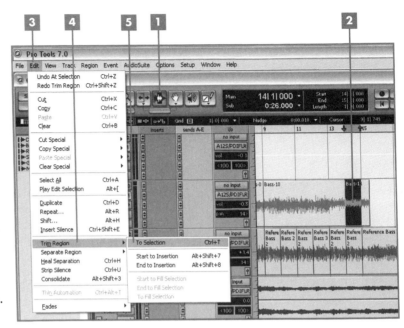

1. Click on the Selector tool. The tool will be selected.

2. Select the area of the audio region that you want to retain.

3. Click on Edit. The Edit menu will appear.

4. Click on Trim Region. The Trim submenu will appear.

5. Because you've made a selection (as opposed to setting a timeline insertion point), the option you'll want to use is To Selection. Click on To Selection. The region will be trimmed to your selection.

Renaming a Region

When you're finished with any of the edit processes we've discussed, you might want to rename the regions you have created. Here's how to rename any region:

1. Click on the Grabber tool. The tool will be selected.

2. Double-click on the region you want to rename. The Name dialog box will open.

3. Type the name you want for the region in the Name the Region text box.

4. Click on OK. The Name dialog box will close and the region will be renamed.

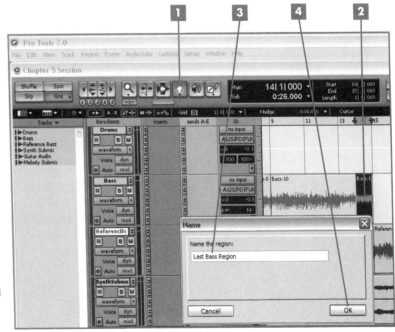

Assembling a Track

After you've created regions, the next step in the process is to organize them on the track. Of course, what you've already learned about the edit modes will aid you greatly in this process, but there are a couple additional tricks that can make the process even easier!

> ❊ **NOTE**
>
> If you're following the examples shown here, you will want to select all remaining regions on the Bass track and remove them from the track, leaving a blank track on which to assemble your newly created regions.

Working in Shuffle mode makes the job easy!

1 Click on Shuffle if you're not already in Shuffle mode.

2 One by one, drag regions onto the desired track in the order that you want them to be played back.

> ❊ **NOTE**
>
> If you're following the example, drag Bass Track Region 1 onto the track six times, and then find the region that matches the region on the Reference track at measure 7 (you'll have to use your ears!) onto the track once. Remember from earlier in this chapter that in Shuffle mode, it doesn't matter where you drop your regions—they'll automatically move to the edge of the preceding region.

Duplicating Regions

Of course, you *could* just drag the same region onto a track over and over and have a repeating loop, but that can get really boring very quickly. Here's another way to make a copy of a region or selection and place it after the original:

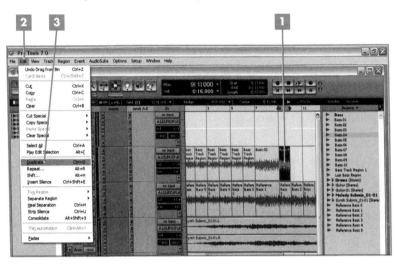

1 Drag and drop **a single** region onto a track, or otherwise select a region.

2 Click on Edit. **The Edit menu will appear.**

3 Click on Duplicate. **The region will be copied immediately after the preceding selection.**

❄ **TIP**

The shortcut for the Duplicate function is Ctrl+D on a PC and ⌘+D on a Mac.

❄ **NOTE**

If you're following the example shown, you'll want to duplicate Bass Part Reassembly 3 (with manual renaming) two times, and then add Bass Part Reassembly 4 at bar 12. Finally, you'll add Bass Part Reassembly 3 another two times, and then Bass Part Reassembly 5. Then you'll be ready to continue. If you have Auto-Naming enabled, you'll have to audition the regions in the Regions list, and really use your ears (which is a *great* way to practice!)

Repeating Regions

Repeating regions is similar to duplicating regions, but with a twist.

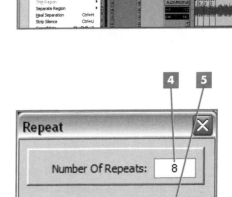

1 Drag and drop **a single** region onto a track or otherwise select a region. In this case, you'll want to place the Last Bass Region onto the end of your bass track.

2 Click on Edit. The Edit menu will appear.

3 Click on Repeat. The Repeat dialog box will open.

4 Type the number of times you want the region to repeat in the Number of Repeats text box (in this case, type 8).

5 Click on OK. The selected region will be repeated the specified number of times, just as if you had used the Duplicate command a number of times.

6 Solo **both** bass tracks (if you haven't already) and play them together. The tracks should sound identical. If they do, then you're done! (If they don't, then it's time to take a close look at the reference track and the track you just created to find where they disagree, and then redo the necessary steps in this section.)

Working with Grids

Hopefully by now you're getting a good idea of the usefulness of working in Grid mode. However, using a grid as wide as a whole measure might not work for you in all situations. You can change the grid and see the possibilities.

If you've listened closely to the melody track, the timing seems a bit off. The good news is that the tempo isn't the problem—the notes have just been shifted—so we can still use the Grid mode; but we'll need to make a finer adjustment that a whole measure grid can accomplish. Read on . . .

❊ ❊ ❊

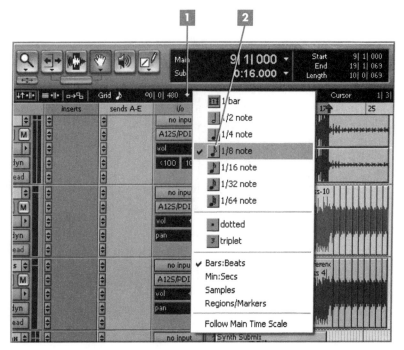

1 Click on the arrow next to the Grid value. The Grid menu will appear.

2 Select the scale (for example, Bars:Beats or Min:Secs) if you want to change the scale of your grid. If you want to continue in the same scale, click on the grid value you want. To fix the melody track, you can choose an 8th note value. The grid will immediately change in the Edit window.

3 Click on Grid if you're not already in Grid mode.

4 Drag a region onto a track. As you drag the region in the track, the region will move in different increments and allow you to drop your region at different locations. This region will sound a *lot* better if it begins at 8|4|480.

5 Drop the region at the desired location. The location, as well as the start, end, and length of the selected region, will be shown in your location displays.

Cutting, Copying, and Pasting

Cut, copy, and paste are pretty tried-and-true staples of most audio software, and Pro Tools is certainly no exception. These processes are very straightforward and easy to use.

Copying a Region

Copying a region can be quite useful—and easy!

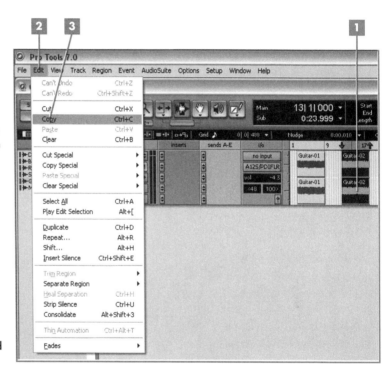

1 Select the region you want to copy.

❋ **TIP**

One of the easiest ways to select a region is to double-click on it if you are using the Selector tool. You can also click on the region if you're using the Grabber tool.

2 Click on Edit. The Edit menu will appear.

3 Click on Copy. The region will be copied to the clipboard.

❋ **TIP**

The shortcut for the Copy command is Ctrl+C on a PC and ⌘+C on a Mac.

Pasting a Region

A copied region means nothing until it's pasted to a new location. Here's how to do this:

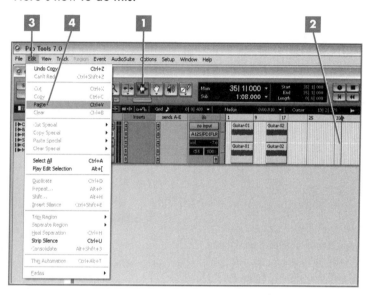

 Click on the Selector tool if it's not already selected. The tool will be selected.

2 Click in a track at the location where you want to paste the region you copied.

3 Click on Edit. The Edit menu will appear.

4 Click on Paste. The region will be pasted at the location you selected.

※ **TIP**

The shortcut for the Paste command is Ctrl+V on a PC and ⌘+V on a Mac.

Cutting a Region

Because you're not going to use that region, go ahead and cut it.

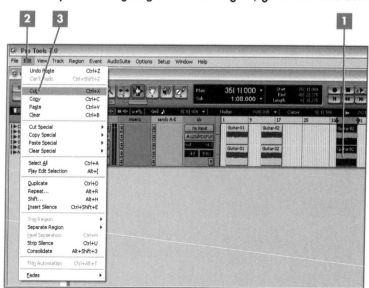

1 Select the region you want to cut. The region will be selected.

2 Click on Edit. The Edit menu will appear.

3 Click on Cut. The region will be cut and placed on the clipboard.

※ **TIP**

The shortcut for the Cut command is Ctrl+X on a PC and ⌘+X on a Mac.

Working with Overlapping Regions

From time to time, you'll have occasion to move one region so that it partially blocks another region. This is absolutely not a problem—happens all the time—but there are some things you should be aware of beforehand. First, you will only ever hear the region "in front," meaning that you won't hear both audio regions play together. Second of all, this sort of action is non-destructive, meaning that when you move the region "in front" out of the way, you'll see the region underneath unchanged.

Before we wrap up this chapter, let's take a look at how you can view and manipulate overlapped regions.

> ❈ **NOTE**
>
> We're going to work with the Guitar track a little bit to show how overlapped regions work, but you don't want to keep this work. If your session sounds good (and it shouldn't sound too bad if you've been following this chapter), you should save your work before moving on with this section.

First, let's take a look at the standard behavior of overlapped regions:

❈ Drag a region over another region using the Grabber tool (in this case, the second of the Guitar regions over the first), and you'll notice that when you play back the track, only the region (and portions of regions) that is immediately visible will be heard.

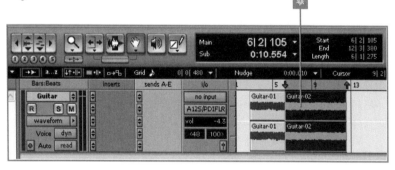

❋ Move the region on top out of the way, and you'll see that the region that has been partially blocked hasn't changed at all!

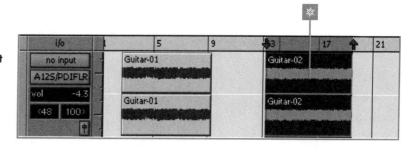

Often, it's hard to visually determine which regions are overlapping and which are simply next to each other. It would sure be easier if there were some sort of visual cue to show an overlap situation. No sooner said than done.

1 Click the View drop-down menu. The View menu will appear.

2 Click the Region menu item. Another menu will appear.

3 This menu is a checklist of region-related aspects that can be shown or not shown. Click the Overlap menu item (it will be checked).

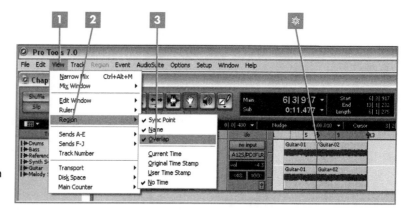

❋ Note that now you'll see a small bevel in the overlapping upper corner of a region that is covering another region.

But wait, there's more! What if you want to change the way the regions are overlapped *without* moving either of the regions?

1 Select the region in front.

2 Click the Region menu. The Region menu will appear.

3 Click Send to Back. The region will now be moved *behind* the first region and will be partially covered by it. Here again, you will not hear any audio except what is "in front," and there will be a beveled upper corner to indicate the overlap (though now it is in the first region, indicating that it is covering another region).

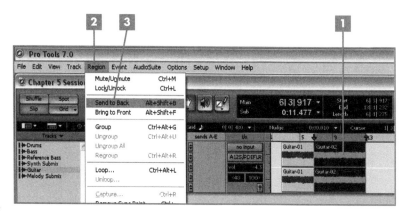

You can similarly choose a region that is in back and choose Bring to Front from the same menu. In either of these ways, the relationship between these two overlapping regions can be reversed, while leaving their timing untouched.

That's it for beginning editing. Now on to some of the more tweaky features!

6 } . . . And More Editing

Although the editing power of a DAW ranks high in the production world, the editing process itself can sometimes be lacking in the way of glamour. A good editor knows that editing essentially boils down to simple functions done many, many times. In the editor's world, patience is a virtue, and it is put to the test when you cut and paste, drag and drop, and perform like functions repeatedly. Indeed, it's not uncommon for a professional editing session to involve hundreds of individual editing operations!

The good news is that you already learned the basics of editing in Chapter 5 (cleverly named "Editing"). Now you're going to learn more efficient and flexible ways to work and expand upon the basic editing tools you've already begun to use. The idea behind these techniques is that the time you save with each editing function will add up. By mastering these new processes, you'll not only save time, but you'll also become a better and more creative editor! In this chapter, you'll learn how to:

❈ Navigate your session with greater ease
❈ Use and customize the zoom tools
❈ Use the variations of the Trim and Grabber tools
❈ Boost your editing efficiency by using the Smart tool
❈ Enhance your system's efficiency when you're playing back your music

More Organization: Memory Locations

As your session gets more complex, organizing and navigating through the maze of times and tracks will become more and more of an issue. Even beyond the editing phase of your project, once you go into the Mix window it will be a little more difficult to navigate through your session Timeline. You won't have the convenience of clicking on a specific time on a track and moving your timeline insertion there (although you will still have the Transport window when you want it). The good news is that you can make navigation more than a little easier by setting up a few memory locations.

Memory locations are presets you can recall at the touch of a button, similar to the zoom presets you created in the last chapter. In this case, though, you can recall specific selections, locations, zoom settings, and more!

❋ **NOTE**

For this section, please use "Chapter 6 (pt. 1)" from the *Pro Tool LE 7 Ignite!* Web page at www.courseptr.com/downloads.

Creating a Memory Location

Of course, before you can use memory locations, you have to create them!

1 Click on Window. The Window menu will appear.

2 Click on Memory Locations. The Memory Locations window will appear.

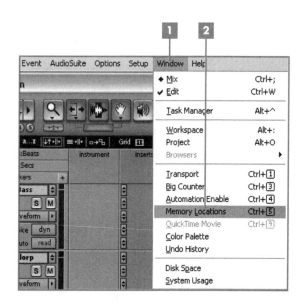

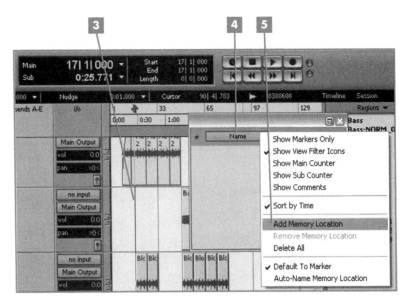

3 Using the Selector tool, place your timeline insertion at a significant point in your session. In this case, I've placed it at the beginning of measure 17, where the "blorp" starts. For this example, also set up any zoom levels, track show/hide settings, and track heights that you wish to recall (refer to the next figure to see how I've set up my window, as a point of reference).

4 Click on the Name button in the Memory Locations window. A menu will appear.

5 Click on Add Memory Location. The New Memory Location 1 dialog box will open, allowing you to set up your memory location.

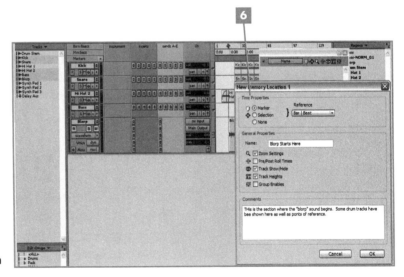

6 Select the time property that you want this memory location to recall. The choices are

❀ Marker. The timeline insertion will jump to a specific location when the memory location is chosen. This is the kind of memory location that I want for this example.

❀ Selection. A selected area will be recalled when the memory location is chosen.

❀ None. The timeline insertion/ selection will not change when the memory location is chosen.

7 Type a descriptive name for this memory location in the Name text box.

8 Check the General Properties boxes that match the settings you want to be recalled with this memory location. The settings will be selected. In this case, when this memory location is recalled, the current zoom settings, track show/hide, and track heights will be recalled. Other characteristics, such as pre/post roll and group enables, will not change when you recall this memory location.

9 This is a newly added feature to Pro tools: Type a descriptive comment in the Comments field to describe or document what you've done.

10 Click on OK. Your memory location will be saved, and the New Memory Location 1 dialog box will close.

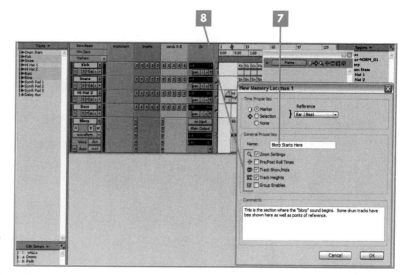

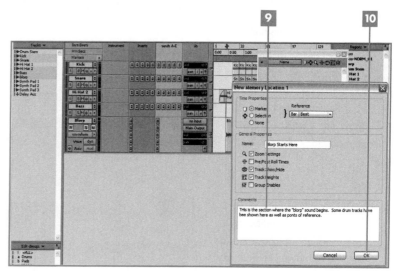

11 Now try setting up a different memory location. Select a different area (in this case I selected from bar 65 to bar 73), different zoom settings, track heights, track show/hides, and this time enable a group.

12 Create and set up a new memory location in the same way that you set up the first one (by clicking on the Name button, selecting Add Memory Location, and setting up the desired parameters of this new memory location). If you're following this example, choose the following settings:

❋ Selection time property. When this memory location is recalled, the selection will be as well.

❋ Zoom Settings selected.

❋ Track Show/Hide selected.

❋ Track Heights selected.

❋ Group Enables selected. This bit is different and will enable the currently enabled groups (in this case, "Pads") when this memory location is recalled.

13 Click on OK when you're finished. The second memory location will be created and the Memory Location 2 dialog box will close.

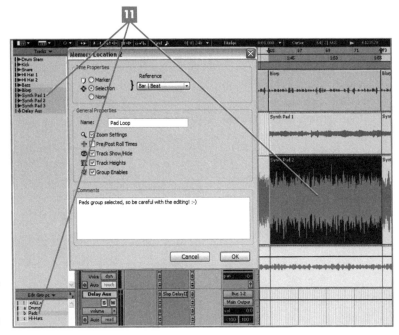

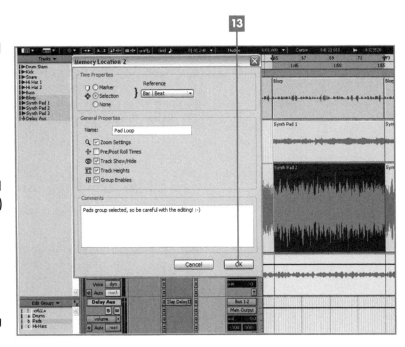

❋❋❋

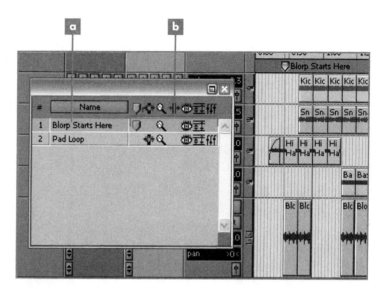

a By clicking on either memory location name, you will instantly recall its location on the time scale, as well as all included parameters, such as zoom settings and track show/hide.

b If you forgot what parameters are enabled, just look to see what icons are included for each memory location. From left to right, the icons are Marker, Selection, Zoom, Pre/Post Roll, Track Show/Hide, Track Heights, and Group Enables.

❄ **TIP**

You can recall any created memory location from your keyboard easily. On the Mac or PC, press the period key, then the number of the memory location you want to recall, and then the period key again.

❄ **TIP**

You can also create memory locations as your session plays by pressing the Enter key. After creating the memory locations on the fly, you can go back and edit them by right-clicking the desired memory location (PC), or double-clicking (Mac).

Using Memory Locations

Beyond this, there's no big mystery to creating and using memory locations; but before you jump into the mix window, take a quick look at some of the other options open to you.

1 Click on the Name button. The Name menu will appear.

❋ When you select the Show Main Counter option, the location of each memory location in relation to the main counter scale will be displayed (as shown at the top of the Edit window).

❋ When you select the Show Sub Counter option, the location of each memory location in relation to the sub counter scale will be displayed (as shown at the top of the Edit window).

❋ When you select the Show Comments option, any comments you've entered for your memory locations will be shown.

❋ When you select the Sort by Time option, your memory locations will be sorted depending on how early or late they are in your session rather than by the order in which they were created.

❋ When you select the Default To Marker option, the Memory Location dialog box will be set to start off with the Marker option chosen.

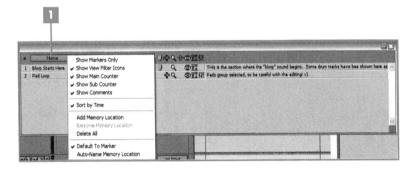

Here's what the window will look like when the two memory location options are selected, as well as the comments. Note the two new columns created, and their time scales reflect the currently selected main and sub counter scales. Each memory location's specific position is shown in these columns. Either or both of these two options can come in mighty handy, particularly when you're working in the Mix window, where it's harder to visualize your time position in your session.

Zoom

Zooming is not only one of the most basic things you'll do in any given editing session, it's also one of the most frequent things you'll do. Of course, the first step down the road of efficient zooming is to learn the shortcuts associated with basic zooming (see Chapter 5). The following sections will discuss other ways to zoom and how to use them.

> ❋ **NOTE**
>
> For the remainder of this chapter, we'll take advantage of what you just learned about memory locations. Please download and use the "Chapter 6 (pt. 2)" session.

More Zoom Tools

Let's start from what you already know and work from there.

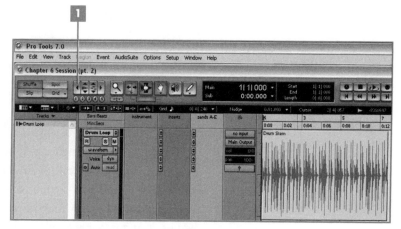

1 Click on the Zoom Out button. As you've seen before, your view of your session's Timeline will expand, and a longer duration will be shown in your Edit window. Note that all tracks, audio and MIDI, are zoomed together.

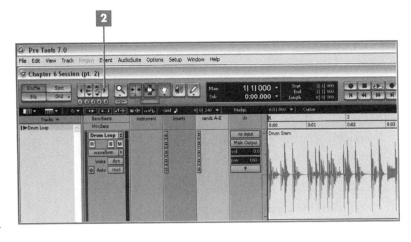

2 Click on the Zoom In button. Again, as you've seen before, your view will narrow in on a smaller slice of time with each successive click of the button. Again, you'll see that Audio and MIDI tracks are zoomed at the same rate. The Zoom In and Zoom Out buttons will allow you to zoom in on the time scale, and, although they won't affect the speed at which your session will play back, they will allow you to view your regions and data differently to suit different kinds of editing.

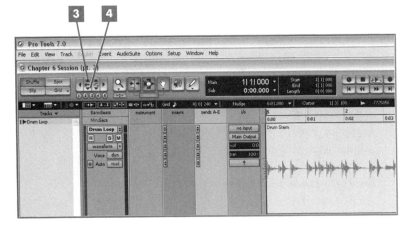

3 Click on the Audio Zoom Up button. With each click of this button your audio data zooms up, allowing you to more clearly see low-level signals. Also, notice that all of your Audio tracks have zoomed up at the same time, but your MIDI data has remained unchanged.

4 Click on the Audio Zoom Down button. The height of your audio waveforms will be reduced with each click of this button.

❋ **TIP**

Although this kind of zooming is not quite as common as zooming in on the horizontal time scale, the shortcut keys are still useful to know. On the PC, it's Ctrl+Alt+] (right bracket) to zoom up and Ctrl+Alt+[(left bracket) to zoom down. On the Mac, the shortcut is ⌘+Option+] (right bracket) to zoom up and ⌘+Option+[(left bracket) to zoom down.

5 Click on the MIDI Zoom Up button. With each click of this button, your MIDI data will zoom up, allowing you to more clearly see individual notes. Note that all your MIDI tracks have zoomed up at the same time, but your Audio tracks are unchanged when you click on this button.

6 Click on the MIDI Zoom Down button. Your MIDI data will zoom down, allowing you to see a greater range of notes at one time in the Edit window.

As you zoom up or down, you will see less or more of the keyboard graphic on the left edge of each MIDI track. You can use this display as a reference point to see how broad (or narrow) of a tonal range you're viewing. Low pitches are displayed toward the bottom of each MIDI track, and high notes are toward the top. You can scroll up and down the MIDI note range by clicking on the up and down arrows at each end of the keyboard graphic.

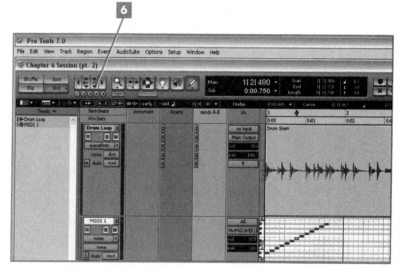

❊ **TIP**

On the PC, it's Ctrl+Shift+] (right bracket) to zoom up and Ctrl+Shift+[(left bracket) to zoom down. On the Mac, the shortcut for MIDI height zooming is ⌘+Shift+] (right bracket) to zoom up and ⌘+Shift+[(left bracket) to zoom down.

Zoom Presets

I'm going out on a limb with this comparison, but go with me on this. Take the average car radio. If you're a music lover, you probably use it quite a bit. On most car radios, there are a number of buttons (usually below the main display) that you can use to set the stations you listen to most often. Once you set them up, you can simply press an individual button and immediately jump to your favorite channel.

Many Pro Tools users find that, although they use all the zoom tools a *lot*, they tend to use certain zoom amounts more frequently than others. Like on a car radio, you can set up your most common zoom presets and jump between them at the click of a single button. In fact, setting these presets is pretty similar to setting the presets on your car radio!

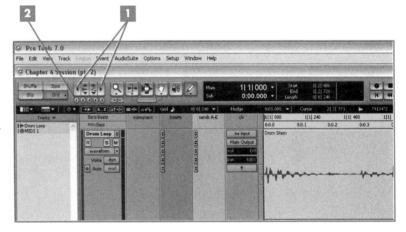

1. Click on either of the time (the vertical axis) zoom tools until you settle upon your most commonly used zoom setting.

2. Hold down the Ctrl key (PC) or the ⌘ key (Mac) and click on the first Zoom Preset button. The button will flash briefly to let you know that the preset has been stored.

3 Repeat Steps 1 and 2 to set a preset for the second Zoom Preset button, using a different zoom level.

4 If you want to go back to your first zoom preset, click on the first Zoom Preset button. Your previously stored zoom preset will be immediately recalled.

From this point on, it's easy. Simply set the five presets for the five zoom settings you use the most. At that point, you can click on the Zoom Preset buttons to switch zoom settings, much like you would change favorite stations on your car radio.

❋ **NOTE**

The Zoom Preset buttons will recall only the horizontal (time) zoom amount, not the vertical zoom levels for Audio and MIDI tracks.

❋ **TIP**

The shortcuts to switch between your presets are pretty straightforward. Just hold the Start (Windows) button (PC) or the Control button (Mac) and press 1, 2, 3, 4, or 5 on your keyboard (above the alphabet section).

More Ways to Work with Selections

After you get comfortable with these more flexible ways of zooming, you'll want to take a look at some different ways of making selections.

❄ **NOTE**

For this section, go to memory location #1—Selections. As you learned earlier in this chapter, you'll simply have to show your memory locations window (from the Window drop-down menu), then simply click on memory location #1.

Making Selections Using the Arrow Keys

In Chapter 3, you saw that the boundaries of your selection were represented in the Rulers area (above the tracks) by a down arrow and an up arrow, representing punch-in and punch-out points, respectively. Using the arrow keys is an easy way to make a selection as your session plays.

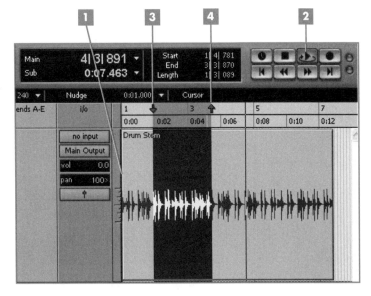

1 Choose a starting point, making sure that it is before the point where you want your selection to start. The starting point will be selected.

2 Start playback. (Remember, you can use the Start button on the Transport window, or you can press the spacebar.)

3 As your session plays, press the down arrow key on your keyboard at the point where you want to begin your selection.

4 While your session is still playing, press the up arrow key on your keyboard when you want your selection to end.

❄ **TIP**

If you're a little late or early on a punch-in or punch-out, don't worry. You can adjust your selection by holding the Shift key while you drag either end with your mouse.

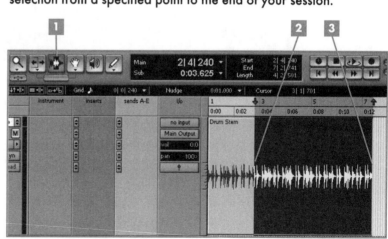

Making Selections Using the Return Key

You've already learned that pressing the Return key (Mac) or the Enter key (PC) will send you back to the beginning of the session. Here's how to use this function a little differently. This method will allow you to make a selection from the beginning of your session to a specified point.

1 Click on the Selector tool. The tool will be selected.

2 Click on the point on a desired track at which you want your selection to end. A flashing timeline insertion will appear at the location you click.

3 Press and hold the Shift key and press the Return key. A selection will be made from the beginning of the session to the timeline insertion that you created with the Selector tool.

Here's a variation of that process that will allow you to make a selection from a specified point to the end of your session.

1 Click on the Selector tool if it's not already highlighted. The tool will be selected.

2 Click on the point on a desired track at which you want your selection to start.

3 Press and hold Control+Shift (PC) or Option+Shift (Mac), and press the Return key. A selection will be made from the timeline insertion that you created with the Selector tool to the end of your session.

Making Selections Using Tab to Transient

The Tab to Transient function is cool for two reasons. First, it's a great concept, although by no means a unique one these days. Second, *it works*, a fact which certainly does distinguish it from similar features in competing software. That being said, the Tab to Transient feature is a great way to make certain kinds of selections, particularly for those of you who enjoy chopping up beats into loopable segments.

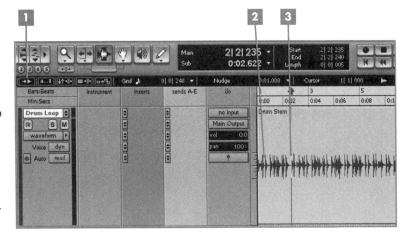

1 Click **on the** Tab to Transient tool. **The tool will be selected.**

2 Use **the** Selector tool **to set a timeline insertion a little before the transient you want to start with. The timeline insertion will be set.**

3 Press **the** Tab key. **As you've seen before, the timeline insertion will jump from transient to transient each time you hit the Tab key. Stop tabbing when you get to the transient that marks the desired beginning of your selection.**

4 Press and hold **the** Shift key and press **the** Tab key. **Again, the timeline insertion will jump from transient to transient, but this time a selection will be made in the process.**

5 When you reach the end of your desired selection, stop pressing **the** Tab key.

A Useful Preference:
Timeline Insertion Follows Playback

Suppose you've selected a nice loopable selection. You'll want to go into Loop Playback mode and hear your work. Sounds great, doesn't it? Then you hit Stop, and the selection goes away! Is this a bug within Pro Tools? Nope—it's the effect of a preference named Timeline Insertion Follows Playback, which you can set in the software. You can either enable or disable this preference. Either mode has its uses, but it's important to understand this preference's functioning so you can know when to use it and when not to!

1 Click on Setup. The Setup menu will appear.

2 Click on Preferences. The Pro Tools LE Preferences dialog box will open.

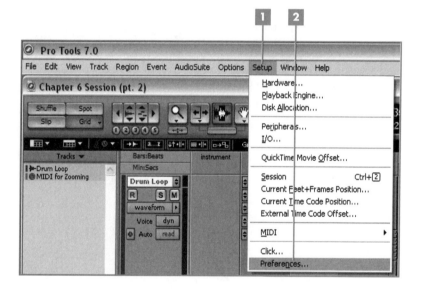

3 Click on the Operation tab. The tab will move to the front.

4 Select or deselect the Timeline Insertion Follows Playback check box. Here's what the options mean:

❀ Checked. Playback will begin wherever the timeline insertion is set. When playback stops, the timeline insertion will jump to the point where you stopped. When you start playback again, it will pick up where you left off. If you have made a selection, that selection will be lost when you hit Stop.

❀ Unchecked. Playback will begin wherever the timeline insertion is set. When play-back stops in this mode, the timeline insertion will stay where it was originally set. When you start playback again, it will start from the original position. If you have made a selection, that selec-tion will be maintained when you hit Stop, making this the ideal mode for editing loopable selections.

5 Click on Done when you've selected the desired prefer-ences. Your preferences will be set and the dialog box will close.

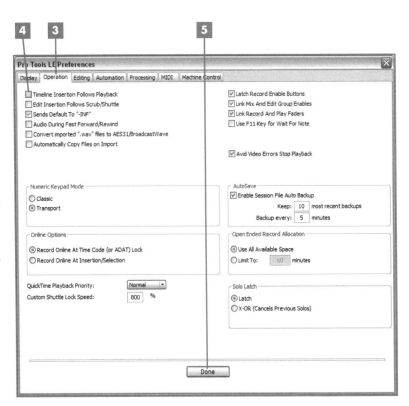

Separate Regions Options

Once you've made your selection, you can separate your regions based upon that selection, as you've done already in Chapter 5. Hang on, though—there are two more new ways to use your selected area to separate your region.

For the purposes of this example, select the entire Drum Stem region shown in memory location 1.

Separate Region on Grid

As the name might suggest, this feature will chop up your region on every grid point. In this session, our grid value is 16th notes, so we will create new regions in 16th-note increments.

1 Click on Edit. **The Edit menu will appear.**

2 Click Separate Region. **A secondary menu will appear.**

3 Click On Grid. **The Pre-Separate Amount dialog box will open.**

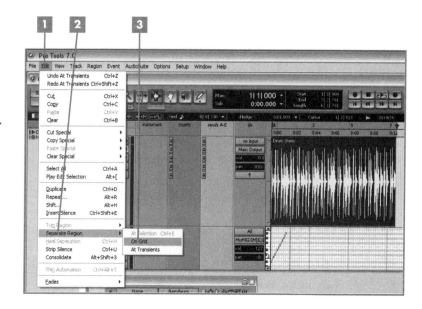

4 Setting any value above zero in the Pre-Separate Amount dialog box will shift the separations earlier. The greater the value, the farther ahead the separations. To separate regions exactly on the grid lines, choose zero. When you're done, click OK.

a Your region will be separated regularly on every grid increment.

b New regions (in this case, *lots* of them) will be added to your Regions list.

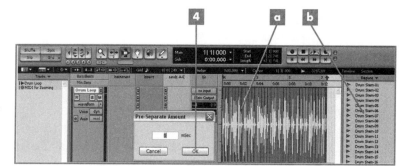

Separate Region at Transients

This is a handy little feature that creates a new region boundary at each detected transient. Take a look.

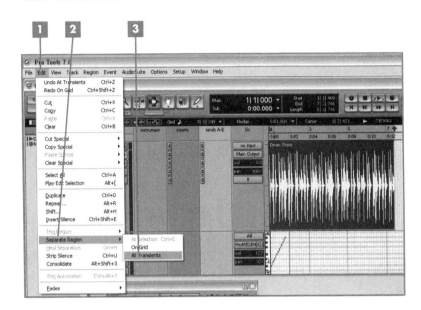

1 Click on Edit. The Edit menu will appear.

2 Click Separate Region. A secondary menu will appear.

3 Click At Transients. The Pre-Separate Amount dialog box will open.

4 Setting any value above zero in the Pre-Separate Amount dialog box will shift the separations earlier. The greater the value, the farther ahead the separations. To separate regions exactly on the transients, choose zero. When you're done, click OK.

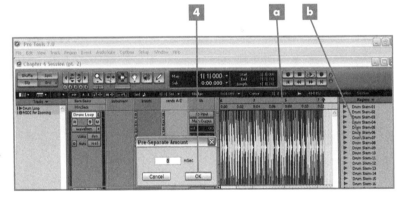

a Your region will be separated regularly at every transient.

b As you saw when you separated on grid lines, new regions will be added to your Regions list.

Navigating and Auditioning a Selection

When you make a selection, the most important parts are the beginning and the end. You'll be listening to the boundaries of your selection many times, just to make sure you've got everything you want and nothing you don't.

> ❄ **NOTE**
>
> For this section, click the second memory location, Navigating a Selection. As you learned earlier in this chapter, you'll simply have to show your memory locations window (from the Window drop-down menu), then simply click on memory location #2.

1 Press the left arrow key. The timeline insertion (and the Edit window's focus) will move to the beginning of the selection.

2 Press the right arrow key. The timeline insertion will move to the end of the selection.

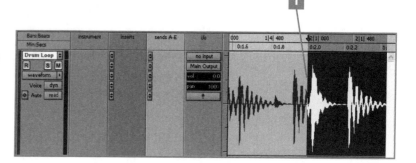

3 Now it's time to audition the boundaries of your selection. Press and hold the Alt key (PC) or the Option key (Mac), and press the left arrow key. Your audio will play up to the beginning of your selection by the pre-roll amount (even if pre-roll isn't highlighted). Since the pre-roll amount is set as one measure (in the lower left of the Transport window), playback will start one measure before the beginning of the selection.

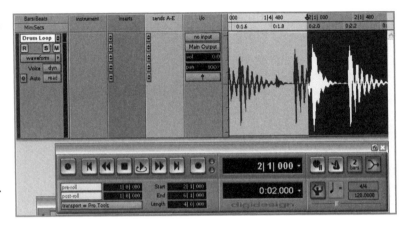

4 Press and hold **the** Alt key **(PC) or the** Option key **(Mac) and** press **the** right arrow key. **Your audio will play up to the end of your selection by the pre-roll amount.**

5 Press and hold **the** Ctrl key **(PC) or the** ⌘ key **(Mac), and** press **the** left arrow key. **Your audio will play from the beginning of your selection by the post-roll amount (even if post-roll isn't highlighted).**

6 Press and hold **the** Ctrl key **(PC) or the** ⌘ key **(Mac), and** press **the** right arrow key. **Your audio will play from the end of your selection by the post-roll amount.**

Beyond the Basics

You've already worked with the basic editing tools, and things like trimming, selecting, and grabbing are starting to become familiar by now. Some of these tools have secondary layers to them, giving them added functionality. And then there's the *Smart tool...* .

The TCE Trim Tool

First on the list is the TCE (Time Compress/Expand) Trim tool. This dandy little tool allows you to stretch or compress the duration of an audio region without changing the pitch!

 NOTE

To follow with this demonstration, go to memory location #3—TCE Trim Tool.

1 Click and hold **the small** down arrow **at the bottom of the Trim tool button until the menu appears. The currently selected version of the Trim tool will be checked.**

2 Click **on** TCE **to change to the TCE Trim tool.**

The icon for the Trim tool will change to reflect this different function. Make sure that it is highlighted. (If it isn't, just click on the icon.)

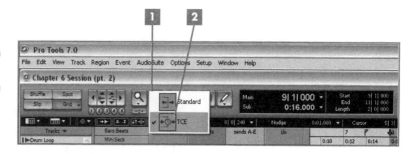

3 Click and hold **either** boundary **of a region.**

4 Drag **the** boundary **in or out, as if you were using the regular Trim tool. When you release the mouse button, a new audio file will be created with a different duration than the original region, but without a different pitch.**

❄ **TIP**

The TCE Trim tool is really useful in Grid mode. Suppose you've imported a drum loop that doesn't match the tempo of the rest of your session. Just make sure your grids are a musical unit (like quarter notes, for example) and use the TCE Trim tool. The edges of the region will snap to the nearest grid point when released, and you'll be perfectly in tempo!

The Object Grabber Tool

Up to this point, the Grabber tool that you have used has moved a block of *time*, and all the regions that are contained within that block, hence the tool's name, *Time* Grabber. But what if you want to select more than one region without selecting all the regions between them? That's where the Object Grabber tool comes into play!

❋ **NOTE**

For this section, go to memory location #4—Grabbers.

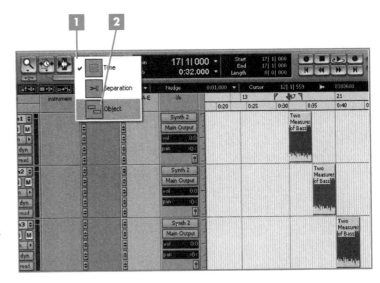

1. Click and hold the down arrow at the bottom of the Grabber tool button until the menu appears. The currently selected version of the Grabber tool will be checked.

2. Click on Object to change to the Object Grabber tool.

3. Click the first region that you want to select. You'll note that when using the Object Grabber the region isn't highlighted, but rather a focus box is displayed around the edge of the region.

4. Holding the Shift key, click additional regions that you wish to move. Note that only the regions (or "objects") that you click are selected, and not the time between them.

5. Drag and drop the regions that you want to move to the desired location. Note that you see an outline of where the regions will be eventually redeposited.

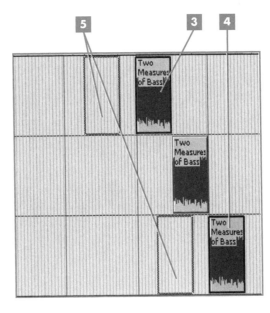

The Separation Grabber Tool

The regular Grabber tool allows you to move regions around in your session. The Separation Grabber tool will let you take a selection from within a single region and move just that selection. This is a cool trick, but you have to go through a few steps first.

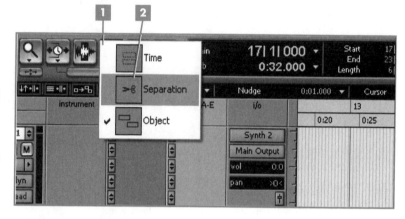

1 Click and hold the down arrow at the bottom of the Grabber button. A menu will appear. The currently selected version of the Grabber tool will be checked.

2 Click on Separation to change to the Separation Grabber tool.

3 Click on the Selector tool. The tool will be selected. (Have faith; we're going somewhere with this.)

4 Select the section of a region that you want to separate. The section will be selected.

5 Click **on the** Separation Grabber tool. **The tool will be selected.**

6 Click and hold **on your** selection.

7 Drag and drop **the** selection **to the desired destination.**

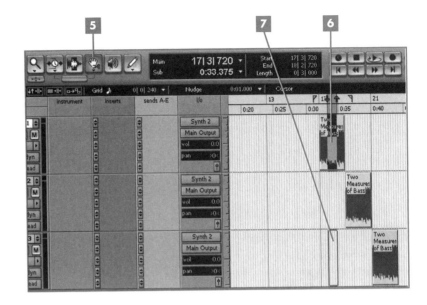

The selection will be removed from the source track and will become its own region, shown in the Regions list.

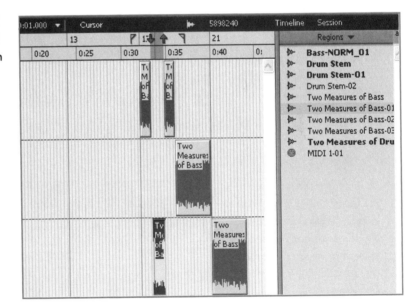

❋ **TIP**

If you want to drag out a selection of a region but leave your source region unchanged, hold down the Alt key (PC) or the Option key (Mac) as you drag.

The Smart Tool

The Smart tool is a real timesaver, combining the use of many editing tools at once and adding some additional functionality for good measure. It might take you a while to get used to using the Smart tool, but once you've got it under your belt, you'll really start saving time.

The idea behind the function of the Smart tool is that when your cursor is in different places on a track, it will take on different tool behaviors.

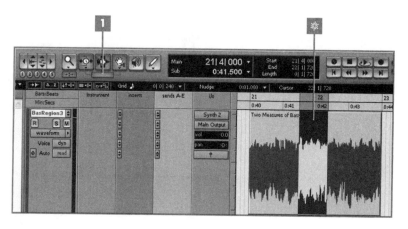

1 Click on the Smart bar below the three primary editing tools to activate the Smart tool. The button will be highlighted, and so will the three tools above it (Trim, Selector, and Grabber), which should give you a hint as to the Smart tool's function.

❋ When your cursor is in the upper half of a track, it will take on the function of the Selector tool.

❋ NOTE

For this part, go to memory location #5—Smart Tool.

❋ When you move your cursor to the lower half of a track, the cursor will take on the behavior of the currently selected version of the Grabber tool (in this case, the Separation Grabber).

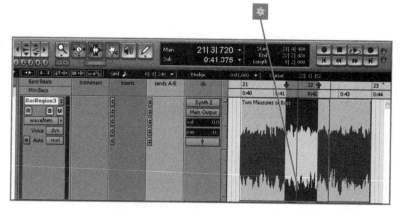

❋ **TIP**

The Smart tool works particularly well when you have the Separation Grabber tool selected. Just move your cursor to the top half of a track to make your selection, and then move your cursor to the bottom half of the track and drag the selection out!

❋ When you move your cursor to either end of a region, the cursor will change its function to that of the currently selected version of the Trim tool (in this case the TCE Trim Tool).

❋ **NOTE**

If you move your cursor to the corners, you'll notice that it will take on a different function, beyond that of the Trim, Selector, or Grabber tools. Be patient—you'll get to the answer in a couple of pages!

❋ **TIP**

Because the position of the cursor within a track is so critical when you are working with the Smart tool, you should take special care with smaller track heights. (Mini height is particularly tricky.)

❋ **NOTE**

For our discussion of fades, go to memory location #7—Fades.

Creating and Customizing Fades

You can use fade-ins and fade-outs to soften the edges of a region. Additionally, you can create crossfades between regions to make a smooth transition from one region to another. Of course, this is nothing new in the world of DAWs, but Pro Tools makes fades easy to create and tweak. You can even use the Smart tool to create them!

Creating a Fade-In

Everybody has heard fade-ins in a mix, when a song starts from a silent beginning and gradually gets louder until it reaches its running volume. In Pro Tools, however, you can create a fade-in for an individual region *within* a mix. Here's how:

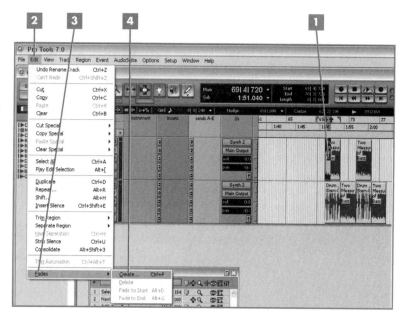

1 Using the Selector tool (or the Selector mode of the Smart tool), select the area of a region that you want to become a fade-in. The area will be selected.

2 Click on Edit. The Edit menu will appear.

3 Click on Fades. The Fades submenu will appear.

4 Click on Create. The Fades dialog box will open.

❄ **NOTE**

It's important to make sure that your selection starts at or before the region boundary and ends where you want the fade-in to end.

5 Click **on the** Waveform Display button **to show a graphic view of the audio you will be fading in. The waveform will be displayed.**

6a Click **on the** Standard radio button **in the In Shape section to select a standard curve. The option will be selected.**

OR

6b Click **on the** S-Curve radio button **in the In Shape section to select an S curve, which rises quickly, evens out, and then rises again to full volume. The option will be selected.**

OR

6c Click and drag **the** Fade curve **to change its shape. The contour of your fade-in will change along with the shape of the fade curve.**

OR

6d Click **on the** Preset Curve Selection down arrow. **A drop-down menu of additional fade-in curve presets will appear.**

6e Click **on the desired** fade-in curve preset. **The option will be selected.**

6f Click **the** Preset Curve Selection radio button **to use your preset shape.**

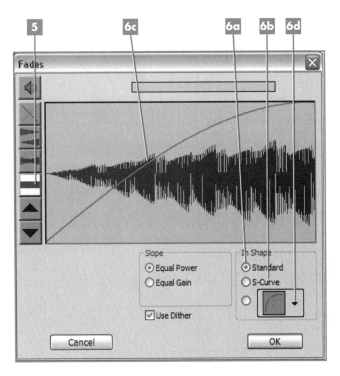

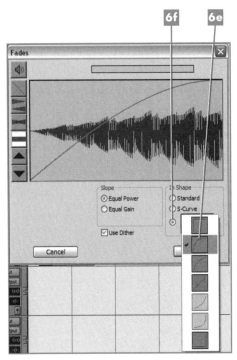

7 Click on OK. **The Fades dialog box will close.**

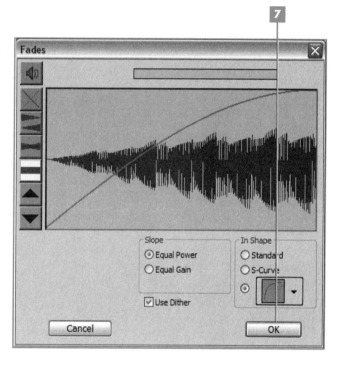

At the beginning of the region, you'll now see a fade region. This section is marked by a vertical line, indicating that it is a fade-in. This fade region represents a fade file located in the Fade Files subfolder. Although this is certainly a region (attached to another audio region) and an audio file, it will not be displayed in the Regions list.

Creating a Fade-Out

After you've created a fade-in, creating a fade-out will be easy.
It really is just a mirror image of the fade-in process.

1 Select the area of a region
that you want to become a
fade-out. Make sure your
selection starts at the point
that you want your fade out to
begin and ends at or after the
region boundary.

2 Click on Edit. The Edit menu
will appear.

3 Click on Fades. The Fades
submenu will appear.

4 Click on Create. The Fades
dialog box will open.

5 Use the options in the Fades
dialog box to customize your
fade-out, just as you did your
fade-in. It still operates the
same, just in the opposite
direction!

6 Click on OK. The Fades dialog
box will close.

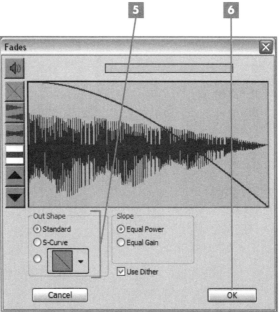

> ❄ **CAUTION**
>
> You've probably noticed that when you use these methods for creating fade-ins and fade-outs, Pro Tools automatically knows whether you want to create a fade-in or a fade-out. Here's something to be careful about when you create a fade-in or fade-out: If you don't select to the end (or beginning) of a region, Pro Tools will get confused about what you want to do. Even if you go to the Edit menu and select Fades, the Create option will be grayed out and unavailable.

Crossfades

Here's how to crossfade between two overlapping regions.

1 Select an area of two overlapping regions that you want to become a crossfade. In this example, I've made a track of overlapping bass and drum regions so that you can easily hear the transition from one region to another.

2 Click on Edit. The Edit menu will appear.

3 Click on Fades. The Fades submenu will appear.

4 Click on Create. The Fades dialog box will open.

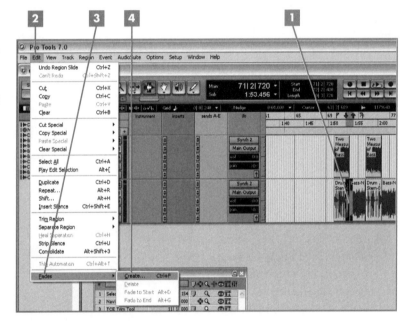

5 Set up the fade-in portion of your crossfade the same way you would a standalone fade-in.

6 Set up the fade-out portion of the crossfade in the same way.

7 Drag the crossing point of your crossfade earlier or later, depending on your preference for this particular crossfade.

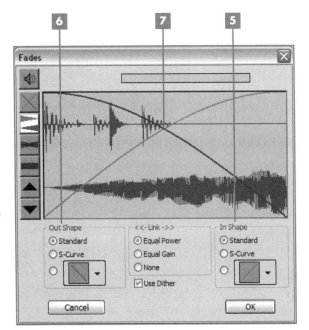

You'll notice that the fade-in and fade-out components of this crossfade are joined, and changes to either aspect will affect the other. Take a look at this linking.

1 Click on the Equal Power radio button in the Link area. The option will be selected. Use this option when you're crossfading audio that is not identical. These curves will prevent the volume drop that can sometimes occur and is commonly perceived as a smooth transition between regions.

2 Move the crossover point from left to right. Notice that it remains at the same position, slightly above the middle of the dialog box.

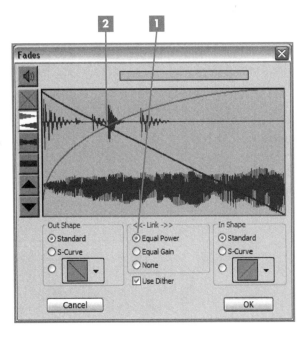

3 Click on the Equal Gain radio button. When you select this as a linking option, your crossover point will not be boosted in any way, although you can still move the crossover point from left to right (earlier to later). When you are crossfading identical or similar audio, this linking will give you the desired smooth transition from region to region.

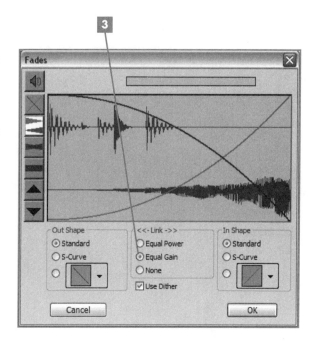

4 Click on the None radio button. This will change one half of a crossfade without changing the other half.

5 Click on the small black handle at the beginning or end of a fade curve. They're tricky to click on with your mouse, but once you do get them, you will be able to drag and drop them anywhere you want, and all other aspects of the crossfade will remain unchanged.

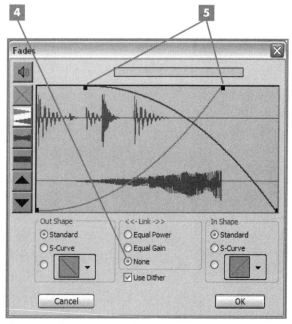

❋ **Note**

Although the None link mode might not be the most commonly used mode of crossfading, it is often the mode of choice if you need a specific non-linear transition.

Creating Fades Using the Smart Tool

In addition to the triple benefit of Trim, Select, and Grabber that you get with the Smart tool, you can also quickly create fade-ins, fade-outs, and even crossfades!

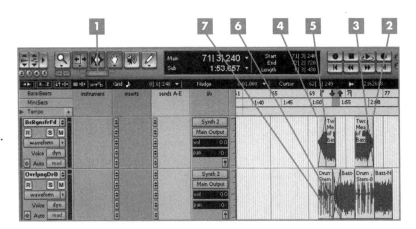

1 Click on the Smart bar to activate the Smart tool. The Smart tool will be selected.

2 Move your cursor to the upper-right corner of a region. The cursor will change to a small square with a diagonal line through it, which looks a bit like a fade-out region.

3 Click and drag your mouse pointer to the left and release the mouse button when you want your fade-out to start to create a fade-out region.

4 Move your cursor to the upper-left corner of a region to create a fade-in.

5 Click and drag your mouse pointer to create your fade-in the same way you created your fade-out (only in the opposite direction).

6 Move your cursor to the bottom corners of two adjacent regions. Now your cursor will be able to create a crossfade!

7 Click and drag your mouse left or right to create a crossfade centered on the regions' boundaries.

So how can you control the contours of your fades when you use the Smart tool to create them?

1 Click on Setup. The Setup menu will appear.

2 Click on Preferences. The Pro Tools LE Preferences dialog box will open.

3 Click on the Editing tab. The tab will move to the front.

4 Click on the Fade In button. The familiar Fades dialog box will appear.

5 Configure the fade-in curve as your default fade-in.

6 Click on the Crossfade button. The Fades dialog box will appear.

7 Configure the crossfade curve as your default crossfade.

8 Click on the Fade Out button. The Fades dialog box will appear.

9 Configure the fade-out curve as your default fade-out.

10 Click on the Done button. Your settings will be saved, and the Preferences dialog box will close.

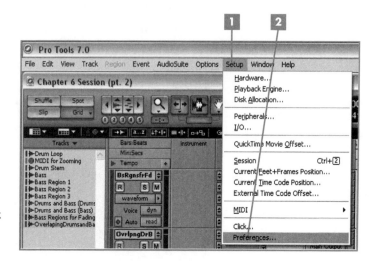

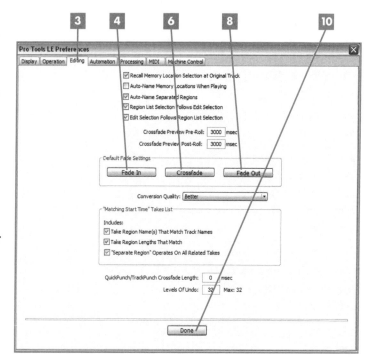

TIP

It's a good idea to set up your most commonly used fade-in, fade-out, and crossfade settings in the Preferences dialog box. Each time you create a fade using the Smart tool, the fade curve will be based upon these preferences.

NOTE

Regardless of whether you used the Smart tool, if you create a fade and you later want to change its contour, double-click on the fade region with the Grabber tool. The Fades dialog box will open again so you can make your changes. Note that any changes you make in this dialog box will not affect your preferences.

Cool Editing Tools

Here are some great new additions to Pro Tools' editing arsenal!

Tick-Based Audio Tracks

Under most circumstances, you'll want your audio regions securely anchored to an absolute time location, right down to the sample. Also, it is pretty customary to have your MIDI data linked to your sessions measures—bars, beats, and *ticks*. Recently, you were given the option of assigning your audio regions to be locked to a tick-based location, which means that as you change your tempo, your regions will move accordingly.

If you go to memory location #9—Tick-Based Audio, you'll see a familiar-sounding drum part, separated at each transient. Basically, each drum hit has been separated. Let's see what can be done.

1 Click the Time Base Selector button. A list will appear.

2 Choose the desired time scale for your track. In this case click the Ticks option.

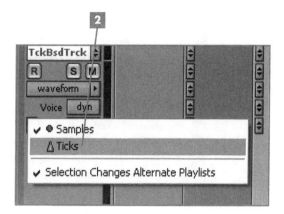

3 With this setting, all the regions on this track are assigned to tempo locations, which means if you change the tempo in your session, each individual region (in this case, each individual transient) will move accordingly. Drag the Tempo slider, and see how your audio changes!

Link Edit and Track Selection

It's a simple enough feature, but definitely worth taking a look at!

❄ **NOTE**

For the purposes of this demonstration, show all the tracks of your session.

1 Click **the** Link Track and Edit Selection button.

2 Select **the desired** track.

3 Using the Selector tool, **make a** selection **on the selected track.**

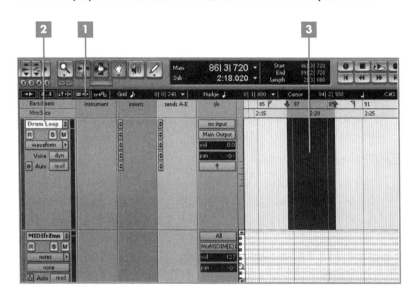

4 Now, select **a** different track. **Note how the selection moves with your track selection.**

❄ **TIP**

If you want to select multiple tracks, and thus make multiple selections, just hold down the Shift key as you select tracks.

Region Groups

NOTE

For this section, go to memory location #10—Region Groups.

Region Groups, a new feature in Pro Tools 7, is another way to link regions together so that they move and change as a single unit, even though they may span multiple tracks.

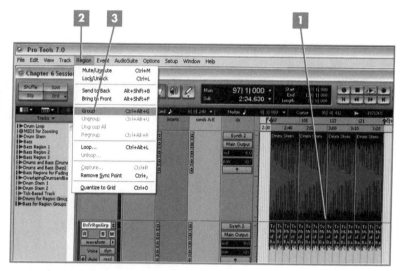

1 Select the regions that you wish to assign to your Region group. In this memory location, your regions have been selected for you.

2 Click the Region menu.

3 Click Group. The regions will be joined into a single larger object.

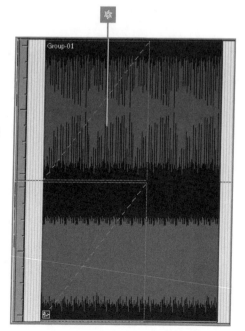

❋ The region group will have its own name, and appear in the Regions list at the right edge of your Edit window. Better than that, though, you'll be able to apply edit processes in a way impossible before, like creating a long fade over the entire region group, as shown here.

❋ **NOTE**

For this last section of the chapter, recall memory location #11— Region Looping.

Region Looping

The ability to loop regions is another brand new feature in Pro Tools 7 and will be a useful new feature for loop-based production. Here's how it works.

1 Select the region(s) that you wish to loop. In this memory location, your region has been selected for you.

2 Click the Region menu.

3 Click Loop. The Region Looping dialog box will open.

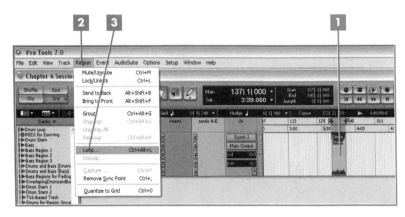

You have a number of choices when it comes to how you want your region to loop:

a Choose the number of repetitions you wish your region to make.

b Specify a length of time (based upon the main time scale) that you want to fill with these loops.

c Loop until the end of the session or until the next region (whichever comes first).

d Check the Enable Crossfade box to create crossfades between each loop iteration. When this option is selected, you can adjust the crossfade curve by clicking the Settings button (the window looks exactly the same as the Crossfades dialog box you worked with earlier in this chapter).

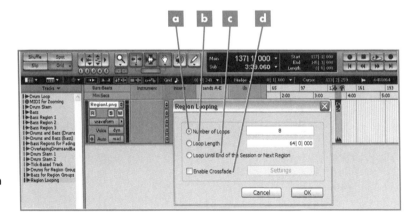

In this example, I've chosen to repeat this region eight times, and here's the result.

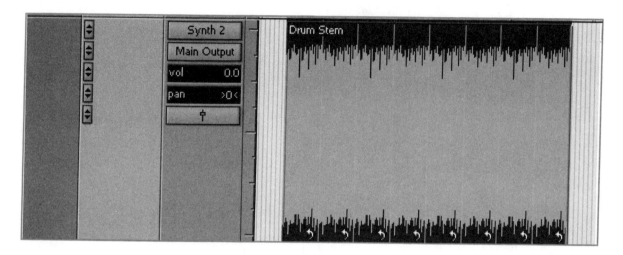

This series of looped regions, like region groups, functions in many ways like a single unit and can be moved and edited with great flexibility.

That's all for now! Next—MIDI!

7 } Using MIDI

MIDI (Musical Instrument Digital Interface) is a language that allows keyboards, synthesizers, and other components to communicate with one another. Since its inception in the early 1980s, MIDI has proved to be an invaluable creative tool to musicians of all kinds, and it has changed the face of the music industry.

Not too long ago, music software worked with *either* audio or MIDI, but certainly not both. Thankfully, those days have changed, and there are a number of products such as Pro Tools that incorporate the creative power of MIDI and all the advantages of digital audio. Pro Tools LE 7 has made particularly impressive gains in its MIDI power, while remaining a solid audio workstation. In this chapter, you'll learn how to:

* ❊ Set up your MIDI studio
* ❊ Route MIDI and audio signals so you can work with synthesizers in Pro Tools
* ❊ Record and edit MIDI data

Setting Up Your MIDI Studio

Just as you configured your audio inputs and outputs before you worked with audio, you'll want to configure your MIDI setup and identify your devices before getting down to work. Don't worry; it's easy!

1 Click on Setup. The Setup menu will appear.

2 Click on MIDI. A submenu will be displayed.

3 Choose MIDI Studio Setup. The MIDI Studio Setup window will be shown.

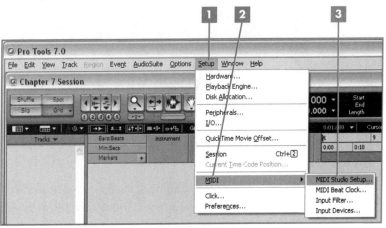

Adding a MIDI Device

Now you can add a synth to your setup.

1 Click on the Create button. A new device, initially named New Instrument 1, will be created.

2 Type a descriptive name for your first device, then press Enter to confirm the name. The name New Instrument 1 will change to reflect your naming.

3 Click on the Manufacturer button. A menu will appear.

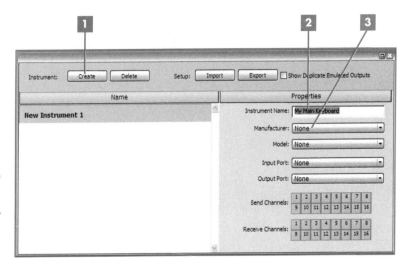

4 Choose **the** manufacturer **that**
matches your device. The
information will be added to
the device description on the
left side of the window.

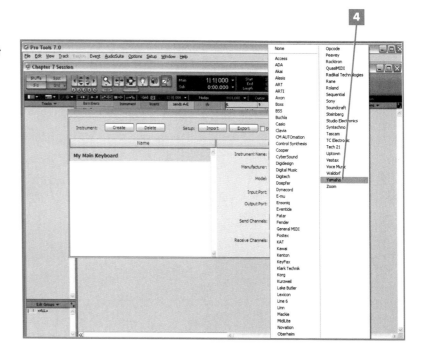

5 Now it's time to choose a
model. Click **on the** Model
button. A menu will appear.

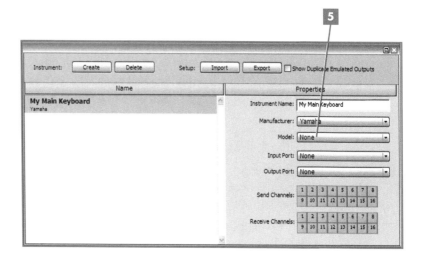

6 Choose the model that matches your device. The information will be added to the device description on the left side of the window.

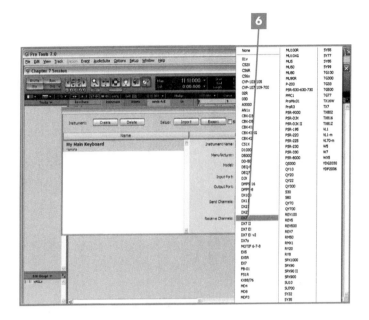

Connecting Your Gear

Now you can connect your gear in a traditional configuration—in other words, connect the output of your MIDI interface to the MIDI input of your device, and connect the MIDI output (*not* the Thru) of your device into an input on your MIDI interface. After you physically connect your MIDI cables to and from your MIDI interface and device, follow these steps.

1 Click the Input Port button. This will allow you to choose the MIDI In connection on your MIDI interface that is accepting data from this device. A menu will appear.

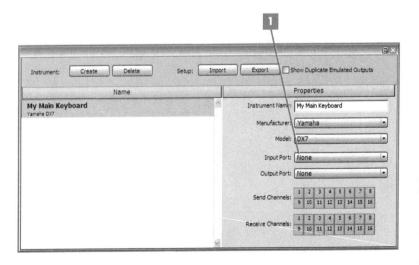

2 Choose the appropriate MIDI In port on your MIDI interface. If you're using a Digi 002 or MBox 2 as a MIDI interface, there's only one MIDI In port, so it's an easy choice!

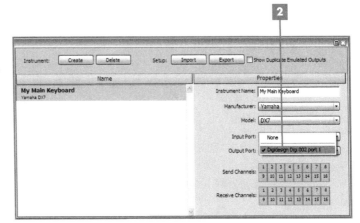

3 Now it's time to choose how you will send MIDI information to this device. Click the Output Port button. A menu will appear.

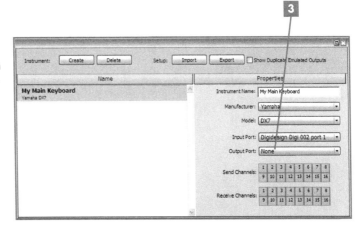

4 Choose the appropriate MIDI Out port on your MIDI interface.

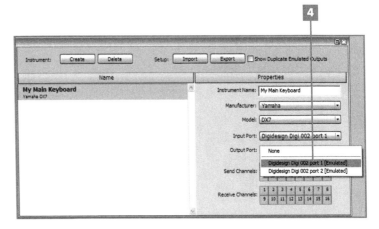

5 By default, a new device is created with all Send Channels enabled, which means that the device can send data on all of the 16 available MIDI channels. Click any numbered box to un-highlight it and remove it from the set of channels that may be used by that device for MIDI transmission.

6 By default, a new device is created with all Receive Channels enabled, which means that the device can accept data on all of the 16 available MIDI channels. Click any numbered box to un-highlight it and remove it from the set of channels that may be used by that device for MIDI reception.

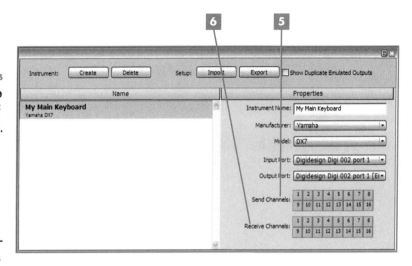

You can repeat this process to include all of the MIDI devices in your system. Before we leave this window, though, let's take a look at some of its other features:

❈ The Import button will allow you to open a MIDI setup file (called a DigiMIDIService Setup file, stored with a *.dms extension) that has been previously created. Be careful, though—this will overwrite your current settings.

❈ Want to store the setup you've got now for archiving or transporting to another system? Just click the Export button. You will be prompted to save a .dms file.

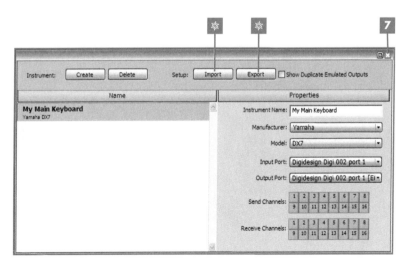

7 When you're done, just close the window, and your settings will be applied to your system.

Signal Flow 201: MIDI versus Audio

Here's the important thing to remember about MIDI as opposed to audio: MIDI is *not* audio. MIDI isn't even audible—it's a digital language that allows musical hardware components to communicate with and control each other on a fundamental level. The common misconception that MIDI and audio are somehow related comes from the fact that the use of MIDI allows musical gear with MIDI connections to make sound.

Given that MIDI and digital audio are fundamentally different (although interdependent), it comes as no surprise that MIDI must have its own rules of signal flow. The good news about this is that you can manage both the MIDI signal path and the audio signal path simultaneously in one session.

Managing the MIDI Signal Path

The good news about MIDI data routing is that the look and feel of a MIDI track is similar to an audio or Aux track.

1 Create a MIDI track and name it descriptively. (See Chapter 3 if you need a refresher on how to do this.)

You'll notice that much of a MIDI track looks like an audio track:

a Track name

b Record, Solo, and Mute buttons

c Input

d Output

e Volume

f Pan

❈ ❈ ❈

2 Click on the Input button. The Input menu will appear, giving you a number of options for the input of the track. These options include the following:

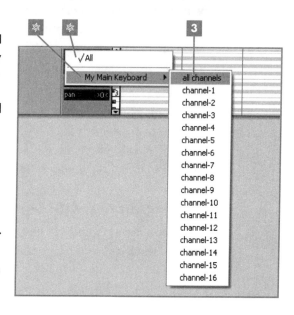

❊ Selecting All as an input will allow the track to accept MIDI data on any channel from any port. This is a particularly efficient way to work if you're a single user in a multi-keyboard studio. With All selected, you can move from MIDI instrument to MIDI instrument without having to change your input selection.

❊ Each input device you create in your MIDI setup will appear as an input option. You can specify a single device or even a specific MIDI channel as an input for your track. This is useful in multi-keyboard setups in which you have multiple musicians at one time. You can assign multiple tracks to accept input from only one MIDI port for each track; this way, you can isolate each musician's performance to a separate track even if all the musicians are playing simultaneously.

3 Select the input that matches the MIDI device you want to play. The input will be selected.

4 Click **on the** Output button.
The Output menu will appear.

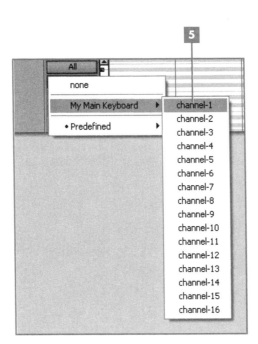

5 Click **on the** device and MIDI
channel **you want to sound
when you play. The device
and MIDI channel will be
selected.**

❋ **NOTE**

The MIDI device that you physically play does *not* have to be the MIDI device
that makes a sound. In this situation, the device you actually play is commonly
called a *MIDI Controller* (not to be confused with controller data, such as
modulation wheel or pitch bend).

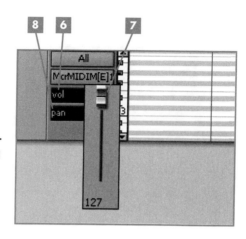

6 Click **on the** Volume display area. **A small fader box will appear.**

7 Click and drag **the** slider **on the fader box to adjust the volume to suit your mix. The MIDI volume will be adjusted.**

8 Click **in the** Pan display area. **A small slider box will appear.**

> ❋ **NOTE**
>
> Note that this fader controls MIDI volume, which is why it has a maximum of 127. MIDI volume has a range of 128 steps, from 0–127.

9 Click and drag **the** slider **on the box to adjust the pan value to your taste. The value will be adjusted.**

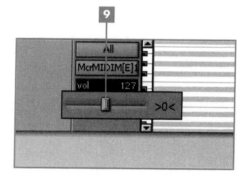

Now your MIDI track is set up to route MIDI data from the master device (controller) to the slave device. When you play your controlling instrument, you should see an indication on the slave device that it is receiving MIDI data. At this point, your slave device should respond to the MIDI data by making sound.

Setting Up an Aux Track to Monitor Your MIDI Gear

So how can you hear your slave device through Pro Tools? First, connect the audio outputs of the slave device to the audio inputs of your Pro Tools interface, and then follow these steps.

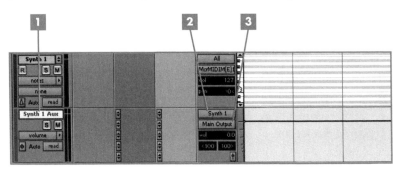

1 Create a new Aux track and name it descriptively. This track will allow you to hear your MIDI device.

2 Assign the input of this Aux track to match the *audio* inputs to which your MIDI slave device is attached.

3 Assign the output of this Aux track to the outputs attached to your monitor speakers.

At this point, you've completely configured your MIDI signal flow, as well as an audio signal routing that will allow you to listen to your gear. Now when you play your controller device, you should trigger your slave device and listen to the output through an Aux track!

Using Virtual Instruments

The latest stage of plug-in evolution is virtual instruments. In a Pro Tools system, these plug-ins are RTAS (Real Time Audio Suite), which you'll work with more in the next chapter, but since these are MIDI-related, we'll discuss them here. Whereas most RTAS plug-ins are audio effects, virtual instruments don't process audio—they *make* audio! Think of them as the marriage between software plug-ins and MIDI synthesizers, taking advantage of both worlds. With virtual instruments, you not only have the power of a MIDI synth without the bulk of physical hardware; you also have the ability to automate its parameters just like any RTAS plug-in. (Don't worry, we'll talk about that in the next chapter.)

The secret to using virtual instruments is in the setup, which really is just a variation of a typical MIDI setup.

As with a typical MIDI setup, you need two tracks to get MIDI data and audio data to work within Pro Tools—a MIDI track (for MIDI data) and an Aux track. In a traditional setup, the Aux track would be used to route audio from an outside source into Pro Tools, and back out through an interface output. In this case, you still need the Aux track, even though there is no outside source involved.

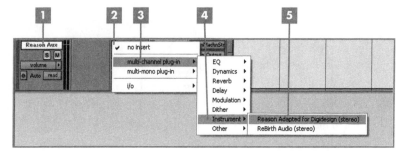

1 After you've set the parameters for a stereo aux input track, click on Create. A new stereo aux input track will be created.

2 Click on an Insert button

3 Select either multi-channel or multi-mono plug-in. A submenu will appear.

4 Click Instrument. Another submenu will appear.

5 In this case, I've opened Reason Adapted, a virtual instrument that is included with many versions of Pro Tools LE (although it is technically a separate application). The plug-in's window will appear.

The virtual instrument will be launched in its own window. In the case of Reason Adapted, a complete virtual synth environment will be instantiated.

The Reason Adapted software communicates with Pro Tools through a bit of software called ReWire, which serves as virtual MIDI and audio communication between the two applications.

6 Click on the Output button in ReWire, and select an output for your software synth.

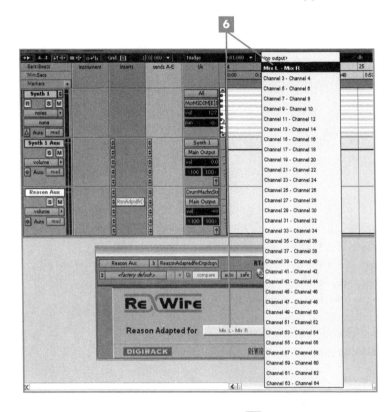

7 Now all you need to do is create a MIDI track and set up the output to be routed to your new virtual instrument. Fortunately, Pro Tools will automatically add the virtual instrument(s) to the list of outputs once the plug-in is instantiated. Click on the Output button of the MIDI track. An expanded menu will appear.

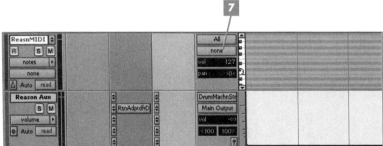

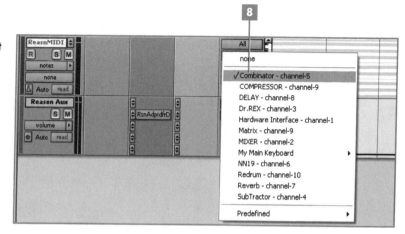

8 Select the instrument you want to control from the drop-down menu.

9 You're pretty much all set, but let's test the setup—here's an easy way, even if you don't have a keyboard: First, bring up the volume level of the Aux track that holds your virtual instrument.

10 Choose the Pencil tool.

11 Click and drag the Pencil cursor in your MIDI track. MIDI data will be created, data will be sent to the virtual instrument, and the instrument will sound.

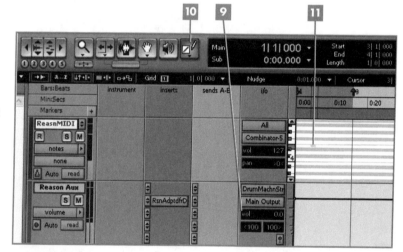

❋ **NOTE**

When you play a session that contains MIDI, you will see MIDI data being played in your MIDI track's level meters. Remember that what you're seeing is not audio, but rather control data being sent to the virtual instrument on your aux input track. The levels you see on the Aux track are the audible signal being routed to your monitor speakers.

New in Pro Tools 7: Instrument Tracks

One of the most exciting new features in Pro Tools 7 is the addition of a brand new type of track, called an Instrument track. This is a real timesaver for MIDI production, as it combines the power of a MIDI track *and* an Aux track in one single strip. Let's delete the *two* tracks you just created in the previous virtual instrument scenario, and do the whole job within just one track. Check it out!

1 Click the Track menu. The menu will be displayed.

2 Click on New. The familiar New Tracks dialog box will appear.

3 Click the Track Type button, and select Instrument Track. When you click Create, a new track will be created.

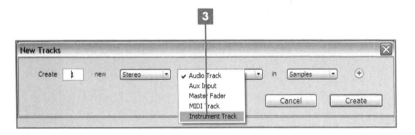

4 Name your track descriptively.

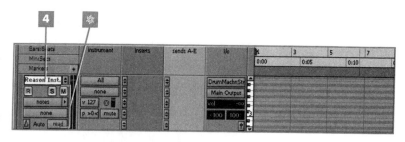

> ❋ Note that the section immediately below the track name is exactly the same as a MIDI track. You have all that functionality, and more. Read on!

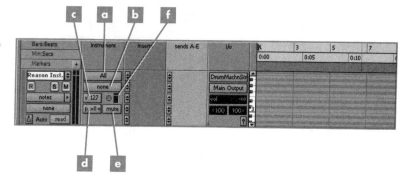

The Instrument column contains the functionality of a MIDI track's I/O column, and then some. . . .

a MIDI Input

b MIDI Output

c MIDI Volume

d MIDI Pan

e MIDI Mute

f MIDI Level Meter

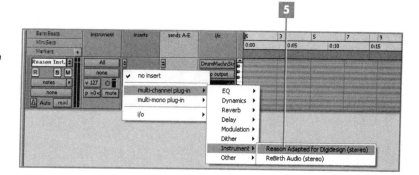

5 The Inserts column of an Instrument track functions like the inserts column of an Aux track. Just instantiate your virtual instrument plug-in on this track just as you did before with an Aux track. Your plug-in will launch, and the plug-in window will be displayed.

6 In the case of any ReWire application, configure the channels for communication between the ReWire application (in this case, Reason) and Pro Tools, as you did before when we were working with an Aux track.

7 Once the virtual instrument is instantiated, you can now choose it from the Instrument column's MIDI Output button.

8 The I/O column of an Instrument track is just like the I/O column of an Aux track, and you'll use it the same way you did before. First, set the output of the track.

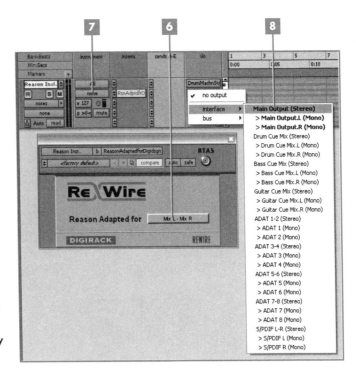

9 Last, but certainly not least, set your track's output level, or you won't hear anything!

10 Now, your track should look something like the example shown here. Use your Pencil tool to test your setup, as you did in the previous section of this chapter. Pretty cool!

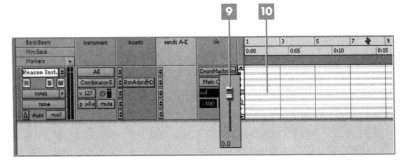

MIDI and Instrument Tracks in the Mix Window

The Mix window is uniquely suited to routing and combining individual signals in order to get a pleasing total "mix" that can be output to a pair of outputs (assuming that your mix is in stereo). Let's take a look at these two new tracks.

❀ ❀ ❀

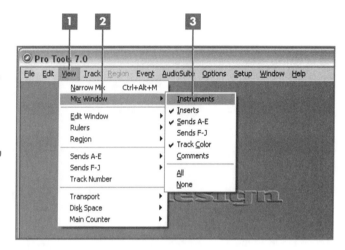

1 First, you need to make sure you're seeing the appropriate characteristics of each track strip in the Mix window. Click the View menu.

2 Choose the Mix Window menu item. A submenu will appear.

3 If the Instruments menu item isn't checked, click it now.

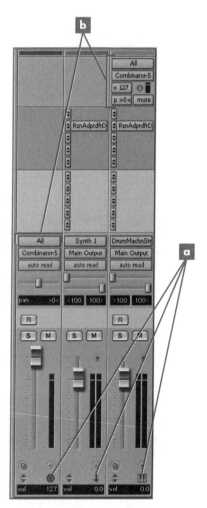

This graphic shows an arrangement of a MIDI track followed by an Aux track, and lastly an Instrument track.

a The icons at the bottom right indicate the type of track (a MIDI plug for a MIDI track, an arrow for an Aux track, and a keyboard for an Instrument track).

b Note that the top section of an Instrument track offers the same functionality as the bottom section of a MIDI track (MIDI input, output, volume, and so on).

c The bottom sections of an Aux track and Instrument track are identical, and it is here where you will set up your Audio Ins, Outs, and more (which you'll learn about in the next chapter).

d All track strips allow the user to adjust positioning with Pan controls, as well as Record (when applicable), Solo, Mute, and Volume controls.

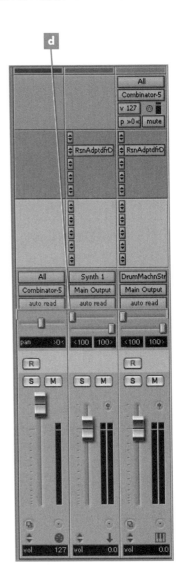

Recording MIDI

Recording MIDI is very similar to recording audio in many respects, but with some extra flexibility. The first step is to pick a sound that you want to use.

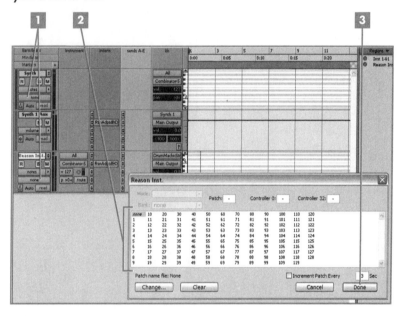

1 Click on the Program Change button (fortunately, it's in the same position on a MIDI and an Instrument track). A dialog box containing a patch list for the MIDI device will open. Depending on the device, the patch list displayed will consist of numeric or text names.

2 Click on the number of the patch you want to use. The patch will be selected.

3 Click on Done. The dialog box will close. The program number or name will appear on the Program Change button.

❋ **TIP**

Here's a useful feature: If you're searching for just the right sound, select the Increment Patch Every *n* Sec check box to cycle through all the sounds in this bank. You can specify the speed at which patches are changed (in seconds) by entering the value in the appropriate field.

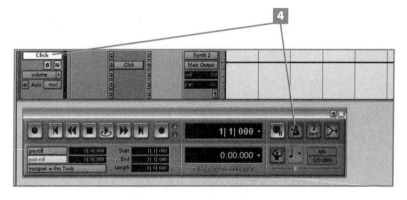

4 Before you start recording, you might want to set up a Click track (which you learned about back in Chapter 4). Remember to click on the Metronome icon to enable your click.

Now it's time to actually record the MIDI. The process of recording MIDI is nearly identical to recording audio.

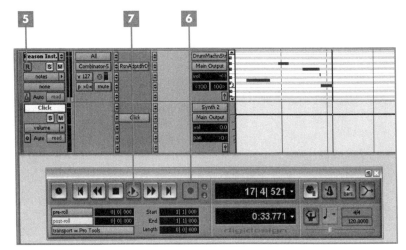

5 Click on the track's R button to arm the recording.

6 Click on the Record button in the Transport window.

7 Click on the Play button. The recording process will begin. It operates the same as when you record audio, with pre-rolls, post-rolls, and so on.

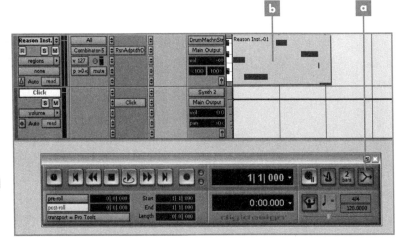

a There's a nifty MIDI feature called Merge that allows you to record over a pre-recorded MIDI track and add to the data that's already there instead of erasing notes that you already played. It's an especially useful feature when you're working in Loop Record mode.

b When you're finished, you'll have a region, as you did when you recorded audio. This time, however, you'll see MIDI note data within the region rather than audio waveforms!

Editing MIDI

There's a whole world of flexibility open to you when you work with MIDI. Operations that are extremely difficult with digital audio, such as fixing one note in a chord, are easy with MIDI!

Editing with Tools

There are many ways to edit MIDI data, and in a very real way you'll have a greater degree of control over specific notes than you might have with audio tracks. To start with, you have all the region editing tools that you've come to know in the previous editing chapters. Selector, Grabber, and Trim (including the TCE Trim tool) will still work with MIDI regions in just the same way that they've worked with audio regions. In the interest of expediency, we won't rehash these basic (but powerful) ways of working in the Edit window, but do take some time to reacquaint yourself with these tools when you get the opportunity.

The interesting thing about working with MIDI is that you have an extra level of control over your data. You can go beyond the relatively large regions and work with individual notes themselves. The good news is that even at this deeper level, you can still use the editing tools that are already familiar to you, though their behavior will be somewhat different. The first thing to do, though, is to change your Edit window's view so that you can actually see what you're working with—you need to look at your tracks in a different way:

1 Click on the Track View Selector on the desired track. The Track View menu will appear.

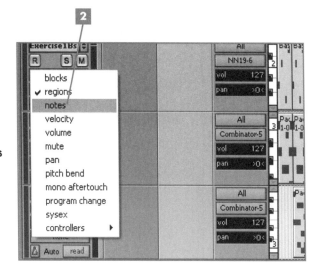

The menu includes options so you can control the kind of data you will view and manipulate. Because this is a MIDI track, the menu will display all editable aspects of MIDI in Pro Tools, including controllers and system exclusive data.

2 You'll be working on note data first, so click on Notes.

The familiar regions will fade somewhat, leaving only a series of small blocks. Each of these blocks represents a MIDI note.

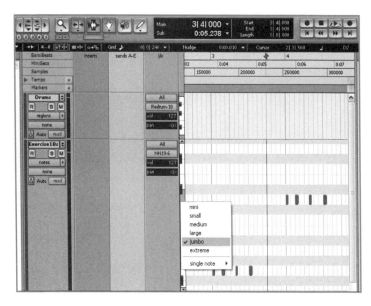

❋ ❋ ❋

On the left edge of the MIDI track's Timeline, you will notice a keyboard graphic. This graphic identifies the pitches of the MIDI notes in the track. Depending upon the kind of music part you're working with, the first thing you'll want to do is get your MIDI data into easy view. Here are a few ways to do it, some of which should look familiar:

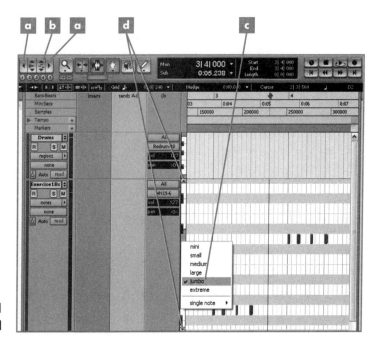

a Use the horizontal zoom buttons to see more or less of your timeline.

b Use the MIDI Zoom buttons to zoom *vertically* on your MIDI data. Note that your tracks' keyboard graphic will expand and contract accordingly, and that these adjustments do nothing to your audio tracks.

c Click within the keyboard graphic to reveal the Track Height menu, and choose the best setting for the job at hand (in this case, Jumbo works well for my Bass track).

d Click on the arrow at either end of the keyboard graphic to scroll up and down the register of the track.

The Grabber Tool

One of the nicest things about Pro Tools is that the basic editing tools are easy to get to, and they're named well. The Grabber tool does just what it says it does—it allows the user to grab objects in the Edit window and move them. In the case of MIDI note data, however, your "objects" are individual notes!

1 Click **on the** Grabber tool. **The tool will be selected.**

2 Click **on a** single note **in your track. The note will be highlighted, indicating that it is selected.**

3 Drag and drop **the** note **to a different pitch or timing, as desired.**

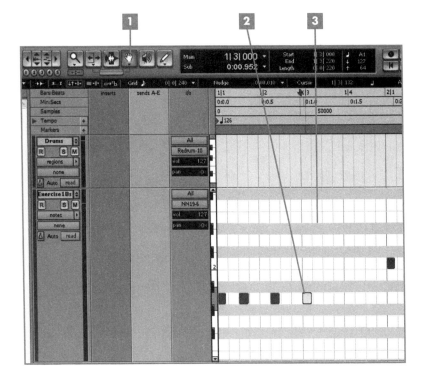

4 **If you want to move more than one note at a time,** drag a box **around the notes you want to change. The group of notes will be highlighted, indicating that they are selected.**

5 Drag and drop **the** group of notes **in the same manner that you moved a single note.**

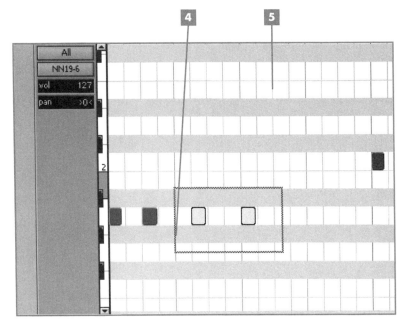

The Trim Tool

The Trim tool, the next of the primary edit tools, allows you to adjust the beginning and/or end of MIDI notes in much the same way you've changed region boundaries when working with audio.

1. Click on the Trim tool. The tool will be selected.

2. Click on either end of a single note in your track. The note will be highlighted, indicating that it is selected.

3. Drag the end of the note as desired. The duration of the note will be lengthened or shortened as appropriate.

The Pencil Tool

The Pencil tool might just be the most useful of all the MIDI editing tools. For example, using the Pencil tool, you can create a MIDI note (or other type of MIDI data). In the Slip edit mode, you can create your data anywhere, but in this case, I want to create a quarter note.

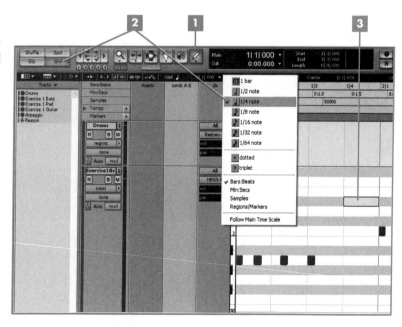

1. Click on the Pencil tool. The tool will be selected.

2. Select Grid mode and set the grid to 1/4 Note.

3. Click on any open area of your track. Wherever you click, a MIDI quarter note will be created.

This mode works well if you want to write notes that have the same duration as your grid, but what if you wanted to write eighth notes, but still use a quarter note grid? No problem. In fact, this is a great way to work with strings of notes—take a look:

1 Click and hold **on the** Pencil tool **icon. The Pencil tool menu will appear.**

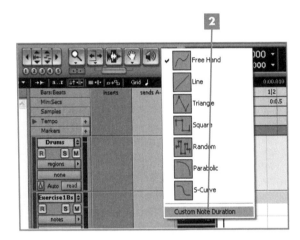

2 Click **on** Custom Note Duration. **A small button below the Pencil tool will appear.**

3 Click **the** Custom Note Duration **button. A menu will appear.**

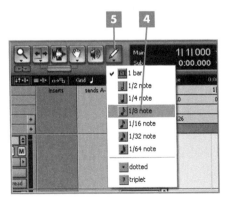

4 Click **the desired** note value. **The value will be selected, and the menu will disappear.**

5 Again, click and hold **on the** Pencil tool icon **to reveal the Pencil tool menu.**

6 To draw a string of notes, click the Line menu item.

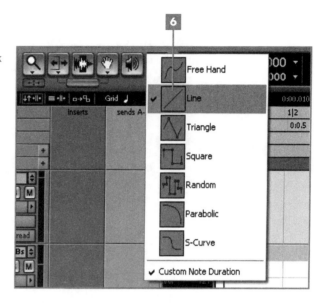

7 Now comes the fun part: Click and hold with your Pencil tool at the point that you want to begin entering new MIDI note data.

8 Drag the Pencil cursor horizontally (left or right) to create a string of notes. Note that in this example, the duration of each note is an eighth note (based upon the custom note duration) and the spacing is every quarter note (based upon the grid value).

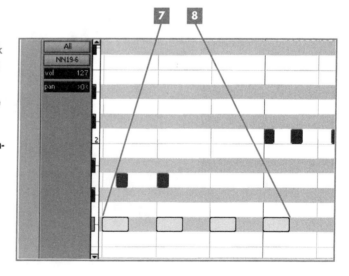

※ **NOTE**

The Pencil tool is great for quick MIDI editing—not only for its Pencil functions, but also for its other functions. If you click in the body of a pre-existing note, the Pencil tool will take on the function of a Grabber. If you move the Pencil tool to either end of the note, it will become a Trim tool.

The MIDI Menu

In addition to editing with tools, you can also powerfully transform your MIDI with functions from the MIDI menu (as of Pro Tools version 7, this menu has been moved under the Event menu). Most of these features are commonly found in most MIDI sequencers and fall into the range of basic operations, but it is helpful to know where to find them and the specific layout of such windows.

Here's how you start the process:

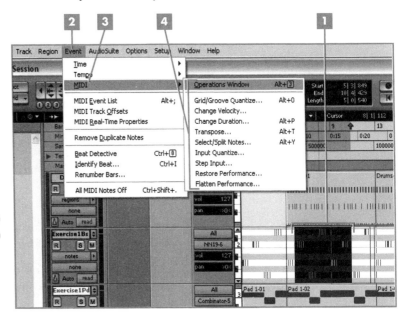

1 Select the group of notes you want to process. The notes will be selected.

2 Click on Event. The Event menu will appear.

3 Click on MIDI. A secondary menu will appear.

4 Choose the process you want to apply to the selection. There are a number of processes you can apply; the next few sections will explain these processes in more detail.

Grid/Groove Quantize

Basically speaking, *quantize* is a MIDI function that aligns the timing of MIDI notes to a grid. It is commonly used to fix timing errors or create a mechanically timed track when the style of music calls for it. Pro Tools' MIDI Operations dialog box for quantization includes all the basic parameters, in addition to Include Within and Exclude Within options, which allow you to set thresholds of notes to be quantized based upon the distance of given notes from the grid.

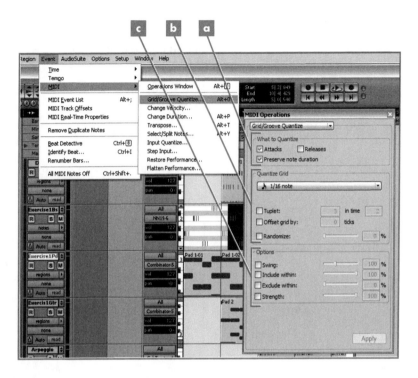

a The What to Quantize section allows you to individually choose which part of your note will be adjusted.

b The Quantize Grid section allows you to choose the resolution of your quantizing. This section also allows you to choose and define tuplet quantization, commonly used to create a triplet-style grid, with three quantize points in the space where there would normally be only two. Finally, there's a Randomize function, which will allow you to add a percentage of timing chaos (see the Tip immediately following this section).

c The Options section allows you to choose how your note data will respond to the quantization operation. Swing will add a triplet-style feel. The Include Within and Exclude Within parameters will allow you to choose which of your data will be affected (including 100% and excluding 0% will insure that all of your MIDI data is quantized). Strength will allow your quantize process to choose how much to correct your timings—for example, if your strength is set to 100%, your notes will be moved all the way to the nearest grid point, whereas at 50% strength they'll only be moved halfway to the nearest grid location.

Beyond basic grid quantizing, there's Groove quantize. When you use Groove quantize, you won't be moving your notes' timing to an equally spaced grid but to a set of complex location points designed to emulate a certain musical feel. The good news is that Groove quantizing is almost exactly the same as regular Grid quantizing. Here's how it works:

1 Click the Quantize Grid button. A drop-down menu will appear.

❊ The first part of this list is a selection of musical note values. Choose the desired note value to change resolution when you are quantizing to a grid.

❊ Listed below are a number of musical grooves for you to quantize to. Choose the desired family of grooves, and a second drop-down menu will appear, allowing you to choose a specific stylistic feel.

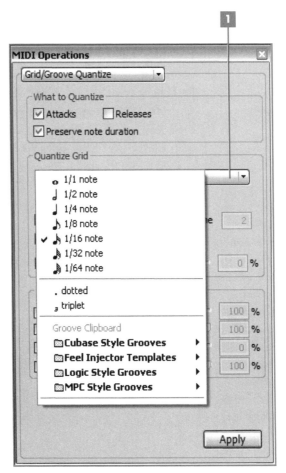

Beyond this difference, the MIDI Operations dialog box functions identically in either Grid or Groove quantize mode.

❊ **TIP**

You can change MIDI processes without going back to the MIDI menu. Simply click on the menu at the top of the MIDI Operations dialog box to reveal a menu of MIDI functions.

Users often apply the Randomize feature to a MIDI drum track in the hopes that it will "humanize" the track. This usually has a negative effect upon the groove. However, used sparingly, the Randomize feature works well when you are dealing with a section of musical sounds (strings, brass, and so on)—it takes the edge off the mechanical accuracy sometimes associated with MIDI.

Restore Performance

Pro Tools' Restore Performance feature is a simple enough operation but a powerful ally when you need it. Think of the Restore Performance option as an improved version of the Undo feature. Consider this: When you save your session, the Pro Tools' undo cue is cleared, which prohibits you from undoing things like audio region edits and so on. What makes the Restore Performance function so special is that it extends *beyond* the last time you saved your session and the levels of undo that Pro Tools already has!

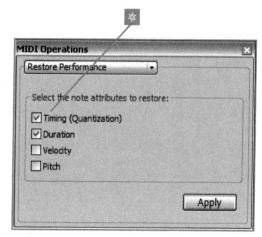

❄ You can selectively restore specific aspects of your MIDI data (timing, duration, velocity, and pitch), so you're not locked into an all-or-nothing situation—you can choose what to recover and what to keep current. When you restore your performance, it will revert to the data's original state, or the last time the performance was flattened (which we'll talk about next), whichever happened most recently.

Flatten Performance

Let's say you've *perfected* your MIDI data, and you want to make sure you can easily recover this ideal state. When you choose the Flatten Performance option, you "print" your MIDI data to your session and remove the option to undo any previous edits that you've performed. If in the future you choose to restore the performance, it will revert to this new flattened state.

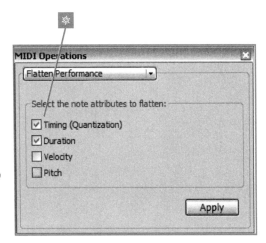

❋ Just as with the Restore Performance option, you can selectively flatten specific aspects of your MIDI data. When you flatten your performance, you will effectively set a new "restore point" that you can recall at will, using the Restore Performance feature discussed in the preceding section.

---

a The Set All To option assigns a single velocity value to all notes.

OR

b You can directly increase or decrease the velocity value by a set amount using the Add or Subtract options.

OR

c You can scale, or proportionally change, the velocity of a set of notes using the Scale By option.

d Finally, you can use the Change Smoothly option to gradually change the velocity from the beginning of the selection to the end, resulting in an increase or decrease in intensity. By using the Change Smoothly by Percentage feature, you can even specify a smooth curve of change.

Change Velocity

The Change Velocity feature sports options with which you can manipulate MIDI velocity (how fast a key is pressed).

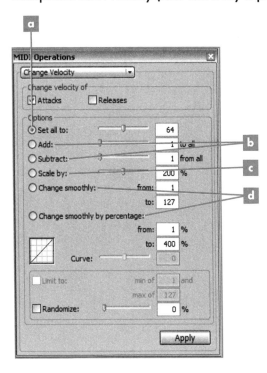

Change Duration

The Change Duration option is similar to the Change Velocity option, but the options affect the length of the selected notes.

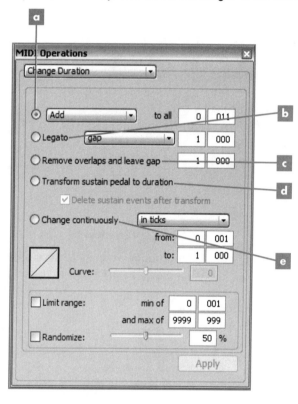

a Click here to set all durations to a single value or add/subtract a fixed value.

b The Legato option will allow you to extend the duration of the selected notes, and the pull-down menu to the right of the radio button will allow you to specify either an overlap or gap between subsequent notes.

c This option can detect overlapping notes (which can be problematic in some circumstances) and change the duration to remove the overlap.

d The Transform Sustain Pedal to Duration radio button will detect pedal data and apply it to the durations of its associated notes.

e The Change Continuously option allows the user to change the durations over time, similar to the Change Continuously feature of the Change Velocity function.

Transpose

Transpose is a MIDI function that changes the note number of MIDI data, effectively changing the pitch of your MIDI music. The options for Pro Tools' Transpose function are very simple and straightforward:

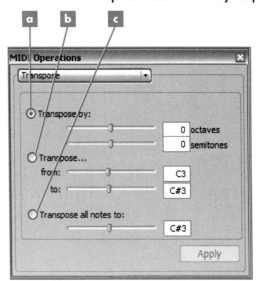

a You can adjust your music by octaves or semitones (also called half steps).

OR

b You can transpose from one reference note to a target note.

OR

c You can change all pitches to a single pitch (particularly useful for changing drum sounds).

❊ **TIP**

Before you change the pitch of an entire section of a song, you might want to exclude your drum tracks from that transposition. Transposing drum kit patches tends to radically change the instrument assignments!

Select Notes/Split Notes

After you've selected notes using the Selector or Grabber tools, you can further logically select notes by setting certain criteria for them. Once you've selected those notes, you can then transform them with another process, or proceed to split the selected notes in a number of ways.

a For both the Select Notes and Split Notes options, you will select notes based on some sort of pitch value. You can set a range (using the Notes Between function), or you can pick out notes starting from the top or bottom of a chord.

b If you don't want to select your notes based upon pitch, you can choose to differentiate your notes based upon velocity, duration, or even the position (measured in beats|ticks) within the measure(s).

c If you choose to select notes for further editing, you're finished. You may, however, choose to split the notes.

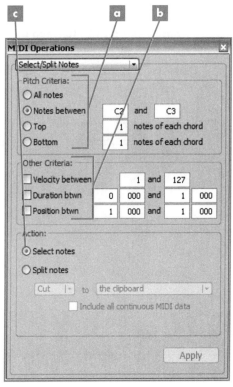

✻ You can choose to either cut or copy the notes by clicking the leftmost button.

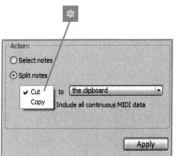

✻ You can choose to cut or copy your split notes to the clipboard (for later pasting) or paste the notes to a track, or series of tracks, based upon pitch (for example, if you split up a 4-note chord, you could create four separate tracks, each with one note).

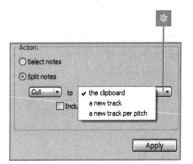

Input Quantize

The Input Quantize feature works exactly like the basic Quantize function except for one thing. Whereas Quantize is applied to MIDI data *after* it has been recorded, Input Quantize processes the audio as it is being played in the session. This feature is particularly nifty for technically challenged people like me because it fixes my timing as I play!

❋ Select the Enable Input Quantize check box to enable the Input Quantize feature. One thing to remember, though—Input Quantize will stay enabled until you turn it off!

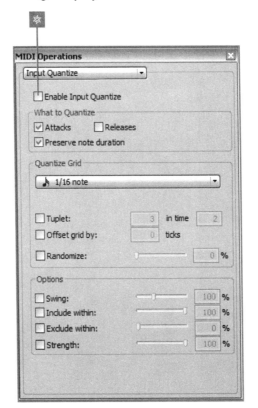

❋ **NOTE**

Newly added to Pro Tools 7, you can now have your Input Quantize use a groove template. Select a groove under the Input Quantize options in the MIDI Operations dialog box , just as you would for the regular Quantize options.

Step Input

If it can be said that MIDI can boost the performance of pedagogi-cally challenged keyboardists (like yours truly), then it might well be said that Step Input is the ultimate expression of this aspect. Forget slowing down the tempo so that you can play a difficult passage slowly; why not instead play *completely* out of time? Recording in Step Input allows the user to set a starting point and note value, and off you go! The really interesting thing about step recording is that you can play as fast or slow as you want, and notes will be sequentially created—here's how.

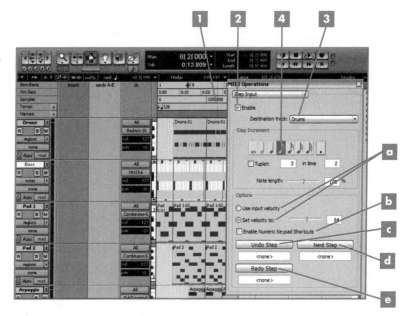

1 Set the session's timeline inser-tion at the point at which you wish to begin creating new data.

2 Enable the Step Input options in the MIDI Operations dialog box.

3 Click the Destination Track button to reveal a list of MIDI tracks in your session, and then choose the track upon which you wish to write your data.

4 Click the note value that matches the value of the notes you wish to create. The Note Length slider will allow you to change the duration of the note (in this case, I've selected eight notes as my step incre-ment, and the 100% note duration specifies that each new note will be a full eighth note).

a You have a choice when it comes to note velocities: You can choose either Use Input Velocity, which will record each note at the velocity at which it was played, or Set Velocity, which will assign all notes to a fixed velocity level.

b Click the Enable Numeric Keypad Shortcuts box to enable your keyboard's numeric keypad to change the step increment settings.

c The Undo Step button will clear your last note entry.

d Next Step will skip the current step and move you to the next incre-ment, leaving a silent increment between notes (also called a *rest*).

e Finally, the Redo Step button will redo the most recently entered step.

1 Click on the Tempo down arrow to reveal the expanded tempo ruler. The horizontal line in the playback shows the tempo of your session over time. This flat line currently represents a static tempo of 126 beats per minute.

2 Changing tempo is very simple in this view. Click the Pencil tool (in this example, with the Line option selected).

3 Just click and drag to create tempo change data. Here's what you'll get:

a The tempo change is represented as a straight ramp (because we were using the Pencil in Line mode), from 126 beats per minute up to 170 beats per minute. With the Pencil tool, you can write (and overwrite) tempo changes with the Freehand, Line, Parabolic, or S-curve settings.

b The tempo changes that were created are also shown as a series of triangular value changes. These values can also be edited by clicking and dragging or even double-clicking and typing a specific tempo value, though the more graphic tempo display as described above is far easier for many Pro Tools LE users to work with.

Tempo Operations

As you learned in Chapter 6, your session's bars and beats time scale is actually a MIDI tempo map. You can control this tempo map quickly and easily from the tempo ruler, or even enter values numerically.

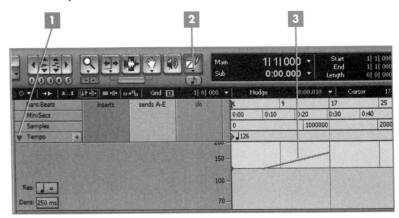

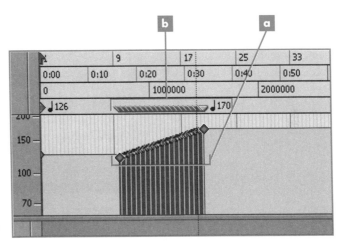

Beyond these easy ways of working with tempo, there are other ways to edit the MIDI tempo map as well.

✽ ✽ ✽

More MIDI Tips

You will be using MIDI tracks side by side with audio and Aux tracks in Pro Tools from this point on, but before we finish our focus on the wonderful world of MIDI, there are a few more key features to take a look at.

The Event List

MIDI tweakers rejoice! In addition to tools and drop-down menu processes, you can use the MIDI Event List window, a simple yet powerful window in which you can type the exact values you want! If you've used a MIDI sequencer before, you have probably seen this kind of window. Here's how to use it in Pro Tools:

1 Click on Event. The Event menu will appear.

2 Click on MIDI Event List. The MIDI Event List window will appear. The following list presents some highlights of the MIDI Event List window.

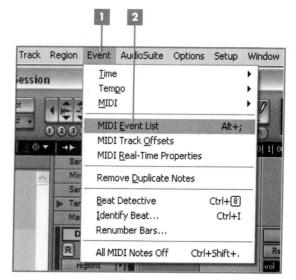

a This button shows the name of the MIDI track being viewed. Clicking this button will allow you to view a drop-down menu of all MIDI and Instrument tracks, where you can choose different tracks.

b You can click on Insert to create a new MIDI event.

c The Start column shows the beginning time for each event, listed sequentially.

d The Event column shows the type of data (note, pan, and so on) displayed by a small icon to the left of the column, as well as the value of that event.

e The Length/Info column shows more specific information about each event.

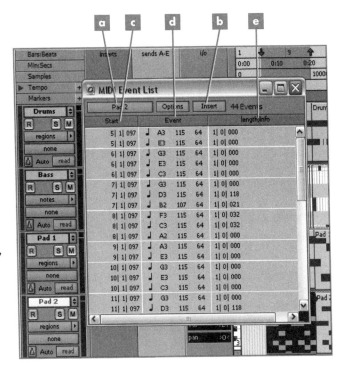

So how do you tweak this data? Easy—just double-click on the value you want to change, type the new value, and press the Enter key!

Removing Duplicate MIDI Notes

From time to time, a MIDI note can be doubly triggered (in my experience, this has happened mostly with MIDI drum controllers). Interestingly enough, this isn't the end of the world and will sometimes go completely unnoticed. Sometimes, though, these duplicate notes can result in erratic behavior from your MIDI devices (notes being cut off prematurely and so on), so Pro Tools has added a new Remove Duplicate Notes command in Pro Tools 7.

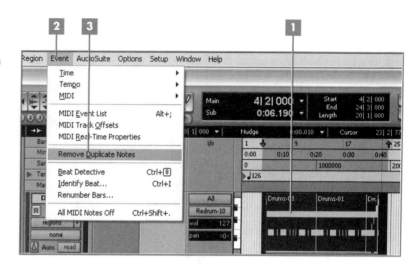

1. Select the MIDI data that you want to clean up through the removal of duplicate MIDI notes.

2. Click on Event. The Event menu will appear.

3. Click on Remove Duplicate Notes. The duplicate MIDI notes will be removed. That's it!

Viewing and Editing Non-Note Data

Of course, you can edit non-note data in the MIDI Event List, but can you edit non-note data (such as volume, velocity, or pan) on the track itself? Sure, but you've got to know how to view it before you can edit it.

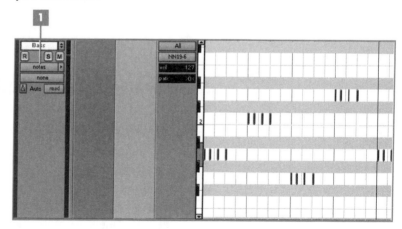

1. On this track, you're looking at (and thus able to edit) note data, as indicated by the label on the Track Display Format button. Click on the Track View Selector button. A menu of other MIDI data you can view will appear.

2 Select the kind of MIDI data with which you want to work. The track to the right will change to show the kind of data you selected.

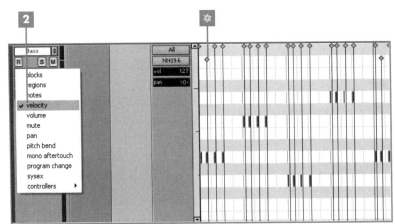

❋ In this case, velocity data is shown. Although you can still see the notes in the background, you see velocity stems for each note event, and that's the only kind of data you can manipulate. It's easy from there because you can use the same tools you used for the note data (such as the Grabber, Trim, and Selector tools, and so on) to change these values.

MIDI Real-Time Properties

The MIDI Real-Time Properties feature is something new to Pro Tools 7 and is already promising to be one of my favorite additions to the DAW. What sets this feature apart from the rest of the MIDI processes we've discussed is that these Real-Time Properties, which are perhaps best described as real-time *processes*, only alter the data as it's being played and don't alter the recorded data in any permanent way.

The Chapter 7 session that I've used for the examples thus far has a bit of a problem that we can use the Real-Time Properties window to fix. The problem is some timing disagreement between the Pad 1 and Pad 2 tracks. Take a look.

1 Select the region(s) or track(s) that need to be fixed.

2 Click the Event menu. The Event menu will be displayed.

3 Click the MIDI Real-Time Properties menu item. The Real-Time Properties window will appear.

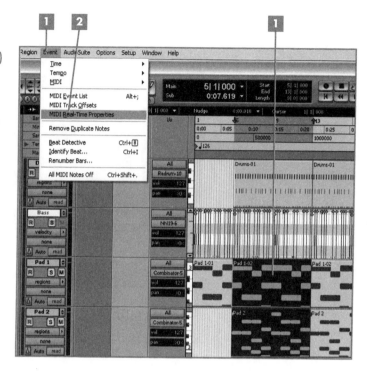

4 The first order of business is to choose what will be processed in real time. Click the Apply To button.

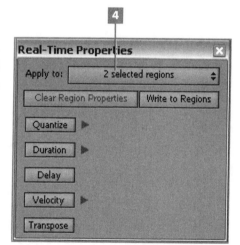

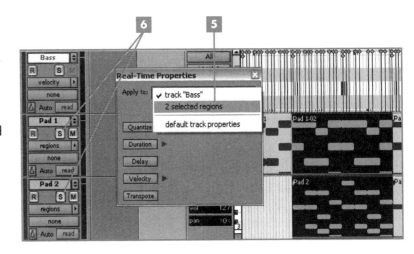

5 The application list will reflect your track and region selections. In this case, the Bass track is selected, as are two regions on the Pad 1 and Pad 2 tracks. For the purposes of this demonstration, choose 2 Selected Regions.

6 This next bit isn't an absolute necessity, but you'll hear the real-time effects better if you solo the tracks you want to hear.

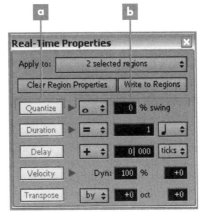

a The different processes that are available as Real-Time Properties are Quantize, Duration, Delay, Velocity, and Transpose. Each of these features is a reduced view of the MIDI Operations dialog boxes that we've discussed earlier in this chapter.

b The next column of buttons, next to each of these processes, is a tiny version of the main parameter(s) that you would otherwise have chosen in the MIDI Operations dialog boxes. This is followed by an extra area to the right that allows you to enter specific values relevant to the process(es) you've chosen.

7 Click the Process Enable button in order to activate any of the available processes. In the window shown here, *all* of the processes are selected in order to show the complete layout of the window. In this example, we'll only need to apply Quantize, so make sure only the Quantize button is selected. Your window should look like this:

a In the figure shown here, Quantize is being applied in real time to the selected regions. The regions that are being processed will be marked by an "R" in the upper-right corner of the region.

b Note that even though you will hear the benefit of quantization, the data itself will not be altered. (If you turn off the real-time process by clicking the Clear Region Properties button, you'll hear the timing problems come right back!)

c If you like the changes you're hearing, you can apply the changes to the data more permanently by clicking the Write to Regions button. Your MIDI data will be changed.

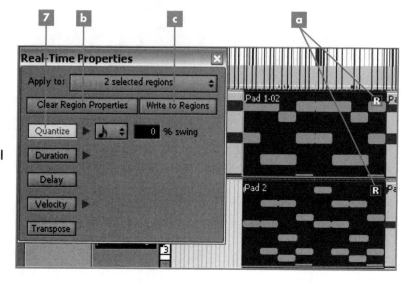

Panic!

Reality check: Sometimes things go wrong. Worse yet, sometimes the things that go wrong can be audible, as in the case of a "stuck" MIDI note that never ends. When that happens, the most important thing to do is stop the data! Whatever you do, don't forget this tip!

1 Click on Event. The Event menu will appear.

2 Click on All MIDI Notes Off (quickly!). A MIDI note-off command will be sent on all channels, on all ports of your MIDI interface, and through the four virtual MIDI connections.

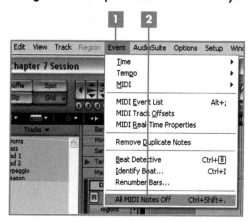

❊ **TIP**

The fastest way to trigger the All MIDI Notes Off function is to use the shortcut keys: Shift+Ctrl+. (period key) will do it on the PC, and Shift+⌘+. (period key) will do it on the Mac.

Importing and Exporting MIDI Data

One of MIDI's greatest advantages lies in its broad compatibility. Regardless of any proprietary file format, nearly every MIDI application can utilize the industry's SMF (*Standard MIDI File*) format. Pro Tools, although a relative newcomer to the world of MIDI, is no exception.

Importing MIDI Data from the File Menu

Just as you can import an audio file to an Audio track, you can import a standard MIDI file to one or more MIDI tracks in your session.

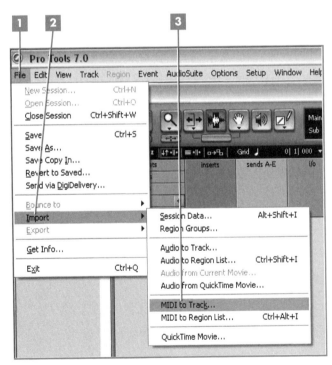

1 Click on File. The File menu will appear.

2 Select Import. A second menu will open.

3 Just as when you imported audio files into Pro Tools back in Chapter 3, you can import your MIDI either to tracks (which Pro Tools will create) or to the Regions list. Either way, you'll get some additional options. For this example, click on MIDI to Track. The Import MIDI Settings dialog box will then open.

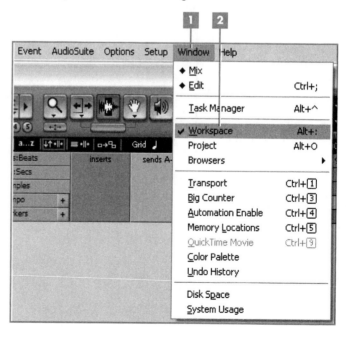

a Click on Import Tempo From MIDI File, depending on your preference. If this box remains unchecked, your imported data will use the existing tempo map from your session.

b You may also have the option to remove previous MIDI or Instrument tracks or MIDI regions, depending upon the initial state of your system. If you don't check any of these boxes, then the imported data will be added to the MIDI data already present in your session.

Importing MIDI Data from the Workspace

Again, just as you can import audio from the Workspace window with ease, you can also import MIDI. With MIDI, though, the news gets even better, as you can import an entire song's worth of material with just a click and a drag. Here's how.

1 Click the Window menu.

2 Click the Workspace menu item. The Workspace window will open, as you've seen before in Chapter 3.

3 Drag the desired MIDI file into your Edit window's timeline.

4 When applicable, a window will appear, allowing you to replace MIDI tempo maps, tracks, and regions, as you've seen earlier in this section.

5 The individual MIDI tracks of the file will be created in your Edit window, and the appropriate regions created.

Keep in mind that even after you import your MIDI data, you have to set your MIDI output and an Aux track before you can play and hear your MIDI data through the Pro Tools mixer.

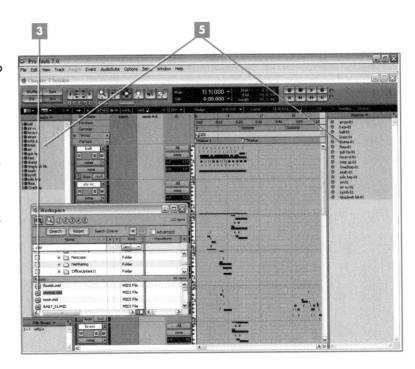

1 Click on File. The File menu will appear.

2 Click on Export. A second menu will appear.

3 Select MIDI. The Export MIDI Settings dialog box will open. This dialog box looks very similar to the session save window, and you will select your destination file and location in the same manner; but before you get to that common window, you'll be able to make a few choices through the Export MIDI Settings dialog box.

Exporting MIDI Data

When you save your session, your MIDI data will be saved in the session file. However, you can also save the MIDI data by itself as a standard MIDI file so you can open it in any MIDI sequencer.

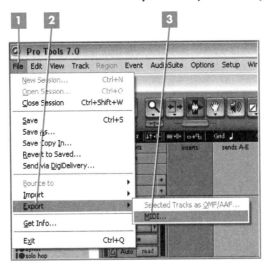

4 Click the MIDI File Format button to reveal a list of saving options:

a Select the 0 (single-track) option to save all of your data as one MIDI track, regardless of how many tracks you have in your session. (This is commonly used in multimedia applications.)

OR

b Select the 1 (multi-track) option to preserve the multi-track organization of your MIDI data. This is the type of Standard MIDI file most used in professional circles, and if you import it into a DAW, your tracks will be recreated.

c Click the Apply Real-Time Properties check box to "print" any real-time operations to your saved Standard MIDI file.

5 Click on OK. The MIDI data from your session will be saved to a Standard MIDI file, whose name and location you can determine according to your operating system.

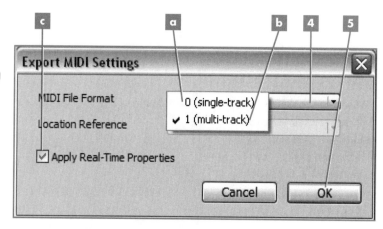

Next stop—mixing!

8 } Basic Mixing

There are two schools of thought when it comes to Pro Tools mixing—mixing *inside* the box or *outside* the box. Mixing inside the box refers to when you use virtual mixer and virtual effects *within* the Pro Tools environment. At any given time, you will listen to the stereo output of your mix from your Pro Tools interface as all the required processing is performed by your computer (the "box"). Mixing *outside* the box refers to the practice of assigning individual tracks to individual outputs of your Pro Tools interface, and from there to the individual channels of a separate physical mixing board. The mixing and automation is performed by this external mixer, and Pro Tools is reduced to a recording, editing, and playback capacity only (which is still a critical role in any production workflow).

There is lively discussion (I'm being polite here) within the professional community regarding the virtues of mixing outside the box versus inside the box. For the end user, the debate boils down to an easy choice: If you've got a sweet-sounding, large-format, external mixing console (for example, an SSL) that you want to use, then by all means mix outside the box and use the board's circuitry to color the sound (kind of like an effect). If you don't have such a console at your disposal, or if you want to preserve the original sound of your tracks, you can feel confident in mixing inside the box. Rest assured, the math behind the Pro Tools mix engine ensures that the integrity of your mix will remain intact!

For the purposes of this book, you'll explore mixing inside the box (a method that has been used on countless professional projects). In this chapter, you'll learn how to:

* Work with the specific layout and function of the Mix window
* Use fader groups
* Use file-based and real-time effects
* Work with traditional mix routing
* Use basic automation techniques

Exploring the Mix Window

You looked at the Mix window before (way back in Chapter 2). Now it's time to dig deeper.... If you're not looking at the Mix window already, the first thing to do is to switch over to the Mix window (which you also learned how to do in Chapter 2). Depending on how you left the Mix window last time, you might see the channel strips appearing rather narrow. Though the Narrow Mix view can certainly be useful in some situations, the normal view will show us more information. Here's how to view the Mix window normally:

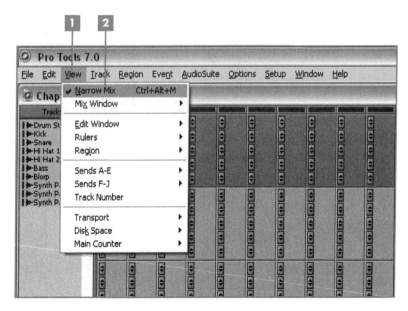

1 Click on View. The View menu will appear, showing the Narrow Mix option checked.

2 Click on Narrow Mix to uncheck it. The channels will be shown in their normal mode.

TIP

There are certainly times when the Narrow Mix mode is desirable. For example, when your session contains too many tracks to be normally displayed at once in the Mix window, switching to Narrow Mix mode will allow you to view more of your mix at once.

Basic Mixer Terminology

Just for a little reminder, this section reviews the basic layout of the Mix window.

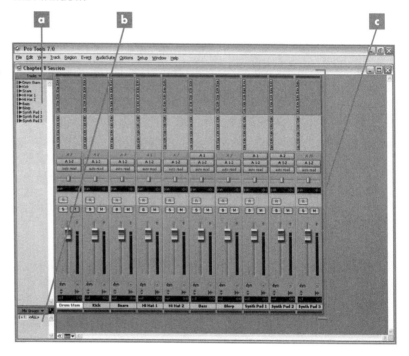

a Tracks list. As in the Edit window, highlighted tracks are displayed as channel strips.

b Groups list. You'll learn more about this in just a few pages.

c Channel strips. There is a separate channel strip for each shown track.

Now take a look at the different sections of each channel strip.

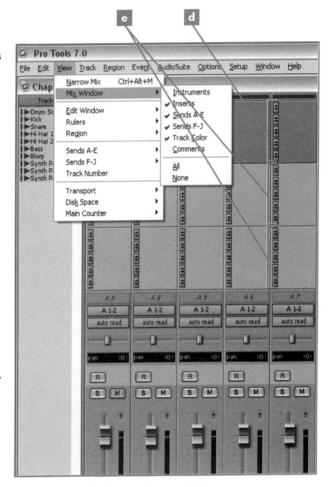

d At the top of the channel strips is the Inserts section. The important thing to remember is that any audio passing through that channel strip will be routed through the inserts first. You've got up to five inserts to use, and it is here that you will launch *plug-ins*, which can be virtual effect units or even virtual instruments.

e Next are the sends. With the introduction of Pro Tools 7, there are now 10 sends for you to use (previous versions had only five), divided into two sections of five sends. You'll use sends to route a portion of your track's processed audio to another destination. Sends are commonly used in conjunction with other tracks to create more complex effect situations.

❋ **NOTE**
MIDI tracks have no inserts or sends, as inserts and sends can route only audio data.

The next section looks and functions identically to the I/O column of a track in the Edit window. It consists of the following:

This section may not look much like anything you've seen in the Edit window, but these functions should be old hat by now.

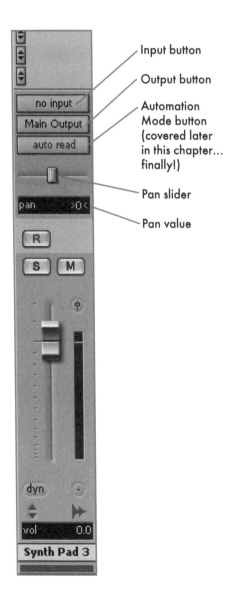

Input button

Output button

Automation Mode button (covered later in this chapter... finally!)

Pan slider

Pan value

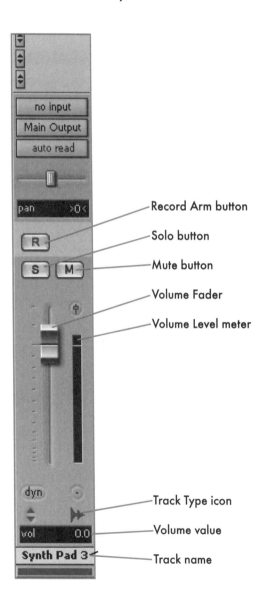

Record Arm button

Solo button

Mute button

Volume Fader

Volume Level meter

Track Type icon

Volume value

Track name

❄ NOTE

The icon at the bottom-right corner of each channel strip will let you know what type of track it is. A waveform indicates an audio track; a MIDI plug indicates a MIDI track. An arrow signifies an aux track, and a sigma marks a Master Fader. For Pro Tools 7's newest addition, Instrument Tracks, a small keyboard symbol is used. The same icons can be found to the left of each track in the Tracks list.

❄ NOTE

You can easily tell whether the track is stereo or mono by taking a look at the volume meters and pan sliders. One meter and pan signifies a mono track, and a stereo track will have two meters and pans. (The top pan is for the left side of the track, and the bottom pan is for the right side of the track.)

More Signal Flow

Whenever you talk about mixing, you're really talking about signal flow. The more complex your mix gets, the more complex the routing of that signal will be. The following list will go through the order of audio signal flow within a track.

1 **Input.** On an audio track, input can be from an interface input (if you're recording), from a bus, or from your hard drive. With aux tracks, the input can only be from an interface input (although you can't record) or a bus.

2 **Insert.** One hundred percent of your signal passes through your insert.

3 **Pre-Fader send.** This type of send makes a copy before the signal hits your volume fader. The destination of this send can be an interface output or a bus.

4 **Volume Fader.** This is where you control the output volume of the track.

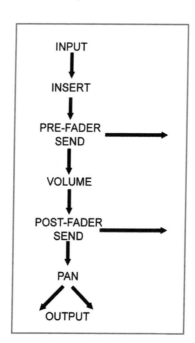

INPUT

INSERT

PRE-FADER SEND

VOLUME

POST-FADER SEND

PAN

OUTPUT

Keep in mind that the volume fader on your track *only* controls the output of that track. That means that the fader has absolutely no effect on the input coming to the track. The net effect is this: If you're recording audio, and see your levels clipping, turn down the output of the instrument. The fader in Pro Tools' Mix window cannot prevent clipping.

5 Post-Fader send. This kind of send makes a copy after the signal has been altered by the volume fader. As with a pre-fader send, the destination can be an interface output or a bus.

6 Pan slider. Panning comes next and allows the signal to be varied between a pair of outputs, usually left and right. This is how you will create a stereo mix of several mono or stereo tracks. If you route your track to a singular output, no pan slider will be needed and you won't see one in the channel strip.

7 Output. After all these stages are passed, the signal goes to the Pro Tools mix engine and out of an interface output pair.

Fader Groups

One neat thing about mixing in Pro Tools is that you can link faders together, so that moving one fader will move a number of faders. This is particularly useful when you have a good relative blend between a number of tracks (for example, a nice balance between all the drums). By making a fader group of these tracks, you can adjust the volume within your entire mix, while maintaining the group's relative levels.

First, though, you should get a feel for what a fader group can do. As luck would have it, Pro Tools automatically creates a group (named All) when a new session is created. Take a look at what it does.

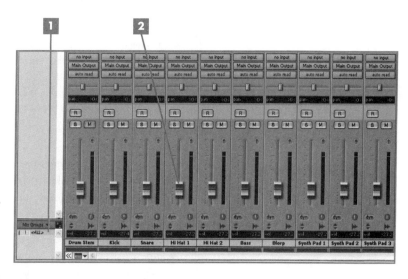

1 Click **on the** All group name. The group name will be highlighted and the group, which includes all the tracks in your session, will be active.

❋ **NOTE**

At the bottom right of each channel strip is a small group icon. When a group is activated, the group's members will display a lit group icon.

2 Click **on any** volume fader and drag it **to change the volume of the track. Because you're using the All group, all the tracks will move proportionally.**

❋ **NOTE**

In a session that uses more than one group, you can highlight more than one group at a time, making multiple groups simultaneously active within your session. Simply click on any group you want to enable, and it will become active.

Creating a Fader Group

You can also set up a new group of your own. In this example, I've set up a blend of my drum track volumes that I find pleasing, and I want to maintain their relative levels.

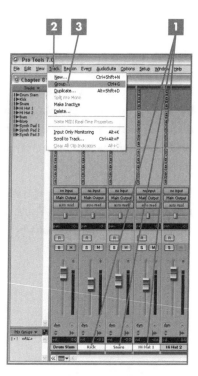

1 Press and hold **the** Shift key, **and** select **any number of** tracks **that you want to group together. The tracks will be selected.**

2 Click **on** Track. **The Track menu will appear.**

3 Click **on** Group. **The New Group dialog box will open.**

4 Type a name for your new group in the Name for Group text box.

5 Click on a Group Type radio button to choose whether the group will exist in the Edit window (see Chapter 6 for more information on edit groups), the Mix window, or both. The option will be selected.

6 Pro Tools will automatically assign a letter to your group for labeling purposes. Click on the Group ID button if you want to select a different letter for the group.

7 Click on OK. Your settings will be saved and the New Group dialog box will close.

8 Go ahead and create another group. This time, select a different set of tracks.

9 Set the group options in the New Group dialog box.

10 Click on OK. Your settings will be saved and the New Group dialog box will close.

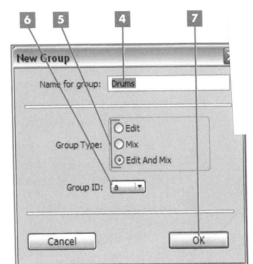

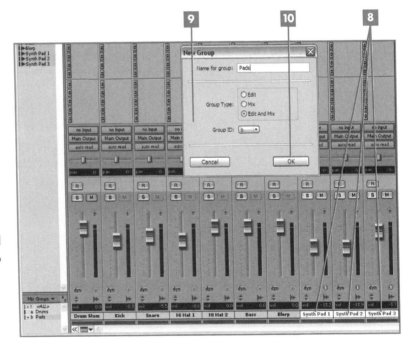

❋ **NOTE**

Pro Tools allows tracks to be members of two groups at the same time. This can be very helpful, for instance, if you want to group your tom-tom tracks together and then group those tracks together with the rest of the drum kit. This is called a *nested* group.

Using Fader Groups

There's just a little more to learn about fader groups before you continue.

a A small dot to the left of a group signifies that some, or all, members of that group are selected. In this case, some members of the All group are selected.

b A larger dot means that all members of the group are selected, plus other tracks. Here all members of the Drums group are selected, plus some other tracks, in this case an additional Hi Hat and Bass track.

c No dot by a group signifies that no members of that group are selected.

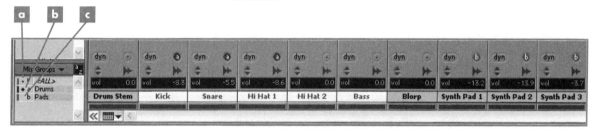

Since it's possible to have a fader group within another fader group (called a *nested* fader group), how do you know if a given track is a member of more than one active group? In this case, I've created a group of my two Hi Hat tracks, but which track is also a member of my Drums group?

d A lowercase letter in a group icon (at the bottom right of the channel strip) shows that the track is a member of only one active (highlighted) group.

e An uppercase letter means that the track is a member of more than one currently active group.

f You can click on the group icon to reveal a menu of all the active groups of which the track is a member.

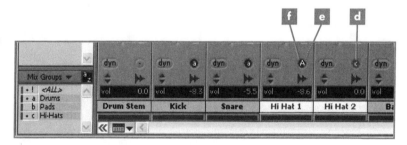

❄ **TIP**

A quick way to select all the members of a group is to click to the left of the group name in the Groups list.

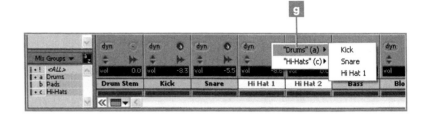

g In this example, the Hi Hat 1 track is a member of two groups. If you move your mouse to either group, a list of all members in that group will be displayed.

Using Effects

Many software applications use plug-ins—programs that run within programs. In word processors, plug-ins can be editing tools or macros; graphics applications have visual effect plug-ins and so on. Pro Tools is no slouch when it comes to plug-ins. Pro Tools plug-ins include all manner of effects processors and even virtual instruments. Because they're software, they have all the benefits and flexibility of software, and they can even save you money and rack space in your project studio!

In a Pro Tools LE system, plug-ins fall into two families—file-based plug-ins (called AudioSuite) and real-time plug-ins (called RTAS, or *Real-Time AudioSuite*). First you will tackle AudioSuite.

AudioSuite

AudioSuite plug-ins are, generally speaking, the most basic of the Pro Tools arsenal of effects. They work directly with files (hence the name *file-based*), and this is *not* done in real-time as your session plays. This means that these plug-ins cannot be automated in your Pro Tools session. It also means that these plug-ins don't consume your session's valuable real-time resources, making AudioSuite a pretty powerful tool to work with. Here's how they work:

1. Select the region or selection you want to process. The region will be selected.

2. Click on AudioSuite. A menu of available AudioSuite plug-ins will appear.

3. Click on the desired effect. The plug-in's window will appear.

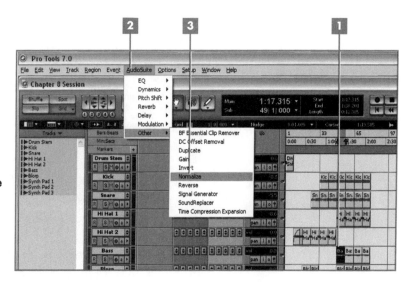

❄ **NOTE**

The effect I've chosen is a handy little process called *Normalize*. This process is a semi-automatic level adjuster that will bring up your entire selection to the point where the loudest level is at its maximum without clipping. The simplicity of the effect window makes it an obvious choice for a book like this one.

Normalize can be very useful in some circumstances, but beware of overusing it! Though levels will be brought up, there can be minor damage done to the accuracy of your audio, and it will bring up ambient noise levels as well. The bottom line is to record at healthy levels, so you won't need to abuse normalization!

Although different effects have different appearances and parameters, they share some common elements.

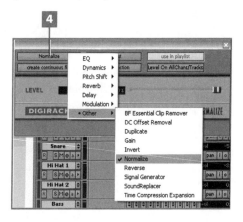

4. Click on the Plug in Selector button (which will show the name of your current plug in, such as Normalize). A list of available AudioSuite plug-ins will appear from which you can change to another plug-in.

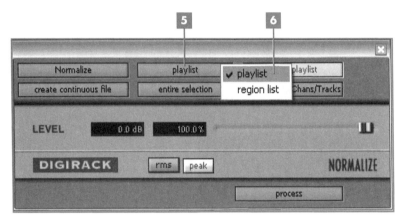

5 Click on the Selection Reference button (which reads "Playlist") to determine which selection will be processed. A menu with two options will appear.

- ❄ Playlist. The playlist option will process the single selection in your track.

- ❄ Region list. The region list option will process the currently selected regions in the Regions list and change all corresponding regions being used in your session.

6 Select Playlist if you want the processed audio to appear in your tracks and also in the Regions list. The button will be highlighted.

7 Click on the File Mode button (which presently reads "Create Individual Files") to determine how the audio will be processed. A menu will appear, showing three different processing options.

* Overwrite Files. This option processes the audio file directly and *destructively*. It *cannot* be undone.

* Create Individual Files. This option is non-destructive and creates separate audio files for each processed region if your selection includes more than one region.

* Create Continuous File. This option will process a selection non-destructively that includes more than one region and create a consolidated single file.

8 Click on the Process Mode button (which currently reads "Region by Region") to determine how your regions will be analyzed prior to processing. A menu will appear, showing two options.

* Region by Region. This option will analyze individually each region within a selection.

* Entire Selection. This option will analyze multiple regions as a whole.

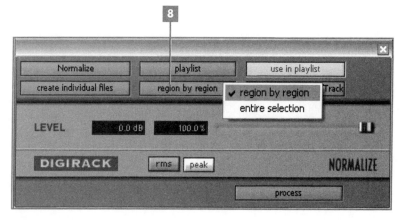

* **NOTE**

The Entire Selection option is commonly used when you are normalizing multiple regions of different volumes. With this mode enabled, each individual region within a larger selection will be analyzed and processed individually.

9 Click on Process to finally apply your effect. The effect will be rendered to a new audio file (or will overwrite your original file destructively if you have chosen the Overwrite Files option in Step 7). A progress window will appear as shown here.

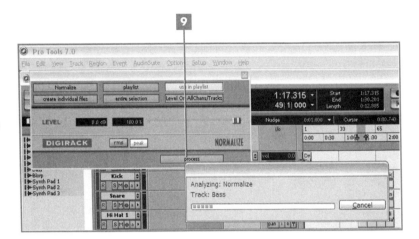

Here's what you'll end with:

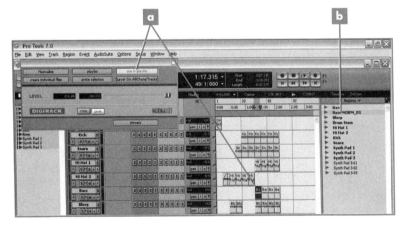

a Since I've set up this AudioSuite process to use in playlist (by highlighting the Use in Playlist button), a new region has been created to replace the previously selected region in the track.

b This new region has also been added to the Regions list and has been named Bass-NORM_01 to indicate that it has been processed by the Normalize AudioSuite plug-in.

RTAS

The next evolutionary step in Pro Tools' plug-in effects is the RTAS (Real-Time AudioSuite) line. A number of RTAS plug-ins have AudioSuite counterparts (the EQs, for example), but the distinction between the two types is an important one. In the case of an RTAS plug-in, instead of processing audio on a file-by-file basis, the plug-in resides on a track's insert and processes the incoming signal as the session is played (in real time).

There are two huge benefits that come with using RTAS plug-ins. First, because the audio is being processed in real time, the audio files on your hard drive won't be changed as the audio plays, which allows you to experiment freely with different plug-ins and settings without worrying about filling your hard drive with tons of edited files. Also, as a result of RTAS's real-time qualities, you can automate the parameters of your plug-in, meaning that your effects can change dynamically over time.

Using RTAS Plug-Ins

The following steps detail how to start using RTAS plug-ins in your session.

1 On an unused insert on the track you want to affect, click on the arrowed Insert button. A drop-down menu will appear.

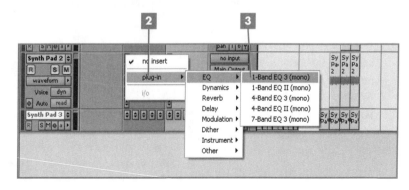

2 Click on Plug-in. The Plug-in menu will appear.

3 Click on the plug-in you want to launch. An effects window will open. This window will appear differently depending on the effect, but there are some common buttons that you should know.

4 Click on the Track Selector button. A list of available tracks will appear.

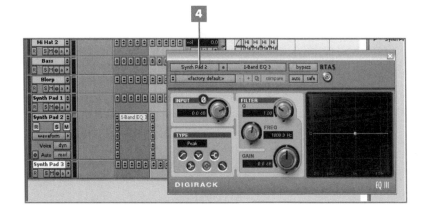

5 This list tells you what track the effect is on. From this list, you can select another track and immediately open the Insert window for that track.

6 The small lettered button to the right of the Track Selector button tells you what insert the effect is on. Click on the Insert button.

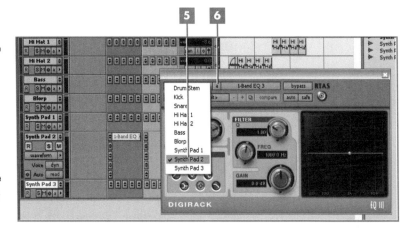

7 A list of all the inserts on the track will appear. From this list, you can select any of the inserts for your track and jump to that insert immediately.

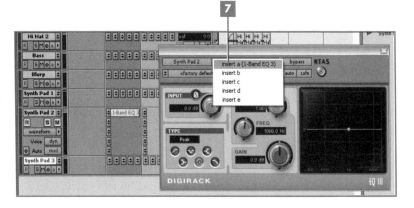

> ※ **TIP**
>
> Because inserts are processed in a series, from top to bottom, the order in which effects are placed in your tracks is indeed significant. For example, a virtual amplifier placed before a reverb will sound a good deal different than an amplifier placed after a reverb. The good news about this is that it's easy to change the order (or even the track assignment) of an RTAS plug-in simply by dragging and dropping the insert icon to a new location in your mixer.

Digging Deeper into RTAS

Okay, so far it's pretty straightforward, but things will get a little more complicated as you continue. For example, when you open a plug-in on a stereo track, you have a few more options. For this example, let's set up a multi-mono reverb on a stereo aux track:

1. On a stereo aux track (in this case, named Delay Aux), click on an Insert button.

2a. Click on Multi-channel plug-in. In the case of a stereo track, a list of stereo plug-ins will appear.

OR

2b. Click on Multi-mono plug-in. This option is available if you have tracks with more than one channel (such as stereo tracks). A list of mono plug-ins will appear. When you select a plug-in, it will be opened twice, although only one plug-in window will be shown. A multi-mono plug-in window has several important features. For the purposes of our example, choose this option.

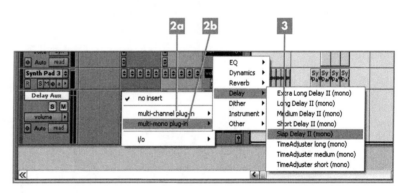

3. For the purposes of this example, choose Slap Delay II. The plug-in will be instantiated, and the plug-in window will open.

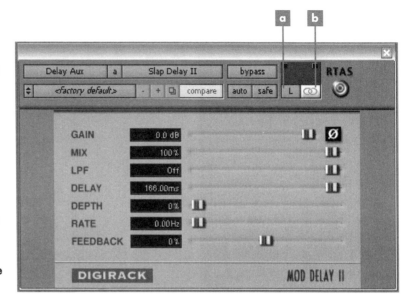

a The Channel Selector button will display either an L or an R to signify the side of the multi-mono plug-in you're presently viewing. When the link button is highlighted, both the left and right sides will appear identical.

b The Link button is unique to multi-mono plug-ins. When the button is highlighted, both instances (left and right) of the mono plug-in will share the same parameter settings. When the Link button is not highlighted, both sides are independently configurable.

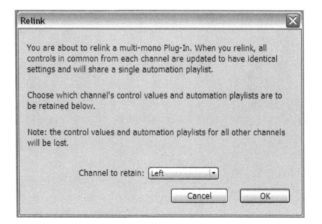

❈ **NOTE**

If you unlink the two halves of a multi-mono effect and then choose to re-link them, the Relink dialog box will appear. This box is pretty self-explanatory. To relink the two multi-mono plug-ins, you have to choose one side's parameters to be applied to the other side. Click on the Channel to Retain button to reveal a drop-down menu that contains both left and right sides. Once you've chosen which side's settings you want to keep, you can click on OK.

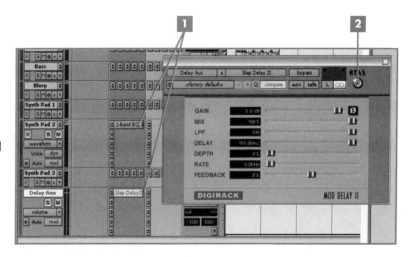

1 Each plug-in you launch (or instantiate, as Digidesign likes to say) will appear as a rectangular button next to its corresponding insert. Click on the desired button to reveal the effect window.

2 The rule for the Target button is that there can only be one active target at a time. Click on the Target button to deselect it. You'll be able to open two (or more) effect windows at a time.

You'll notice that by default, only one effect window can be open at a time. (Clicking on a new plug-in will replace the previous plug-in window with the new one.) So what if you want to view more than one plug-in window at a time? That's when the Target button comes into play.

❄ **NOTE**

If you're using a control surface (a Digi 002 or Command | 8, for instance), only the effect with the active Target button will be accessible from the surface's knobs and faders. Your mouse, however, will still manipulate all the open effect windows, regardless of the Target button's status.

❄ **TIP**

You can also open more than one plug-in window at a time by holding down the Shift key while you click on a plug-in button on an insert. However, there can still be only one targeted effect at a time. (The first plug-in you opened will retain the active target.)

Mixing Tips

The point of the mixing process is to achieve just the right blend of audio elements in your session. Over the years, certain conventions have arisen to help mixing engineers work more efficiently, and these conventions have become something of a tradition. Let's start out by learning some traditional effects routing.

Using Dynamic-Based Effects

Traditional effects tend to fall into one of two categories—*dynamic*-based effects or *time*-based effects. Let's begin our discussion with dynamic effects. Dynamic-based effects change the volume level without changing its duration in any way. Some of the most common examples of dynamic effects are equalizers, compressors, and limiters.

The setting up of a dynamic-based effect is very simple—in fact, you've done it once already with the Synth Pad 2 track if you've been following the examples shown in this chapter. Traditionally, you'll want these types of effects to process 100 percent of the track's audio, with little thought of creating a wet/dry kind of mix with these processes. Here's the traditional routing for dynamic effects:

1 Click on an insert on the track you want to affect and select a dynamic-based effect (such as the EQ shown here). The plug-in window will appear.

2 Adjust the parameters of the effect to suit your mix's needs.

When you're finished tweaking the effect, you're finished with the routing. Although it is simple enough, this sort of routing works well with dynamic effects because 100 percent of the signal to the track first passes through the insert. This example shows a classic model— the entirety of a track's signal passing through an equalizer.

Using Time-Based Effects

Time-based effects *do* affect the duration of the sound beyond that of its original waveform. This family includes effects such as reverb, delay, and echo. In these cases, you generally will want to have some sort of a wet/dry mixing situation (*wet* meaning an affected signal and *dry* referring to an unaffected signal). The generally preferred way to mix these two signals is with two separate faders in your Mix window.

1 Create a stereo aux track. In this example, you can use the aux track (Delay Aux) that you created earlier in this chapter.

2 Click on a Send Selector button on the "dry" track (in this case, let's use Synth Pad 3). A drop-down menu will appear.

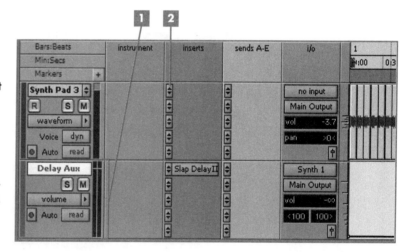

3 Because you'll be routing
audio from one track to
another within Pro Tools, you'll
use a bus. Click on Bus from
the drop-down menu.

4 Select an unused stereo bus.
(Buses used in the session will
be shown in bold.)

5 After you've sent a copy of
your audio track through a bus,
you need to set the input of
the aux track. Set the input to
match the same stereo bus you
chose for your audio track's
send. The input will be set.

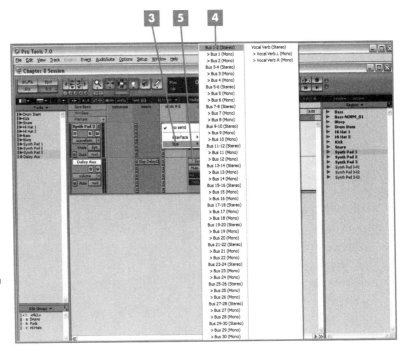

6 Drag the volume fader on
the send's output window
to increase the volume. The
volume will be adjusted
accordingly.

7 Click the volume display on
the destination aux track, and
drag the volume slider to the
desired level.

8 Click on an Insert arrow button
on the aux track, and select a
time-based effect from the menu.
In this case, you can use the
delay that has been previously
set in this chapter. Adjust the
initial settings for the plug-in.

9 Play your session to test your
connection. If you've routed the
audio signal correctly so far,
signal that is shown in the audio
track's meter will also be shown
in the send's output window
and the aux track's meter.

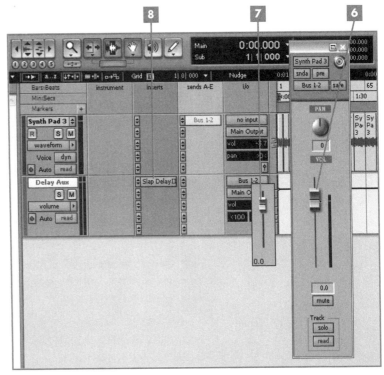

10 Only one more thing: When the Pre button is highlighted on the send's output window, the send will be a pre-fader send, meaning that the output of the send will not be affected by the audio track's volume fader. When the Pre button is not highlighted (the Pro Tools default mode), the send is a post-fader send, and the volume fader of the audio track will affect the volume going out of the send, and from there to the aux track.

❊ **NOTE**

Although a post-fader send is generally more common (hence it is the default in Pro Tools), both pre- and post-fader sends have their uses. It all depends on the results you want. Choose Post-fader if you want to have your dry track (the audio track) and your wet track (the aux input) blend and then have the dry track's level affect the wet track's output. This way, when you raise and lower the volume fader on the dry track, you'll raise and lower the signal being routed to the aux. If, however, you want the wet and dry tracks to be completely independent, use a pre-fader send. Because signal will be routed to the aux track *before* the dry track's fader, a full signal will be sent to *both* faders. Experiment!

❊ **NOTE**

Most plug-in effects have a mix parameter that allows you to blend a dry and wet signal. Often this setting defaults to 100 percent wet, but not always. Be sure to check your plug-in's mix parameter; in a mixing situation like this, you'll want the mix to be 100 percent wet.

✻ Here's a way to make production much simpler and get more performance out of your DAW in the bargain. You can have multiple sources and destinations for each bus in your system. That means that you can create sends on a number of tracks, assign them all to the same bus(es), and route all those signals to the input of a single aux track, as shown here. It's important to note that you can independently control the levels and panning of each of your sends, which will let you tailor the signal going to the Aux track.

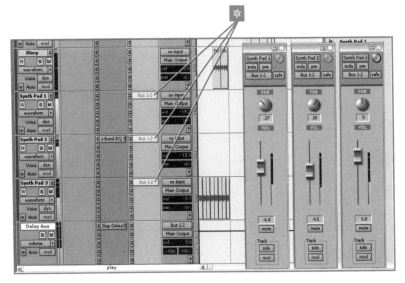

That's it! Now you have dry faders (the audio tracks) and a wet track (the aux track), and you can adjust the balance as you want. Remember, *all* of the parameters that you've just set up (send levels, aux levels, plug-in parameters, etc.) are a starting point only, and you can tweak them to your heart's content.

But wait, there's more . . . .

Automating Your Mix

Automation is truly one of the coolest things about mixing in Pro Tools. Automation basically refers to the ability to record parameter changes over time, to be recalled when you play your mix again. You'll find that the ability to control multiple volume and pan changes in real time as your session plays will be a huge advantage to your mix. Better still, not only can you automate faders and pans (features traditionally reserved for expensive mixing consoles), but you can even automate plug-in parameters!

✻ **NOTE**

Before you start dealing with mix automation, you should get some terminology straight. Audio and MIDI data are *recorded*, and automation is *written*. This might seem like a matter of semantics, but you'll see the differences as you read on.

The Automation Modes

There are five automation modes, which determine the way your fader, pan, and other motions will be written into the session. Understanding the distinction between the modes is the best way to start working with automation.

1 Click on the Automation Mode button on a track (labeled "Auto"). A drop-down menu of the five automation modes will appear.

The modes are as follows:

※ Auto Off. In this mode, automation cannot be written or played back, even if automation has been previously written.

※ Auto Read. Automation cannot be written in this mode, but previously written automation will be played back.

※ Auto Touch. Only the parameter that is "touched" (by clicking with your mouse or using a control surface) will write automation. When the parameter is released, it will return to any previously written automation.

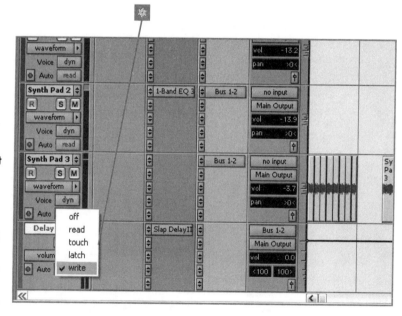

※ **NOTE**

With all of these modes, automation can only be written during playback, and writing will stop when playback is stopped or, in the case of Auto touch, when you let go of the parameter you are automating.

❊ **Auto Latch. This mode is similar to auto touch—only the parameter that is "touched" will write automation. When the parameter is released in this mode, however, it will remain at the last value and continue to write automation at that position until you stop the transport.**

❊ **Auto Write. In this mode, automation will be written on all enabled parameters, regardless of whether the parameter is being touched.**

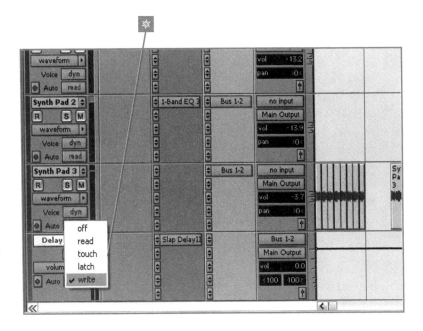

Here's an example of how to use the automation modes together:

1 Click the Track View Selector button to graphically view the parameter you wish to automate.

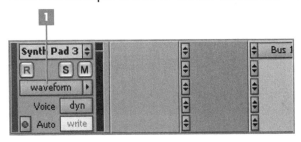

In this example, I want to work with Synth Pad 3 and change the track's volume over time.

2 Choose the track parameter that you wish to view. In this case, I've chosen Volume.

❊ Note that when an automation parameter is selected, it is displayed in that track as a line.

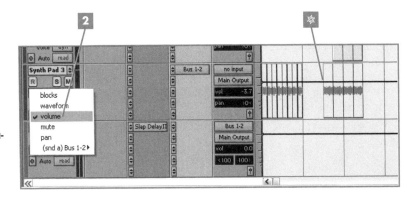

❊ ❊ ❊

3 Choose the Write automation mode from the Automation Mode button menu. You can access the menu either from the track itself or the bottom of the output window. For the purposes of this example, let's start with Write mode, which will create new automation data for all automatable parameters.

4 Begin playback of your session.

5 Click on a mix parameter (such as volume or pan) and move it to create automation data.

6 When you're done writing automation, stop your session's playback.

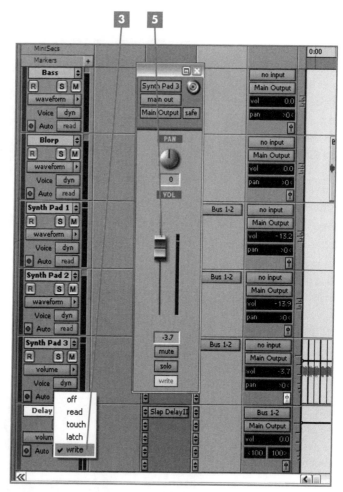

TIP

You can choose a different automation mode for each track.

You'll note that new automation data has been written, like this volume change that I created here. So what if you want to change things?

7 Select the Touch automation mode from the Automation Mode button menu when you're finished writing automation. Auto Touch, like Auto Latch, is commonly called an "update" mode, as it is most commonly used to over-write specific parameters.

8 Play your session. Your parameters will read back the automation you have just written, and the appropriate controls will move.

9 When you want to change your data, just click on the appropriate control and adjust it. Let go of the control when you want to return to the previously written automation, then stop playback. Here's what you'll get:

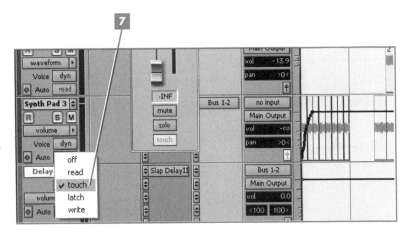

a Automation was played back as originally written until this point, when I began moving the volume fader.

b At this point, I released the fader. Since I was in Auto Touch mode, the fader began to move back to the previously written automation as soon as I let go of the fader.

c Auto Touch mode will take a little time to go back to the previously written automation (a parameter called AutoMatch time).

✳ CAUTION

Be careful of following an Auto Write pass with another Auto Write pass. Remember, this mode overwrites *all* enabled parameters (volume, pan, plug-ins, etc.), and will overwrite all these parameters at the same time. Auto Touch and Auto Latch, on the other hand, only operate on the specific parameter(s) being changed, and leave any others alone.

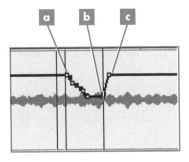

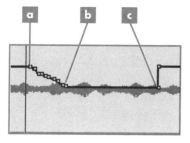

The previous example shows Auto Touch as an update mode, but there is another update mode, Auto Latch, that is also available. Auto Latch works exactly the same way, except that the adjusted control won't go back as soon as it is released, but will rather retain its value until playback is stopped. Here's how a similar update pass would look with Auto Latch mode:

a Automation was played back as originally written until this point, when I began moving the volume fader.

b At this point, I released the fader. Since I was in Auto Match mode this time, the fader stays put when I let go of it.

c When playback is stopped, the automation will stop being written.

Plug-In Automation

Virtually every knob or button of a plug-in can be automated. There are two methods by which you can do this.

Method One

1 Click on the plug-in you want to automate. The plug-in window will appear.

2 Click on the Auto button. The Plug-In Automation dialog box will open.

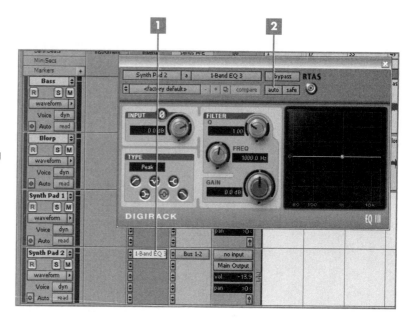

3 Highlight the effects parameters you wish to automate.

4 Click on the Add button. The selected parameters will be shown in the list to the right of the button.

5 When you're finished, click on OK. Your settings will be saved, and the Plug-In Automation dialog box will close.

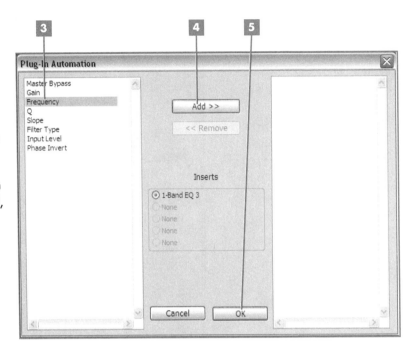

Method Two

1 Press and hold the Ctrl+Start (PC) or Control+Option+⌘ (Mac) keys, and click on the parameter you want to automate. A menu will appear.

2a Click on Enable Automation for <parameter name>. The parameter will be ready to be automated.

OR

2b Click on Open Plug-In Automation Dialog. The Plug-In Automation dialog box you saw in method one will open. At this point you can follow Steps 3 through 5 from the "Method One" section.

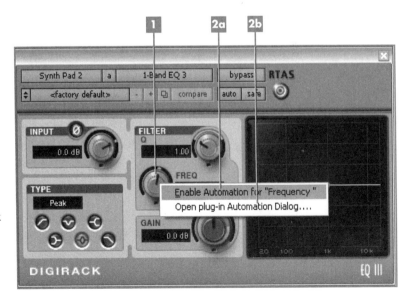

❋ Parameters armed for automation will be identified with a red color (sometimes it's an outline, a box, or in this case a small light beneath the parameter). In Auto Read mode, the label will be green; in any of the Write modes, the box will be red.

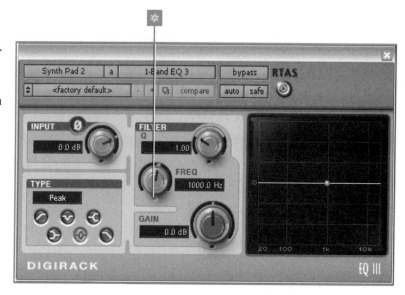

Next stop ... the mixdown!

9 } Finishing Touches

Almost done! Now that you're at the threshold of finishing your first project, it's interesting to look back at all you've accomplished to get here, from setting up your system to recording, and then editing (and more editing) to mixing. Now you're at the stage of creating a deliverable product—good job! Okay, break's over.

Before you can truly consider a project finished, there's usually some tweaking to be done. Then, when you're satisfied with the mix, it's time to mix it down to a file or pair of files that you can actually listen to on something other than your Pro Tools rig, like a CD player for example. Last but absolutely not least, there's the business of archiving your files. In this chapter, you'll learn how to:

* ❋ Tweak your mix automation in the Edit window
* ❋ Use a Master Fader
* ❋ Bounce to disk in a CD-ready format
* ❋ Back up your session efficiently

More Fun with Mixing

Though you've certainly gotten a solid start with mixing in the previous chapters, there are a few more techniques that you might find useful.

More Fun with Plug-ins

Learning more about managing your plug-in effects will save time and boost creativity!

Recalling Settings

In addition to setting and automating your plug-ins with ease, you can also recall previously created preset settings. This can work with both AudioSuite and RTAS—here's how:

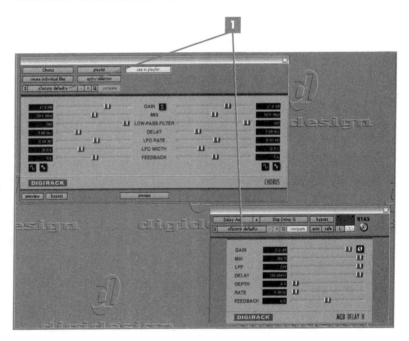

1 Click the Librarian button (it will show the currently selected preset, like "Factory Default" in this case). A list of available presets, specific to that particular plug-in, will be displayed. The location of the Librarian button is nearly identical for AudioSuite (Chorus in this example) and RTAS (Slap Delay II).

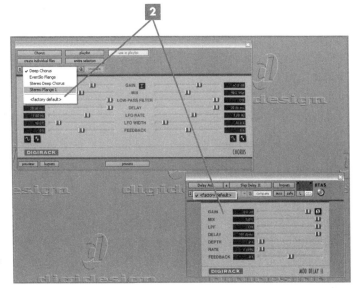

2 Select the desired preset from the displayed list.

a Use the plus (+) and minus (–) keys to increment or decrement through the available presets.

b Click the Plug-in Setting Select button to reveal the plug-in setting window, shown here.

c From the plug-in setting window, click the desired preset.

d Click the Increment Setting box (the box will appear checked) to automatically cycle through the available presets according to the value entered in the Seconds box. In this case, the Chorus plug-in will cycle through all four of its presets, changing settings every 3 seconds. This is a handy way to choose the appropriate setting for your effect (especially when there are a large number of presets).

e When you settle upon the desired setting, click Done, and the setting will be applied to your effect.

Notice that there are no presets associated with the Slap Delay II plug-in. When there are presets listed (as with the Chorus in this example), there are a number of other ways that presets can be accessed (again, this works for both AudioSuite and RTAS):

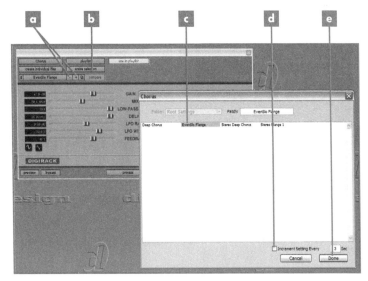

Creating Presets

Let's say that you created the *perfect* Slap Delay, and you'd like to use the same settings in future projects. No problem—it's nearly as easy as recalling presets!

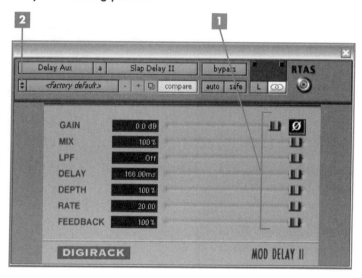

1. Adjust the settings for your effect (notice the subtlety of the ones I used for this example!).

2. Click the Settings Menu button (the small arrow button immediately to the left of the Librarian button). The Settings menu will appear.

3. Choose the Settings Preferences menu item. A submenu will appear.

4. Choose the Save Plug-in Settings To menu item. Another submenu will appear.

  a. Choose Root Settings Folder to save your settings to your host computer's root settings folder. With this option selected, you'll be able to recall these settings with any other sessions you create or open on this computer.

  b. Choose Session Folder to save your settings to a subfolder of the session you've currently working in.

5. For the purposes of our example, choose Root Settings Folder.

Before we go any further, there is a setting that you should check on:

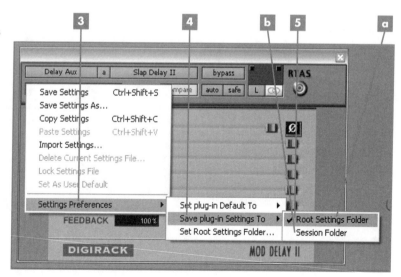

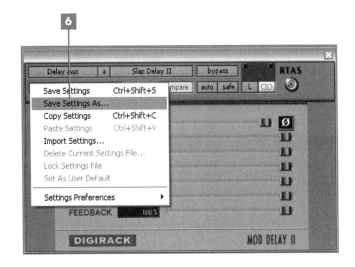

6 Click the Settings Menu once more, then choose Save Settings As. **The Save Effects Settings As dialog box will open.**

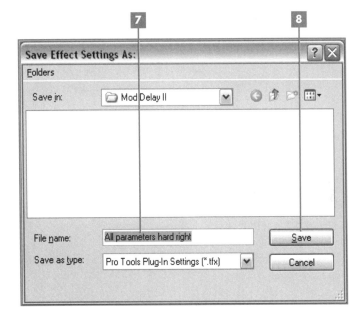

7 Type a descriptive name for your effect (such as "All Parameters Hard Right").

8 Click Save. **The parameters will be saved, and the dialog box will close.**

Here's what you'll end up with:

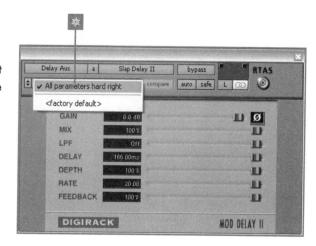

※ You'll note that your saved preset will be added to the list of available presets. The more presets you save, the longer that list will become!

More Fun with Automation

Creating mix automation by manipulating knobs, sliders, and faders with your mouse is a great feature, but it'll only take you so far. If you want to get really specific with your automation, sometimes the only place to do that is back in the Edit window.

1 If you're not already there, go to the Edit window. In this screen, you're looking at your regions, with waveform data inside. To edit your automation data, you have to see it first.

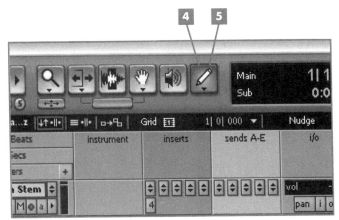

2 Click on the track display format button. The button will display the currently selected display format (in this case "Volume") for easy visual reference. A drop-down menu will appear, displaying available data that can be shown.

3 Click on the data you want to edit. (For this example, take a look at volume.) The volume data will appear.

4 Click on the Pencil tool. The tool will be selected, and you will be able to write new automation or overwrite previously written automation.

5 Click and hold the small arrow at the bottom of the Pencil tool button. A drop-down menu will appear. Just like the Trim and Grabber tools, the Pencil has some interesting options. For example, suppose you want to change this automation from the curve that it is now into a straight linear ramp (which, when you're looking at volume automation, would be a linear increase in volume). The best version of the Pencil tool to use for this would be the Line option.

You can see a line that represents the movements that you wrote during your earlier automation session for the mix parameter you selected (in this case, volume). Note that you can still see your regions and waveforms in the background, but in this mode you cannot edit them in any way.

6 Click on the option you want to use. The option will be selected.

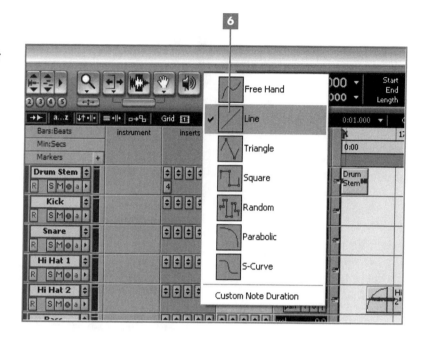

7 Click and hold the Pencil tool at the point at which you want to begin writing new automation.

8 Drag the mouse to the right. The Pencil tool will progressively write new automation over what was previously written. In this case, a straight line will be drawn because the Line option for the Pencil tool was chosen.

9 Release the mouse button. Your new automation line will be written.

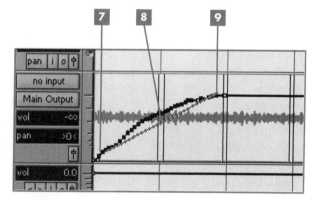

Of course, you can write more than just volume automation in a straight line. Go ahead and try some pan automation that ping-pongs from the left to the right side.

1 Click on the track display format button and choose Pan. The pan data will appear as a line along your track, looking a lot like volume automation. With pan, though, you're not getting louder and softer as your curve moves higher and lower—you're panning from right to left.

2 Although you *could* draw a straight line from left to right over and over again, there's an easier way to do it. Click and hold the small arrow at the bottom of the Pencil tool button. A drop-down menu will appear.

3 Click on the Triangle option. The option will be selected. Note that the pan automation line is flat. This means there is no panning change over time on this track.

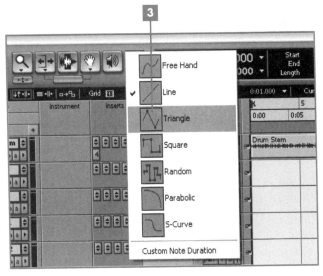

4 When you're dealing with the Triangle, Square, or Random Pencil options, the Grid setting will determine the frequency of the curve (even if you're not in Grid mode). In this case, you want to pan from side to side every measure, so choose 1 bar as your grid value.

5 Click and hold the Pencil tool at the point at which you want to begin writing automation.

This time, as you drag to the right, a triangle wave will be drawn across the track. The frequency of your panning will be one measure, as set up in your Grid value. The severity of the ping-pong is determined by your cursor's height in the track. In the case of pan automation, a higher and lower triangle wave will translate into a more extreme pan from left to right.

6 When you're finished, release the mouse button. The pan automation will be written to your track.

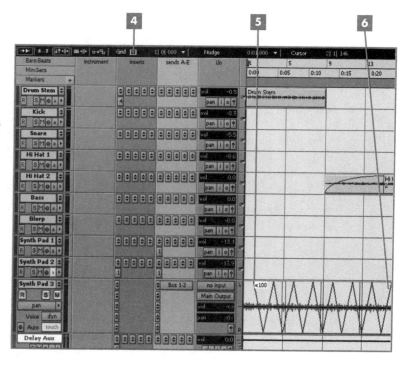

❄ NOTE

Although the triangle wave will change based upon the Grid value in any mode, if you want the apex of the triangle wave to fall on a grid line, you must be in Grid mode.

Copying and Pasting Automation

Once you've got a segment of automation that you like, you can cut and paste that automation from one location to another. It's easy!

1 Click on the Selector tool. The tool will be selected.

2 Select the area of automation that you want to copy, just as if you were selecting a segment of audio. The area will be selected.

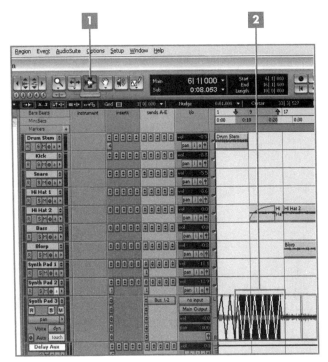

3 Click on the Edit menu and choose any of the basic editing functions (such as Cut, Copy, Paste, or Duplicate) you've used before.

❋ **TIP**

Remember, you can use the regular shortcut keys instead of clicking on the Edit menu.

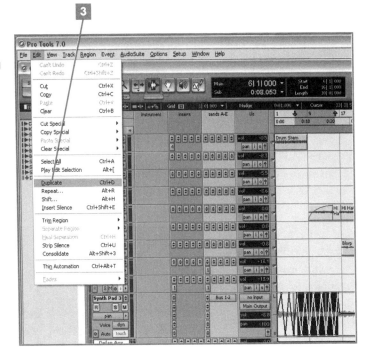

❋ ❋ ❋

After you perform the editing functions, you'll be able to see that the automation curve has been edited. One thing to keep in mind, though: Any edits you do for a specific automation parameter (pan, for example) will not affect any audio or any other automation parameters; they will only affect the parameter you're looking at right now.

> ❄ **NOTE**
>
> Another thing to keep in mind when you work with moving regions: When you move (or copy) a region in the Edit window, all the automation associated with that region will also be moved (or copied), even though that automation is not visible at the time.

More Mixing Power with Subgroups

Subgroups can be a *powerful* ally when mixing, for a number of reasons. First though, what's a subgroup? Simply put, a *subgroup* is an arrangement whereby the output of a number of tracks is routed to the input of a single track. This has the effect of "funneling" the audio through the single track, which can make levels and effects easier to manage. Take a look:

1 Create a track to be your subgroup master (in this case, I've chosen to create a stereo aux track) and name it appropriately.

2 Since you'll be using internal routing for this sort of situation, choose an available bus for the input of the subgroup master. In this case, I've used buses 1 and 2 already, so I've chosen buses 3 and 4.

3 Assign the outputs of the tracks to be grouped (in this case, I've chosen the drum tracks in this session) to the same bus(es) as you've chosen for the input of your subgroup master.

4 Your subgroup master is now in control of the overall volumes of your subgouped tracks. Note that the relative blend of the drums remains consistent and that the subgroup master controls the overall output.

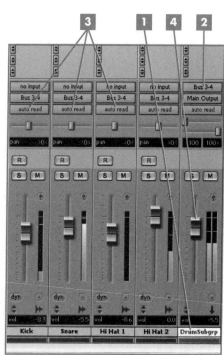

❋ In addition to making your levels more manageable, subgroups can also help you work smart with plug-ins. Suppose you want to apply a compressor to your drums (a very common thing to do). One way you could go is to instantiate a compressor on each of the tracks, but that would be unwieldy to work with and wasteful of your limited processing resources. Instead, just launch one effect on an insert of the subgroup master. Only one plug-in to adjust, and thrifty use of your CPU!

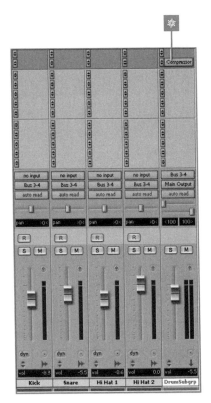

Using Master Faders

There's one kind of track we haven't touched on yet, called a *Master Fader*. Although it looks similar to an audio track, its function is substantially different than anything you've seen up to this point.

A Master Fader is a way to control output. This output can be the signal of a bus, in the case of complex mixing, but most commonly, a Master Fader is used to control the output of an interface. With this simple but powerful track, you can control the level of your session globally. The following sections will show you how a Master Fader works.

Creating a Master Fader

First things first...you need to create a Master Fader.

1 Click on Track. The Track menu will appear.

2 Click on New. The New Tracks dialog box will open.

3 Create a stereo Master Fader. The new Master Fader will be created below the currently selected track. The Master Fader looks similar to any other track, but don't be fooled—it's significantly different!

a You'll notice that the position on the track that would normally display an Input button is conspicuously blank. That's because there is no input on a Master Fader; it is only a way to control an output.

b Notice also that there are no sends on a Master Fader. That's because a Master Fader is a last step in the signal path, so there's nowhere to send a signal to.

c You cannot place regions on this track (similar to an aux track).

4 Click on the Output button and select the interface output you are using to listen to your mix. The interface output will be selected.

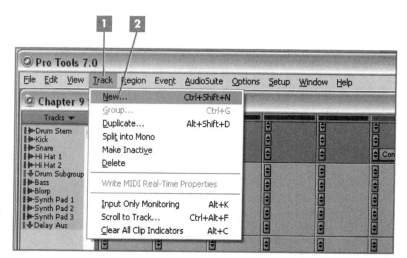

Controlling Your Mix with a Master Fader

Now you can use your Master Fader to control your entire mix.
For example, the following steps will show you how to create a
fade-out for your entire mix in one easy process.

1 Select the Pencil tool and
choose the Line option to
create a straight fade-out.
The option will be selected.

2 Write the automation on the
track as if you were editing
prewritten automation. You'll
hear a linear change in the
volume of your entire mix,
starting at the point at which
the Master Fader's automation
begins.

❁ **NOTE**

If you want to write automation onto your Master Fader in the Mix window,
it's no problem. Simply write automation (in any of the automation modes)
just as you would on any other type of a track!

Basic Mastering Techniques Using a Master Fader

Mastering is a post-mix process that further refines a mix to a professional quality. It is such an exclusive and important process that there is an entire segment of the professional audio community dedicated to the specific task of mastering others' mixes. That being said, the task of professionally mastering a mix is certainly not recommended for the non-specialist.

You might, however, want to try your hand at a little basic mastering to punch up your mix for your own enjoyment or to make an evaluation mix a little more palatable for your client. That's where Master Faders really shine. You see, there's another interesting difference between a Master Fader and any other track—one that may not be initially apparent. This difference is in the area of signal flow, making the track more functional as a mastering device. The inserts are *after* the fader in the signal chain. Read on....

> ❄ **NOTE**
>
> The discussion in this section relates to mastering a mix in your own studio (as opposed to having your mix professionally mastered). If or when you decide to have your mix professionally mastered, the mastering engineer will want to do this job himself, usually with highly specialized (and costly) gear specific to the process of mastering. It's always a good idea to consult your mastering engineer before submitting your mix so you can find out what they want from a mix.

Adjusting Dither

Dither is a common mastering tool used to offset some of the negative sonic qualities of digital audio. In simple terms, it is a very low-level noise that may be added to your digital audio to combat distortion introduced in the signal when the bit depth is reduced. For example, if you're working in a 24-bit session but you will be creating a 16-bit file for an audio CD, you can greatly improve the quality of your audio by applying a dither plug-in on a Master Fader. You can adjust the dither for your Master Fader by following these steps.

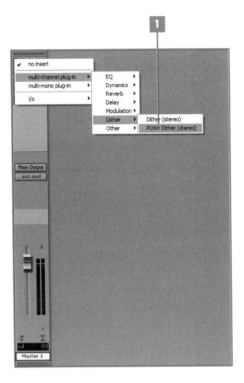

1 On the Master Fader's insert, select the POWr Dither (stereo) option from the multi-channel plug-in menu. The POWr Dither window will appear.

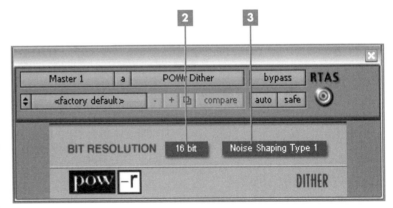

2 Click on the Bit Resolution button and choose the final resolution of your mix. For example, if you want to make an audio CD of the mix, you would choose the 16 bit option.

3 Noise shaping will help make the dither noise less audible. Select a Noise Shaping option. (For now, you can stick with the default shaping, but be sure to listen to different mixes with different noise shaping later.) The option will be selected.

Punching Up Your Mix with Compression—Two Ways

Another common process in mastering is compression. Applying compression to a mix is a tried-and-true method employed to narrow the music's dynamic range, thereby maximizing the overall power of the audio. Give it a try in the following steps.

1 On your Master Fader, instantiate a compressor plug-in on an insert before (above) the one you used for dither. The Compressor plug-in window will appear.

2 Adjust your compressor's parameters to punch up your mix to suit your taste. It'll take some experimentation to find your ideal settings, of course. You can start with a preset configuration specifically for mastering a mix, like the one shown in this example.

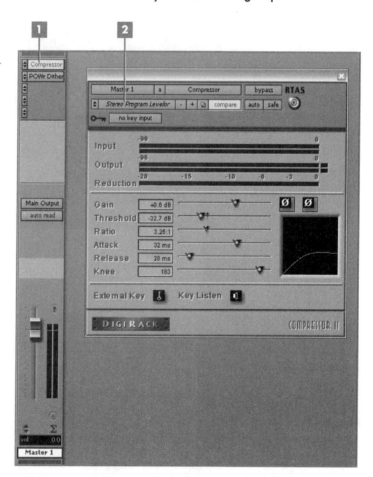

NOTE

If you're using dither *and* a compressor on a Master Fader, you'll want to arrange your inserts so that the dither is the last plug-in (on the lowest insert). Don't worry if your dither is on the top insert; you can just drag it down to a lower insert (and later in the insert's signal path) with your mouse, and then create your compressor above it.

Now, those of you with mixing experience might notice a problem with this sort of routing. You see, a compressor operates by attenuating (or reducing) any level above a certain *threshold*, which you set in your effect window. Any incoming signal that falls below that threshold will not be affected by a compressor. As long as you don't use your master fade-ins or fade-outs, there's no problem with using a compressor on the Master Fader, *but* if you do use the Master Fader for such things, you'll hear your compressor kick in or out, depending on whether you're fading in or out. How do we get around this problem? I'm glad you asked!

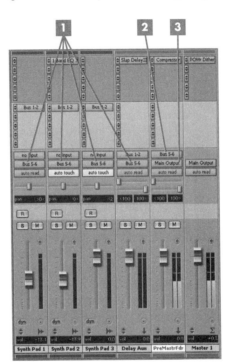

1. Re-assign the output of all tracks previously assigned to Main Output to an available pair of buses (in this case, buses 5 and 6). Your session will now be inaudible, but wait!

2. Create a stereo aux track, assign the input to the same pair of buses (in this case, buses 5 and 6), and drag the compressor plug-in to that track's insert.

3. The output of this aux track, Main Output, will then be routed to the Master Fader. Bear in mind that the inserts of the aux track are *pre-fader*, and so the signal going to the compressor will be affected by neither the Master Fader volume level *nor* the aux track's output level, meaning you can apply your global fade automation on either track. That's it!

Bouncing to Disk

When you're working in a Pro Tools session, you're in a multitrack environment. Even though you're listening through stereo monitor speakers, you're hearing many component tracks, artfully mixed together by Pro Tools' software mix engine. From a production standpoint, it's a pretty cool way to work, but if you ever want to hear your song outside of the Pro Tools environment, you'll have to somehow render the mix down to a format that is compatible with the outside world.

The Bounce to Disk function is the right tool for this job. It will mix down your session as it plays in real time and create a new audio file of your entire mix. It's a simple process, but one that demands attention to detail to be done just right, so I'll go over all the steps carefully. For example, here's how to go about bouncing to disk so you can burn an audio CD (red book format) of your entire mix.

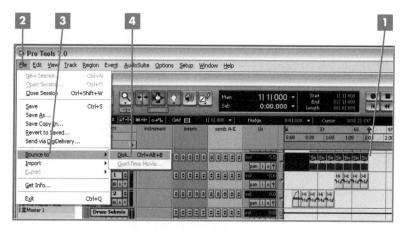

1. Using the Selector tool in the Rulers area, select the area of the session you want to bounce to disk. The area will be selected.

2. Click on File. The File menu will appear.

3. Click on Bounce To. A submenu will be displayed.

4. Click on Disk. The Bounce dialog box will appear.

5 Select the output you are using to listen to this mix from the Bounce Source menu. This is perhaps the most important step in this process.

❋ **TIP**

If you bounce to disk and then later find that your bounce is a silent audio file, you probably chose the wrong bounce source.

6 Click on the File Type arrow. The File Type menu will appear, displaying a list of available formats for your mixdown.

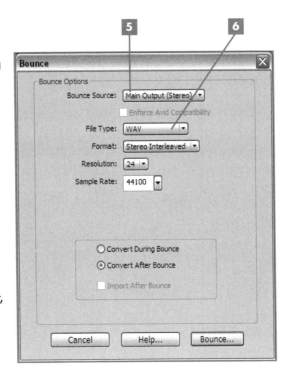

7 Choose the file type that suits your needs. The first two formats (WAV and AIFF) involve no data reduction, so they're well suited for tasks such as continued production or CD burning. The next three formats (MP3, QuickTime, and Windows Media) offer lossy data reduction, which will result in smaller file sizes.

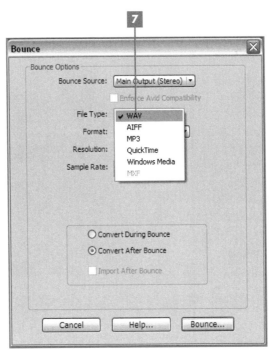

8 Click on the Format arrow. The Format menu will appear.

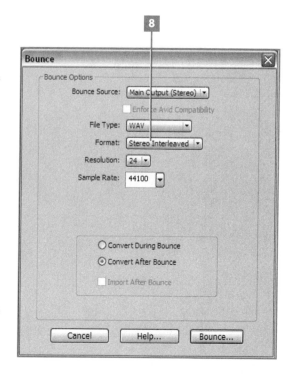

9 Select the file format that suits your purposes. Here's a brief rundown of the available formats:

a Mono (Summed). With this option, your mix, even if it is stereo, will be mixed down to a single mono file.

b Multiple Mono. With this option, your mix will be output to a pair of mono files—one for the left side (with ".l" after the file name) and one for the right (with ".r" after the file name). This is particularly useful for bounces that you intend to use in future Pro Tools sessions.

c Stereo Interleaved. Use this option is for tracks destined for CD burning. Your mix will be rendered to a single stereo file.

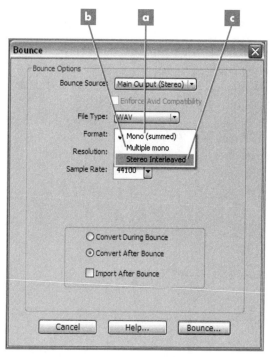

10 Click **on the** Resolution arrow. **The Resolution menu will appear, displaying the bit depths to which you can bounce.**

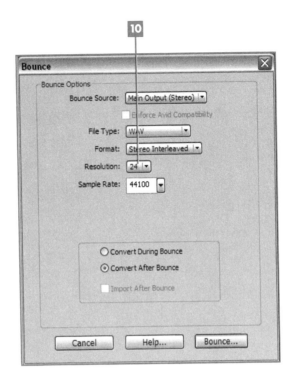

11 Select **the** bit depth **you want your bounced file to be. The bit depth will be selected.**

❈ **NOTE**

For the purposes of CD burning, the bit depth must be 16.

12 Click **on the** Sample Rate arrow. **The Sample Rate menu will appear, from which you can choose your bounce's sample rate.**

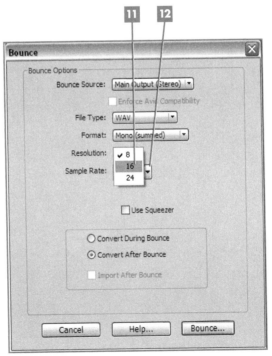

13 Click on the desired sample rate for your mix.

❄ **NOTE**

For CD burning, the sample rate for your bounced file must be 44.1 kHz.

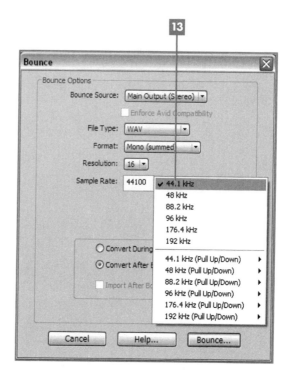

14 If the sample rate or bit depths you've chosen for your bounce file are different from those of your session, you will need to convert the bounce file. Click on the Conversion Quality arrow. The Conversion Quality menu will appear.

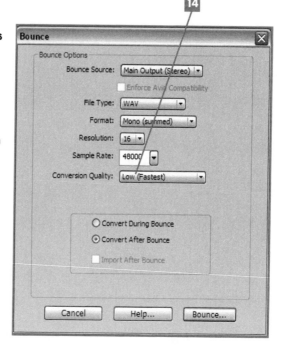

15 If you need to convert in any way, you have a few options:

a Convert During Bounce. This option allows you to convert during the bounce process (as your session plays).

b Convert After Bounce. This option allows you to convert after your bounce pass is completed.

c Import After Bounce. This option allows you to import your bounced file back into your session on an audio track.

16 Click on Bounce. The Save Bounce As dialog box will open.

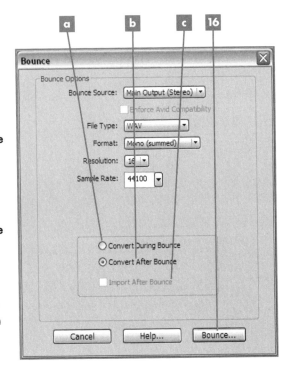

17 Save your file using the options in the Save Bounce As dialog box. You can save your file under any name you want, in any drive, and in any folder. For the purposes of illustration, I'll stick with the default location, which is within the session's Audio Files folder.

18 Click on Save. Your bounce will begin.

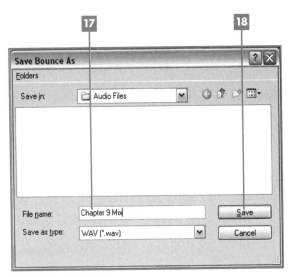

Your session will begin playing, and a small countdown window will indicate that bouncing is occurring.

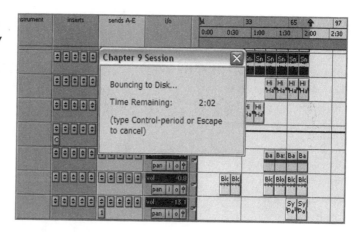

If conversion is necessary (and assuming you chose to convert *after* the bounce), you'll see a quick conversion process after your session finishes the bounce.

Here's an example of what you'll end up with. It's important to know exactly where your files are created. If you followed the default location, your bounced file will be

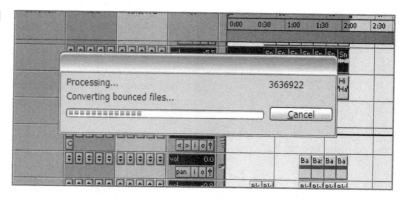

* In the hard drive that holds your session.
* In any folders that house your session's folder.
* In your session's folder.
* In your session's Audio Files subfolder.
* An audio file, with the name you created.

NOTE

As you can see, your bounced file can get hidden quite well beneath layers of folders on any number of drives. The point I want to emphasize is that it is extremely important to know exactly where and under what name your files are saved. (This goes for session files and other audio files as well.) You can save your bounced file anywhere you choose in your system, but with this great flexibility comes the added responsibility of using this power wisely.

Enjoy your final mix—you've earned it!

10 } Moving to the Next Level: Tips and Tricks

Pro Tools is a complex, professional application, and mastering it is a lifelong pursuit for industry professionals. This book is meant to provide you with a solid basic understanding of how to use this powerful product—a strong foundation upon which to build greater knowledge over time. The good news is that by mastering the previous chapters, you've attained that basic understanding.

Now, here's a laundry list of next-level functions, designed to allow you to be even more productive! In this chapter, you'll learn how to:

✳ Work more efficiently in the Edit and Mix windows

✳ View data more specifically

✳ Import and use movie files

✳ Boost your session's efficiency

> ✳ **NOTE**
>
> To follow along with the examples shown in the screenshots of this chapter, download, set up, and open the folder named "Chapter 10 Session." You'll note that in this session (as in Chapter 6) the features are demonstrated through a series of memory locations. Also, you'll note that even though the session is extensive in its tracks and complexity, it's only using a few different audio files, keeping the overall session folder small!

Making the Most of Editing

The follow sections detail processes that will make your editing even more efficient and fun!

Zoom Toggle

Here's a cool little trick that will allow you to toggle between two zoom settings quickly. This is particularly useful when you're working with a specific selection, then zooming out to see your selection in the context of the rest of your session.

1 Make a selection in the Edit window.

2 Press Start+E (PC) or Control+E (Mac). Your selection will zoom in to fill the Edit window.

3 Press Start+E (PC) or Control+E (Mac). You will toggle back to the previous zoom level.

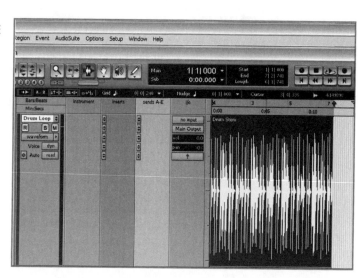

❋ **NOTE**

To follow along with these first sections, go to memory location #1—Identify Beat. From the Window menu, open the Memory Location window, and simply click location #1 (for more on how to use memory locations, please refer to Chapter 6).

The Identify Beat Function

One of Pro Tools' greatest strengths is its ability to use MIDI and audio in the same environment. Before they'll work together, though, their tempos must agree. You can use the Identify Beat function to tell Pro Tools the tempo of your audio! This memory location (#1–Identify Beat) shows a great example of a very common dilemma. Listen to the region—sounds like 8 full measures of drums, correct? Okay, now look at the selection length *according to the Pro Tools Tempo Ruler*—it says that the region is 6 measures, 1 beat, and 741 ticks! Obviously, your judgment is correct, and here's how to clue Pro Tools in!

1 Make a selection of a specific musical length. (In this case, it's 8 measures that loop perfectly.) Use your ears to make this loopable selection—*not* your MIDI tempo or session grid.

2 Select the Conductor icon if it isn't already lit. The icon will be selected.

3 Click on Event. The Event menu will appear.

4 Click on Identify Beat. The Add Bar | Beat Markers dialog box will open.

5 Type the location that your ears tell you is the beginning of the selection in the Location text box in the Start area.

6 Type the location that your ears tell you is the end of the selection in the Location text box in the End area. In this case, since we hear an 8 bar selection, it ends at the beginning of bar 9 (9|1|000).

7 Click on OK. The Add Bar | Beat Markers dialog box will close, and your tempo will change to match your audio.

> ❄ **TIP**
>
> You can use the Identify Beat function at any point in a session. For example, if you have a live drummer who gets a little faster during the chorus, just select the chorus and enter your loopable selection in the Add Bar | Beat Markers dialog box.

Relative Grid Mode

New with Pro Tools 6! In the normal Absolute Grid mode, you made regions snap to grid lines. If your grid resolution was set to 1 bar, for example, regions (and MIDI notes) snapped to the nearest bar. Relative Grid mode, on the other hand, will move the object not to the nearest grid, but by the selected grid resolution. For example, if you have a grid resolution of 1 bar, and a region is off the grid by, say, 10 milliseconds, the grid will always maintain its 10-millisecond distance from the nearest measure.

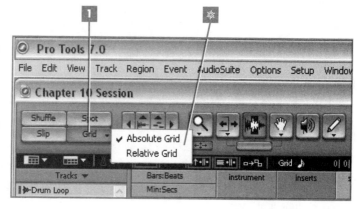

1 Click on the down arrow in the lower-right corner of the Grid button. The following options will appear:

❄ Absolute Grid. This is Pro Tools default mode. It is based on the absolute values that you set as your Grid value. When you move regions or notes, they will snap to the grid lines.

❄ Relative Grid. In this variation of the Grid mode, regions and notes will move by grid *amounts* while maintaining a consistent distance from the closest grid line.

Tips for the TCE Trim Tool

The secret behind the TCE Trim tool is that it operates on the same software code as the AudioSuite Time Compress/Expand plug-in. Because of this, there are ways that you can customize its effectiveness. To do so, you first need to open the AudioSuite plug-in.

1 Click on AudioSuite. The AudioSuite menu will appear.

2 Click on Other. Another menu will appear.

3 Click on Time Compression Expansion. The Time Compression/Expansion window will appear.

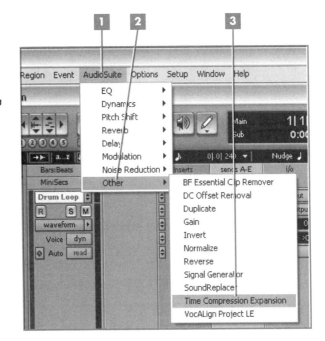

4 Set the plug-in's parameters to commonly used settings. For example, setting the Accuracy parameter to Sound is useful for minimizing phasing and other sonic artifacts.

5 Click on the arrow button to the left of the preset name. A menu will appear.

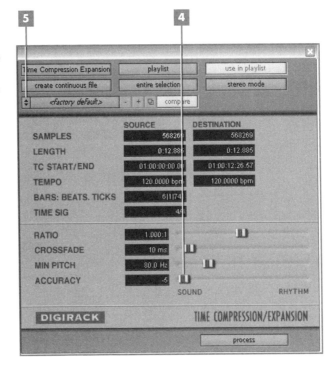

6 Choose Save Settings As.
The Save Settings As dialog box will open.

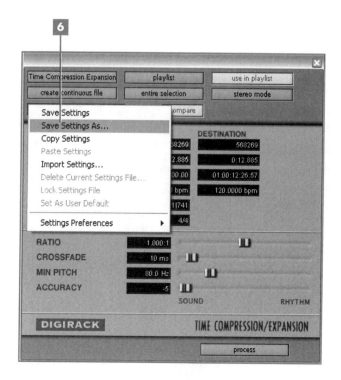

7 Type a descriptive name for this preset in the File Name text box.

8 Click on Save. The preset will be saved.

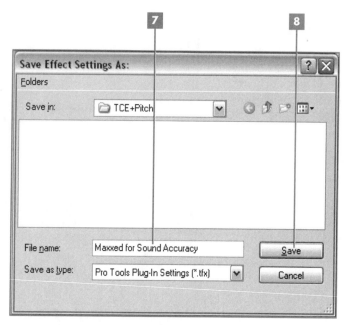

❋ NOTE

Make sure you save your settings in the root settings folder. (Pro Tools defaults to this.) If you're not sure where you're saving your settings, click on the Settings menu (the arrow button to the left of the setting's name in the plug-in window) and click on the Settings Preferences option. From there, go to the Save Plug-in Settings To option and make sure Root Settings Folder is checked.

9 Just for example's sake, create another commonly used preset. In this example, I've set up a preset optimized for rhymic accuracy. When you're finished adjusting the settings, save the preset.

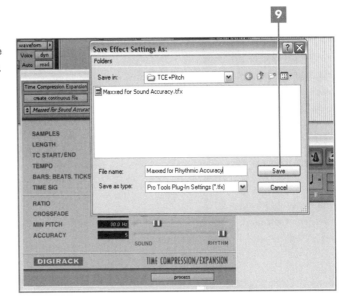

10 Now it's time to change the Trim tool. Click on Setup. The Setup menu will appear.

11 Click on Preferences. The Preferences dialog box will open.

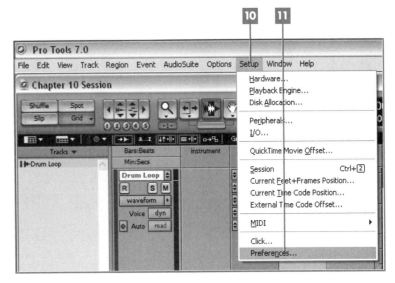

12 Click on the Processing tab. The tab will move to the front.

※ The TC/E area will display the AudioSuite plug-in currently used for the TCE Trim tool. On a basic Pro Tools system, it should read Digidesign TC/E; however, if you install other third-party time compression/ expansion plug-ins, you can change the software that the Trim tool will use by clicking on the down arrow and selecting the desired software.

13 Click on the Default Settings down arrow. The Default Settings menu will appear.

14 You'll see the presets you created in AudioSuite, available for you to choose as the TCE Trim tool's default settings.

15 Click on Done. The Preferences dialog box will close. From now on, until you change the default settings, the TCE Trim tool will have the chosen preset's parameter settings.

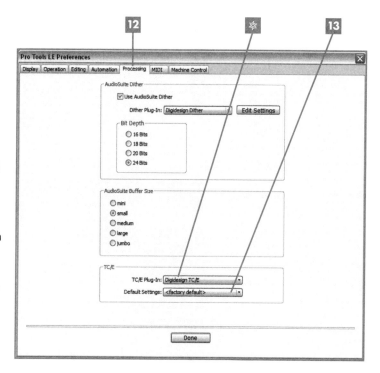

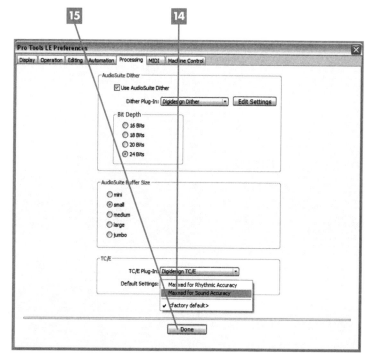

Edit versus Timeline Selection

Throughout this book, whenever you have made a selection on a track, that selection has been reflected in the Rulers area (or the Timeline) and vice versa. Normally this is the way to work, but these two selections don't *need* to be linked.

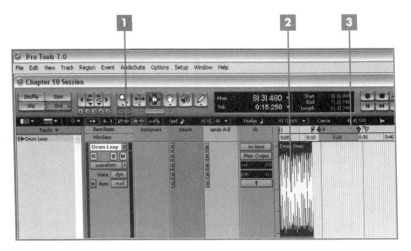

1. Click on the Link Timeline and Edit Selection button to deselect it. The button will be deselected.

2. Make a selection on any track.

3. Make a different selection in the Rulers area. Note that the two areas do not reflect each other.

It's important to take a moment to see just how Pro Tools acts in this situation. If you try to play back your selection, note how what plays back is your *timeline* selection. In truth, this always has been the case, though most users don't make any distinctions between the edit selection and the timeline selection, and they leave the linking enabled all the time.

Unlinking your edit and timeline selections can be nifty when you want to hear a different part of your song than the part you're editing— for example, you want to hear a little *before* the region that you're working with, so unlink your edit and timeline and make a timeline selection that reflects what you want. Just be careful to *relink* when you're done with this unusual mode of operation. You can either click on the Link Timeline and Edit Selection button again to reactivate it, or go into your menus.

4 Click on Options. The Options menu will appear.

5 Click on the Link Timeline and Edit Selection option to re-enable it. The button will be enabled.

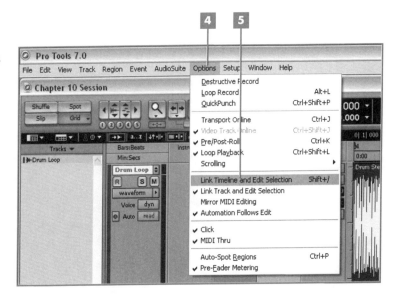

Samples versus Ticks

You learned back in Chapter 6 about the advantages of tick-based audio tracks, but there's a little more to the story! Let's take a look at audio and MIDI track timing properties.

Track Timings

a Audio tracks, by default, are created as *sample-based* tracks, which means that each region is anchored to a specific sample location. What that means is that tempo changes and other MIDI functions will have no effect upon the regions of the track.

b MIDI tracks, on the other hand, are created by default as *tick-based* tracks, which means that regions on this track *will* respond to tempo and meter changes. Speed the MIDI tempo and the MIDI notes will speed up accordingly.

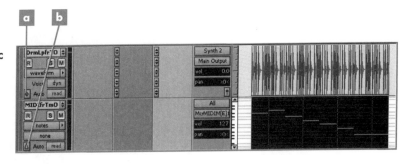

❄ NOTE

For this section, go to memory location #2—Tempo Operations.

Even though these are the *default* states for each kind of track, there are advantages to working unconventionally!

a As you saw in Chapter 6, changing an audio track to tick-based timing (as shown by the Metronome icon) will allow you to put your region timing under the control of your MIDI tempo map. In this example, if you were to change the tempo of your session, your regions would move and change your drum audio's "tempo" as a result.

b Less common, but no less possible, is the practice of changing a MIDI track to sample-based timing, as shown here. To do it, just click the track's Time Base Selector and choose Samples. In this mode, your MIDI track takes on a very interesting behavior, as your MIDI data will *not* change when you change tempo and meter in your session. You might ask, "Why would I want to do this, since MIDI is a musical tool?" Well, for starters, you might be using a MIDI note to trigger a sound effect that needs to be synched to video and is not being used in a musical way—this is a great way to keep that specific MIDI data in place!

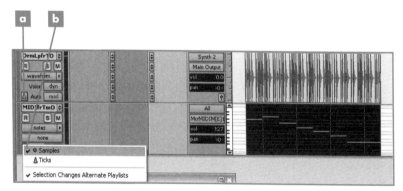

Session Linearity

This next bit can get a bit tricky, so stick with me here. By default, the rulers of your sessions are evenly spaced (or *linear*) based upon real time, which can be broken down into hours, minutes, seconds, frames (for timecode use), and *samples*. This means that when you change tempo, a MIDI operation, your real-time display will remain evenly spaced, and your MIDI tempo spacing will expand or compress according to your tempo changes. Take a look:

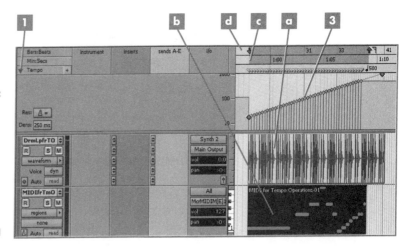

1. Click the Tempo Editor down arrow. Your tempo ruler will expand to show you a graphic display of your tempo changes.

2. For the purpose of our example here, choose the Pencil tool with the Line option selected.

3. Draw a tempo change, starting from a lower tempo, then ramping up to a faster tempo.

You'll notice a few things:

a. Your sample-based tracks (in this case, an Audio track), will not react to the tempo change.

b. Your tick-based tracks (in this case, MIDI), will change based upon your tempo change.

c. Your real-time rulers will remain evenly spaced.

d. Your tempo ruler will change its spacing based upon your temp changes.

You'll also note that as a side effect of this tempo change, the spacing of the notes has changed radically; and even though all the notes on this track are half notes, their appearance has really been altered. Often, this is a bit of an annoyance when working with MIDI data, and it's desirable to be able to see your note values displayed more consistently, regardless of tempo changes. It's very easy to do, and it makes quite a difference in your Edit window's view.

4 Click the Linearity Display mode down arrow. A menu will appear.

5 Click on Linear Tick Display. Notice how your screen changes (though the *sound* of your session does not—this is *only* a display change).

a Note that the spacing of both your audio and MIDI tracks has changed. The time base of each track hasn't changed, but the overall linear display of the session has been changed from real time to tempo linearity. Note that the sample-based Audio track is now not as evenly spaced as it once was, whereas the MIDI track (despite the tempo change) is perfectly spaced.

b Your rulers have also changed. Your bars and beats ruler (top) is now evenly spaced (again, despite the tempo change), and the minutes:seconds is now unevenly spaced. As you listen to and watch the playback of your session, you'll see that the *only* change made to your session has been visual. This change in linearity is simply for your ease of use.

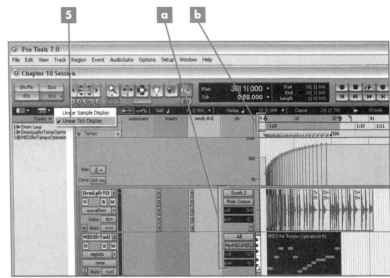

Cool Editing Tools

Strip Silence and Beat Detective have recently been added to Pro Tools LE—let's take a look.

Using Strip Silence

Strip Silence is a nifty little editing tool that acts upon regions in a way similar to how a noise gate acts upon audio. Simply stated, when you use the Strip Silence feature, any audio below a specified volume threshold will be removed from your selection, leaving discrete regions that you can move and edit separately.

1. Click on Edit. The Edit menu will appear.

2. Click on Strip Silence. The Strip Silence window will appear.

❄ **NOTE**

Please go to memory location #3— Strip Silence.

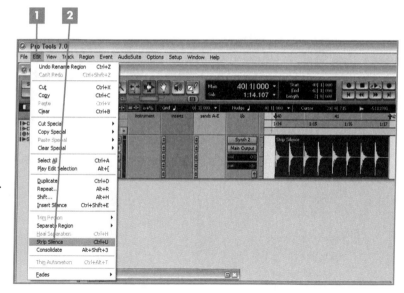

3 Select the area in your session that you would like to strip. The area will be selected.

4 Adjust the parameters in the Strip Silence window until you achieve the desired separation. (Before the regions are processed, you will see where new region boundaries will be created.) The available parameters include the following:

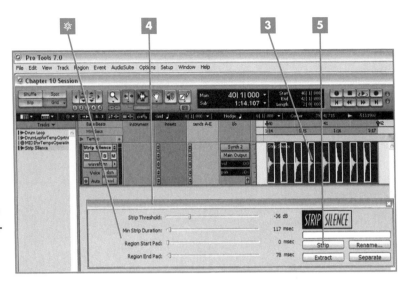

* Strip Threshold. Any volume level under the strip threshold will be removed from your selection.

* Min Strip Duration. This value determines the shortest region able to be created by strip silence.

* Region Start Pad. This slider will move the front region boundaries earlier in time.

* Region End Pad. This slider will move the back region boundaries later in time.

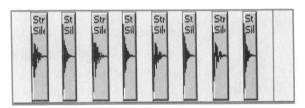

5 Click on Strip. Your selection will be chopped into discrete regions, and the audio below your threshold value will be removed from the track altogether. These new regions will be shown in the Regions list.

Don't worry, you haven't deleted any audio. In fact, you can use the Trim tool and drag any region boundary out to recover the audio that has been stripped.

There are a few other options regarding the Strip Silence window that are available to you:

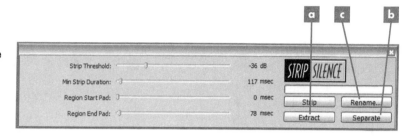

a Extract. This does the opposite of the Strip function and will leave only regions of "silence."

b Separate. This mode will not actually strip any audio, but will leave regions of "sound" and "silence," based on your settings.

c Rename. This option will allow you to custom name the regions that will be created when you strip.

Beat Detective

One of the most interesting music production tools in Pro Tools' array is Beat Detective. Based on the same technology that makes the Tab to Transient feature work so well, this process has different kinds of applications. Generally speaking, it is used in conjunction with drum tracks, but it can be applied with any audio with clearly defined transients (or MIDI).

The first of these applications is based on the idea that a musical groove (from swing to rock to polka and everything in between!) is by definition *not* mathematically uniform. This "human" element is in opposition to the mathematical precision of a static MIDI tempo. What this means is that in order to get your audio and MIDI to groove together, you'll have to create a more complex MIDI tempo map, which is exactly what Beat Detective does!

 NOTE

For the first part of our Beat Detective discussion, go to memory location #4— Beat Detective (pt.1).

1 Select **the** segment of drums that you wish to analyze.

2 Click on Event. **The menu will appear.**

3 Click on Beat Detective. **The Beat Detective window will appear.**

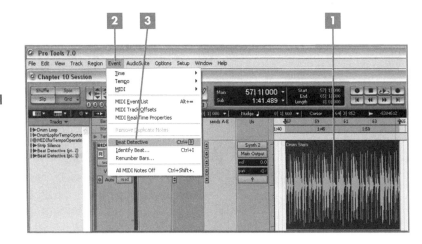

4 The mode for this sort of operation is Bar|Beat Marker Generation. Click its radio button to enter this mode.

5 This step is very important: Make sure that your values in Beat Detective's Selection area correctly reflect the same selections in your session. (Notice how the Selection area in Beat Detective *and* the Edit window's selection display match.)

6 Choose **the smallest** musical note value of your audio (in this case, 16th notes) from the Contains button.

7 Click Analyze. **Your audio will be examined by Beat Detective, which will look to detect transients.**

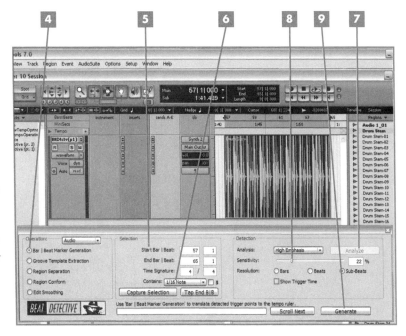

8 Slowly raise the Sensitivity slider from zero. You will notice that as your sensitivity increases, you will see vertical lines intersecting the transients of your audio. Once you are satisfied that the important transients have been marked (and no others), stop moving the slider.

9 Click Generate. **The Realign Session dialog box will open.**

❄ **TIP**

Assuming that your selection is known to be in general agreement with the MIDI tempo, you can click the Capture Selection button in the Selection area of Beat Detective. This is an easy way to go with audio in which the beat has already been identified.

Thankfully, this dialog box is fairly self-explanatory. Basically, what will happen in the next step is that a very complex tempo map will be created, which, as you have learned, will have no effect on sample-based tracks, but which can have a *big* effect on tick-based tracks.

a If you have tick-based data (let's say, a drum part on a MIDI track), and you want the timing of that data to move to match the timing of this audio track, choose Preserve Tick Position.

b If you have tick-based data that doesn't need to be conformed to the groove of this audio, choose Preserve Sample Position.

10 In this example, where we have no other tracks, either option is fine. Click OK.

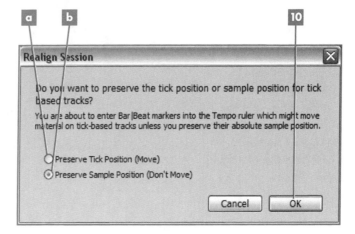

You will see now that a great number of small tempo changes have been added to your tempo ruler (each shown as a blue triangle). What you've done is create a tempo map that changes constantly to match the groove of the drum audio, which has effectively created a MIDI *grid* that also reflects these changes. Since things like Grid mode and MIDI Quantize rely on this grid for their timing, you can now conform any additional MIDI and audio to this original drum beat, and they will all groove together!

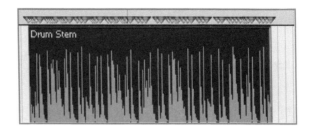

Here's a variation on that same sort of logic.

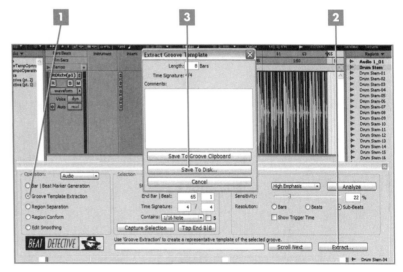

1 Click the Groove Template Extraction radio button.

2 After going through the same selection and analysis process that you used earlier in Steps 5 through 8, click the Extract button. The Extract Groove Template window will appear.

3 In this window, you can either save to a clipboard for immediate use or to disk for more long-term use. What are you saving? Well, what you have extracted is the same sort of timing information that you used in Bar | Beat Marker Generation, except that by extracting this information, you've added it to your list of usable MIDI Groove Quantize options. More simply put, you will now have the option to quantize future MIDI data to have the same feel as these drums here!

1 Select the segment of drums that you wish to analyze.

2 The mode for this sort of operation is Region Separation. Click its radio button to enter this mode.

3 Again, make sure that your values in Beat Detective's Selection area correctly reflect the actual selections in your session. Be careful—Beat Detective does not automatically update its selection values, and this memory location is at a different section of your session!

4 Choose the smallest musical note value of your audio (in this case, 16th notes) from the Contains menu button.

5 Click Analyze. Your audio will be examined by Beat Detective, which will look to detect transients.

6 Slowly raise the Sensitivity slider from zero. You will notice as your sensitivity increases, you will see vertical lines intersecting the transients of your audio. Once you are satisfied that the important transients have been marked (and no others), stop moving the slider.

7 Click Separate. Your region will be separated into a number of smaller regions.

But that's not all Beat Detective can do—not by a long shot. Let's reverse the equation: Let's say that instead of creating a new tempo map so that the rest of my session can conform to my drum audio, I want to conform my audio to the current tempo of the session. Beat Detective can do that, too. In this example, we'll take our familiar Drum region and conform it to the mathematically static tempo of the session.

NOTE

Please go to memory location #5—Beat Detective (pt. 2).

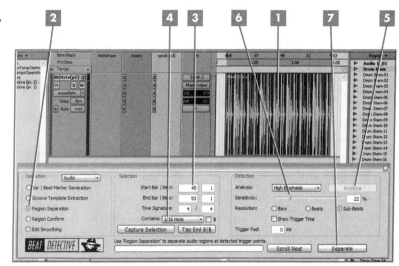

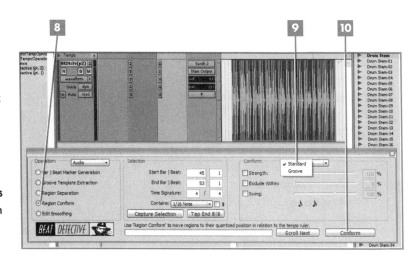

8 Now that you've chopped up your larger region, it's time to get the smaller regions in line: Click the Region Conform radio button.

9 If you click on the Conform Mode button, you'll see that you can conform your regions in a standard way, or through Groove Conform (which will allow you to use the groove templates included with Pro Tools *in addition* to any grooves you may have extracted). For our purposes, choose the Standard mode.

10 Click the Conform button. The regions will move subtly to match the existing tempo. Listen to the region, and you will hear a slight change in the feel.

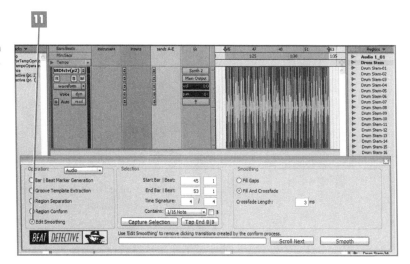

11 As a by-product of the conforming process, some gaps will be produced between the regions and commonly some clicks and pops (as you will hear in this example). That's where the final mode comes in: Click the Edit Smoothing radio button.

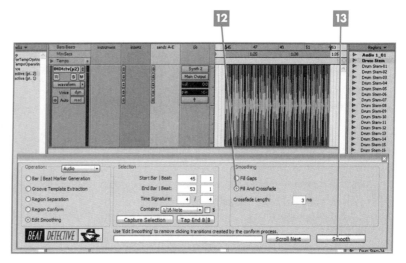

12 This last mode is very straight-forward—it will eliminate the gaps between regions. If there is no problem with clicks or pops, click the Fill Gaps radio button. If there *are* clicks and pops (as there are in this example), a small crossfade between regions will fix the problem. Set the Crossfade length to a reasonable amount (this will change from situation to situation—in this case, 3 ms sounds good), then click the Fill and Crossfade radio button.

13 Click the Smooth button.

Your audio will now have a significantly different feel and with no gaps!

 TIP

Beat Detective can also analyze MIDI data and perform similar operations—a new addition to the Beat Detective process. To use Beat Detective with MIDI, just click the Audio button in the upper-left corner of the Beat Detective window. Some subtle changes in the window will be shown, but the general workflow is the same.

 TIP

Before I close the discussion on editing, I want to show you a useful shortcut. On either a Mac or a PC, hold the Shift key and press the spacebar to play back your session at half of real-time speed. This feature comes in particularly handy when you're setting punch-in or punch-out points for a particularly tight spot. (Just make sure not to record that way, or your audio will be twice as high in pitch!)

Making the Most of Mixing

Here are a couple of tips to make your mixes rock!

Using the Edit Tools

So far, you've only used the Pencil tool to edit your automation. This section will show you how to use a couple of other tools.

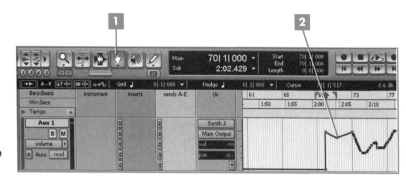

1 Click on the Grabber tool. The tool will be selected.

2 Click on the automation line. A new breakpoint will be created. From that point, you can drag the breakpoint to the desired location.

❋ **TIP**

Hold the Option key (Mac) or the Alt key (PC) and click on a previously written breakpoint to remove it.

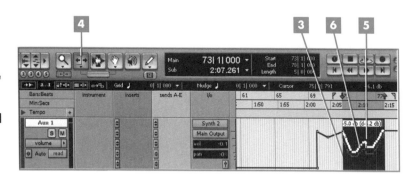

3 Make a selection on a track you want to change (using the Selector tool).

4 Click on the Trim tool. The tool will be selected.

5 Move the Trim tool into the selected area. The Trim icon will appear on its side.

6 Click and drag your mouse up or down to change any prewritten automation proportionally. The amount of change effected upon your automation will be shown in the delta value.

7 Release **the** mouse button. **The automation will be proportionally changed in the selected area.**

Toggling Groups

This section will show you how you can temporarily suspend fader groups so you can quickly change the balance of the fader group.

✳ NOTE

For this section, please go to memory location #7–Mixing (pt. 2), and switch to the Mix window.

In this example, we've got four vocal parts that are grouped together. Here's a way to change the balance of the group without the hassle of deactivating the Mix group!

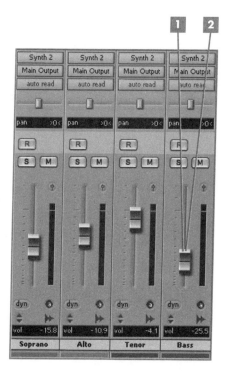

1 Press and hold **the** Start (Windows) key **(PC)** or the Control key **(Mac), and** click and drag **the** fader you wish to change. **You can change the volume of a track without affecting other tracks in the group.**

2 Release **the** key. **Your group will be re-enabled.**

> ❄ **TIP**
>
> Before you leave the task of mixing, here's one more tip for your considera-
> tion. Remember when you used a send from a dry Audio track to a wet Aux
> track back in Chapter 8? Guess what? You can send from multiple tracks to
> a single aux. Just create identical sends on each track you want to route to
> a single aux, assigning each send to the same bus. This method is commonly
> used for assigning many tracks (such as drums, for example) to a single
> reverb. It's a simple and convenient way to work, and it conserves your
> CPU's resources as well!

How to Consolidate (and Why)

One way to increase the efficiency of your system is to minimize its
edit density. *Edit density* refers to the number of times your system
must acquire data from your hard drive during playback. If you
have many small regions (such as drum loops, for example), it can
increase your edit density. In extreme cases, high edit density can
cause playback errors.

The trick is to decrease the number of regions without changing the
sound of your session, and the consolidate function is the key.

> ❄ **NOTE**
>
> For this demonstration, go to memory location #8—Consolidation. You'll see a
> section of drums to which Beat Detective has been applied to conform it to an
> even grid—*lots* of regions!

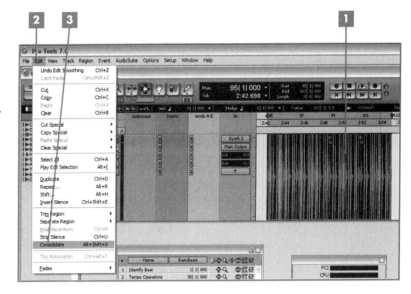

1 Select a section of your session that is particularly dense with regions (this has been done for you in this example).

2 Click on Edit. The Edit menu will appear.

3 Click on Consolidate. Your selection of multiple regions will be rendered into a single region.

A window will display the progress of the rendering process.

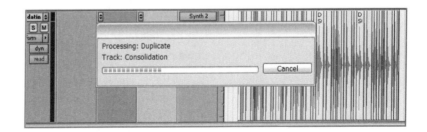

Your selection will be replaced with a single region that sounds identical to the original selection.

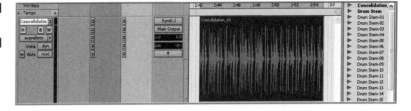

❄ **NOTE**

When you consolidate, any selected space that is not occupied with a region will be rendered as silent audio, as will any gaps in between regions in your selection.

Working with Movies

Although Pro Tools is certainly an audio program, there is a degree of support for incorporating video into your session. Let's have a look at the process of importing a QuickTime Movie, which couldn't be easier.

1 Click on File. The File menu will appear.

2 Click on Import, and another menu will appear.

3 Click on QuickTime Movie. The Choose a QuickTime File dialog box will open.

4 Navigate to the file you want to use and click on Open. A new track will be created in your session. Although it's not an audio track, you'll see it displayed in your Edit window and the Track Show/Hide list. You can arrange the track in your session just as you would any other track. Additionally, a video window will appear.

5 If your movie window doesn't
appear, click on QuickTime
Movie from the Window
menu. The Movie menu will
appear.

6 If you want to export your
movie with the audio you've
created, click on QuickTime
Movie from the File and
Bounce to menus. This option
is similar to the Bounce to Disk
function, except it bounces the
mixed audio into a QuickTime
movie file.

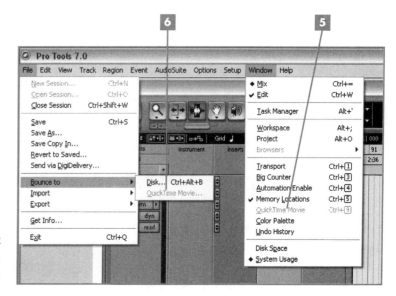

Interoperability: Making Shared Sessions Work

Perhaps the most compelling reason to learn and use Pro Tools is
the fact that it is a worldwide standard in the DAW world. From
bedroom studios to multi-million dollar studios, Pro Tools allows
greater mobility for amateurs and professionals alike than perhaps
any other application. Take your humble author, for example—I
wrote a good portion of this book in airports with an Mbox 2 LE
system, and I could easily open the exact same work in any pro
studio with a minimum of muss and fuss!

It bears mentioning at this point that for the LE user, this interoperability has been enhanced with version 7. In addition to full audio
and MIDI import and export, Pro Tools can now support Rex and
ACID files. For those readers who have had experience with beat-
based production, you'll recognize these two formats as long-time
tools of the trade, and now you will be able to use them in the Pro
Tools environment. For those of you who haven't had any direct

experience with these, Rex and ACID files are loop segments that may be imported into your session and will follow tempo changes in your session, similar to the tick-based audio that you have already worked with.

The best way to maximize the interoperability of Pro Tools is to make every effort to ensure that your session can be opened and heard properly on every system and that collaborators can easily get around in your work. Here are some recommendations on how to make this happen:

✳ Name all tracks *before* recording, and name them in a way that anyone can understand.

✳ Use your comments. The Comments column of every track, and the comment field of Markers, are valuable sources of information to others.

✳ Use your memory locations. Identify each section of your work, and descriptively name it so that anybody can understand the overall layout of your work.

✳ Internally record (using a bus) all your virtual instrument tracks to audio tracks. This insures that even if your collaborator doesn't have your virtual instruments in their systems, they will still be able to hear them.

✳ Use AudioSuite when appropriate. Just as with internal recording, this will create a new file that can be played back in any Pro Tools situation, even if the actual plug-ins don't exist on the other system.

✳ Use a Click track. Recording a great beat is all well and good, but if you're not in sync with the MIDI tempo of your session, operations like Quantize, Beat Detective, and Grid mode will do more harm than good!

✳ Before you archive your session, or whenever moving it from one system to another, do a Save Copy of your session and click all options for saving. This will ensure that all your audio, video, and plug-in settings will be saved in one central location. *That's* the file you should archive or move to another system for further work.

Good Luck

Congratulations—you made it! You've gone through a solid introductory tour of Pro Tools' basic operations and features; and although this discussion of Pro Tools is certainly not a comprehensive listing of *everything* that Pro Tools can do, you can rest assured that your creative journey has started well. Over time, you'll not only learn more about Pro Tools, but undoubtedly you will find your own working style—a process that will be constantly refined as you gain experience and speed.

You've begun a great exploration and a worthwhile endeavor, in my humble opinion. I personally believe that artistic pursuits nourish not only the soul of the patron but of the artist as well. It's my wish that this product and the technology to come serve to inspire you to push the limits of your creativity. Good luck!

A $\}$ Review Questions

Now it's time to put your money where your mouth is! Just kidding—there'll be no trick questions here, and it's not about passing or failing. I've just created a few questions based on each chapter so you can make sure you're getting the really important points. Good luck!

Questions

1. Physical audio connections, which allow for audio to be recorded and played back, are connected to the _____.

2. Because a Pro Tools session refers to audio files that are stored elsewhere on your hard drive, Pro Tools is a _____-based application.

3. When audio files are recorded into your session, the files are stored in the _____ folder.

4. The Open Session and Close Session commands are located in the _____ drop-down menu.

5. The two primary windows used in Pro Tools are the _____ and _____ windows.

6. True or False: The Save Copy In command can copy your entire session, including audio files, to another location.

7. The _____ list allows you to control what tracks in your session will be displayed

8. The _____ list shows audio files and regions.

9. The _____ view will allow you to see more channels at one time in your Mix window.

10. What keyboard shortcut is used when you're changing the heights of all shown tracks at once?

11. When you create a session in Pro Tools, one group is created automatically and will be shown in the Groups list. What is the name of that group?

12. Can two active paths both use the same physical output?

13. Can two sub-paths use the same physical output?

14. What's the shortcut for creating a track?

15. True or False: Once tracks are created, they cannot be rearranged in the Edit window, so take special care in how you create them.

16. True or False: There's only one way to import audio into your session, and that's to the Regions list.

17. What are the buttons in the I/O column of an audio track (medium track height), from top to bottom?

18. What kind of track should you use for the Click plug-in?

19. What is the name of the mode in which you can create multiple punch-in and punch-out points for a single take?

20. True or False: Recording audio in Pro Tools is always non-destructive.

21. What will happen to your plug-ins when you go into Low Latency mode?

22. How many edit modes are there, and what are their names?

23. Which edit tool do you use to adjust the beginning or end of a region?

24. Which edit tool do you use to move a region to another location?

25. What is the shortcut for duplicating a selected region?

26. How are overlapping regions visually represented?

27. You can create memory locations while Pro Tools is playing by pressing the _____ key.

28. How many zoom presets are there?

29. What's a transient in Pro Tools?

30. Which tool will allow you to change the tempo, but not the pitch, of an audio region?

31. The _____ tool will allow you to move a selected area of audio from within a region.

32. The _____ tool combines many of the most common editing functions (like Trim, Select, and Grab) into one tool.

33. True or False: MIDI is not audible.

34. The Edit MIDI Studio Setup window can be opened from the _____ drop-down menu.

35. What type of track (new in Pro Tools 7) allows you to work with MIDI and audio in one track?

36. The _____ function can change the timing of your MIDI notes to snap to a grid.

37. The _____ tool is useful for editing MIDI notes because it takes on different functions, depending on the position of the cursor.

38. Of the two kinds of plug-in effects available on an LE system, which one is real-time?

39. Of the two kinds of plug-in effects available on an LE system, which one is not real-time?

40. What is the name of the component within Pro Tools that routes audio like a virtual cable?

41. True or False: You can select a bus as an input on a Master Fader.

42. An insert on a Master Fader is a _____-fader.

43. True or False: Bouncing to disk happens in real time (for example, bouncing a three-minute song takes three minutes).

44. True or False: When you clear regions from your tracks, they will automatically be removed from your hard drive.

45. True or False: Audio can be deleted when you compact your session.

46. What is the shortcut key combination for toggling zoom levels?

47. The _____ feature allows Pro Tools, with your help, to compute the tempo of a selected area of audio.

48. Beat Detective operates by analyzing _____.

49. You can make an active plug-in inactive by holding which keys and clicking on the insert?

50. The option of bouncing to a QuickTime file is found in which drop-down menu?

Answers

1. Audio interface

2. Pointer

3. Audio files

4. File

5. Edit, Mix

6. True

7. Track Show/Hide

8. Regions list

9. Narrow Mix window

10. Hold the Option key (Mac) or the Alt key (PC) while you change the height of any one track, and the heights of all shown tracks will change at once.

11. The All group

12. No

13. Yes

14. Shift+⌘+N (Mac) or Ctrl+Shift+N (PC)

15. False. You can drag a track up or down (in the Edit window) or left and right (in the Mix window) by clicking on the track name in the Track Show/Hide list or by clicking and dragging the track name in the track itself.

16. False. You can import to the Regions list or straight to an audio file, or you can drag and drop from the workspace! No matter which method you use, though, the region will be added to the Regions list.

17. Input Selector, Output Selector, Volume, Pan, Output Window Selector

18. An auxiliary input track

19. QuickPunch

20. False. Although most record modes will not overwrite audio files on your hard drive, Destructive Record mode can.

21. They will become inactive.

22. There are four edit modes: Shuffle, Slip, Grid, and Spot.

23. The Trim tool

24. The Grabber tool

25. ⌘+D (Mac) or Ctrl+D (PC)

26. A beveled upper corner in the overlapping region

27. Enter

28. Five

29. A transient is the initial high-energy peak at the beginning of a waveform.

30. The Time Compress/Expansion (TCE) Trim tool

31. Separation Grabber

32. Smart

33. True

34. Setups

35. An Instrument track

36. Quantize

37. Pencil

38. RTAS

39. AudioSuite

40. A bus

41. False. There are no inputs on a Master Fader.

42. Post

43. True

44. False. Audio files will not be automatically deleted when you clear them from your Regions list, but it is an option when you choose the Clear Selected function (when your selected regions include whole files). Think twice before choosing to delete audio files—it can't be undone!

45. True, so be careful!

46. Control+E (Mac) or Start+E (PC)

47. Identify Beat

48. Transients

49. ⌘+Control (Mac) or the Ctrl+Start key (PC)

50. File > Bounce to

Keyboard Shortcuts

For increased operational speed and ease of use, there are many Pro Tools keyboard shortcuts to give you fast access to a wide variety of tasks. This appendix details the many keyboard shortcuts that are not shown within Pro Tools menus. The shortcuts are grouped by functional area for your added convenience and quick reference.

The first section details shortcuts for Pro Tools on the Mac OS.

Mac OS Keyboard Shortcuts

Global Keyboard Commands

Function	Key Combination
Change all audio channel strips	Option+applicable function
Change audio channel strip and all selected audio channel strips	Option+Shift+applicable function
Toggle item and set all others to same new state	Option+click on applicable item
Toggle item and set all others to opposite state	⌘+click on applicable item
Fine Tune	⌘+click on control slider/pot/breakpoints

Mix and Edit Groups

Function	Key Combination
Temporarily isolate channel strip from group operation	Hold down Control+any operation that affects groups
New group	⌘+G (with two or more tracks selected)
Suspend/resume all groups	⌘+Shift+G or ⌘+click on Groups pop-up menu
Rename group	Double-click to far left of group name in the Groups list
Group enable/disable	Type ID letter on keyboard. (To enable keyboard selection of groups, click box at top right of Groups list.)
Hide all tracks	Click on track symbol in Show/Hide menu
Show group members only	Control+click on group(s) in Groups list (Control+Shift+click for multiple groups)

Edit Selection Definition and Navigation

Function	Key Combination
Locate play/edit cursor to next region-boundary/sync point	Tab
Locate play/edit cursor to previous region-boundary/sync point	Option+Tab
Go to and select next region	Control+Tab
Go to and select previous region	Control+Option+Tab
Extend selection to next region-boundary	Shift+Tab
Extend selection to previous region-boundary	Option+Shift+Tab
Extend selection to include next region	Control+Shift+Tab
Extend selection to include previous region	Control+Option+Shift+Tab
Return to start of session	Return
Go to end of session	Option+Return
Extend selection to start of session	Shift+Return
Extend selection to end of session	Option+Shift+Return
Set selection start/end during playback	↓ / ↑
Set selection start/end to incoming time code while stopped	↓ / ↑
Select entire region in Edit window	Double-click with Selector
Select entire track in Edit window	Triple-click with Selector / ⌘+A
Extend selection to a memory location	Shift+period key+mem loc number+period key (The first period key press is not required with Classic numeric keypad mode selected in Preferences.)
Place play/edit cursor or create selection across all tracks	Option+click in Rulers
Extend play/edit cursor or selection across all tracks	Enable All edit group (! key) and Shift+click on any other track. (To enable keyboard selection of Groups, click box at top right of Groups list.)

Record and Playback

Function	Key Combination
Open New Track dialog box	⌘ - Shift+N
In New Track dialog cycle through track type	⌘+</>
Cycle up/down through New Track options	⌘+↑ / ↓
Start record	⌘+spacebar/F12
Stop record	Spacebar
Stop record and discard take	⌘+period key
Start/stop playback	Spacebar
Half-speed record	⌘+Shift+spacebar
Half-speed playback	Shift+spacebar
Pause (pre-prime deck for instant playback)	Option+click on Transport play button
Pause (pre-prime deck for instant record)	Option+click on Transport play button during recording
Enable/disable online record	⌘+Option+spacebar
Enable/disable online playback	⌘+J / Option+spacebar
Toggle record modes (normal/Destructive/Loop/QuickPunch)	Control+click on Transport record button
Loop playback toggle	⌘+Shift+L or Control+click on Transport play button
Record-safe track	⌘+click on Record enable button
Solo-safe track	⌘+click on Solo button
QuickPunch	⌘+Shift+P
Enter/exit record during playback in QuickPunch	⌘+spacebar/click Transport record button
Set and enable pre-/post-roll time	Option+click with Selector before/after selection
Disable pre-/post-roll time	Option+click within selection closer to front/back
Scroll to selection start/end	← / → (when selection exceeds window view)
Toggle Transport Master (Pro Tools/Machine/MMC)	⌘+\

Auditioning

Function	Key Combination
When Transport = Pro Tools:	
Play by pre-roll value up to selection start/end	Option+ ← / →
Play by post-roll value after selection start/end	⌘+ ← / →
Play by pre- and post-roll value through selection start/end	⌘+Option+ ← / →
Play by pre-roll value to current location counter time	Option+ ← / → (when no selection)
Play by post-roll value from current location counter time	⌘+ ← / → (when no selection)
When Transport = Machine/MMC:	
Cue Transport to selection start/end	⌘+ ← / →
Cue Transport with pre-/post-roll to selection start/end	Option+ ← / →

Scrub (Jog)/Shuttle

Function	Key Combination
Temporary Scrub mode when using Selector	Control+click+drag
Extend selection while scrubbing	Shift+click+drag with Scrubber (also in temporary Scrub mode)
Shuttle	Option+click+drag with Scrubber (also in temporary Scrub mode)
Shuttle-lock	Control+number key (1–9, where 5 = real-time, 9 = max speed)
Change direction during Shuttle	+/– (e.g., shuttle backward = Control+number key+minus key)
Shuttle-lock stop	0 (press number key to resume Shuttle)
Exit Shuttle-lock mode	Spacebar or ⌘+period key

Editing, Nudging, and Trimming (+/– Key Usage Is on Numeric Keypad Only)

Function	Key Combination
Change Grid value	Control+Option++/–
Change Nudge value	⌘+Option++/–
Nudge selection or region right/left by Nudge value	+/–
Nudge data within current region to right/left by Nudge value (keeps region start/end and moves underlying audio)	Control++/–
Nudge left selection boundary right/left by Nudge value	Option+Shift++/–
Nudge right selection boundary right/left by Nudge value	+Shift++/–
Nudge back/forward by next Nudge value	See "Commands Focus Mode" section below
Trim left edge of region to right/left by Nudge value	Option++/–
Trim right edge of region to right/left by Nudge value	++/–
Reverse Trimmer direction when trimming region	Option+Trimmer
Trim up to, but not over, adjacent regions	Hold down Control key while trimming
Duplicate region(s) in Edit window	Option+click selection and drag to destination
Delete selection in Edit window playlist	Delete
Constrain audio region to vertical movement	Control+move audio region with Grabber
Snap region start to stationary playhead or edit selection start	Control+click new region with Grabber
Snap region sync point to stationary playhead or edit selection start	Shift+Control+click new region with Grabber
Snap region end to stationary playhead or edit selection start	⌘+Control+click new region with Grabber

Zoom

Function	Key Combination
Horizontal zoom in/out (audio and MIDI)	⌘+] / [
Vertical zoom in/out (audio)	⌘+Option+] / [
Vertical zoom in/out (MIDI)	⌘+Shift+] / [
Fill window with selection	Option+click on Zoomer or Option+F
View entire session	Double-click on Zoomer or Option+A
Zoom vertical and horizontal axis	Hold down ⌘ key while using Zoomer
Zoom to previous horizontal zoom value	Option+click on display scale arrows
Max zoom before waveform drawn from disk	⌘+click on Zoomer (faster drawing from RAM)
Select five preset zoom levels	See "Commands Focus Mode" section below

Memory Locations

Function	Key Combination
Create memory location	Enter
Reset a memory location	Control+click on memory location button
Delete memory location	Option+click on a memory location button
Recall a memory location	Period key+memory location number+period key (or click on memory location button). (The first period key press is not required with Classic numeric keypad mode selected in Preferences.)

Select Edit Tools/Modes

Function	Key Combination
Shuffle	F1 or Option+1 on alpha keyboard
Slip	F2 or Option+2 on alpha keyboard
Spot	F3 or Option+3 on alpha keyboard
Grid	F4 or Option+4 on alpha keyboard+repeated pressings toggle between relative and absolute Grid mode
Zoomer	F5 or ⌘+1 on alpha keyboard
Trimmer	F6 or ⌘+2 on alpha keyboard
Selector	F7 or ⌘+3 on alpha keyboard
Grabber	F8 or ⌘+4 on alpha keyboard
Scrubber	F9 or ⌘+5 on alpha keyboard
Pencil	F10 or ⌘+6 on alpha keyboard
SmartTool	(F6 and F7) or (F7 and F8) or ⌘+7 on alpha keyboard
Cycle through edit tools	Escape key
Cycle through edit modes	~ key

Commands Focus Mode

**To use single keys on the commands below, click the A...Z button
in the Edit window or use the Control key in combination with the single keys below.**

Function	Key Combination
Zoom level 1–5	Alpha keys 1/2/3/4/5
Play to/from edit start by pre-/post-roll value	Alpha keys 6/7
Play to/from edit end by pre-/post-roll amount	Alpha keys 8/9
Copy edit selection to timeline selection	Alpha key 0
Copy timeline selection to edit selection	0
Track View toggle	- (minus key)
Capture timecode	= (on numeric keypad)
Center timeline start	Q
Center timeline end	W
Zoom toggle	E
Zoom out horizontally	R
Zoom in horizontally	T
Snap start (of selected region) to timecode	Y (Only available in Pro Tools HD)
Snap sync point (of selected region) to timecode	U (Only available in Pro Tools HD)
Snap end (of selected region) to timecode	I (Only available in Pro Tools HD)
Snap start (of selected region) to playhead	H
Snap sync point (of selected region) to playhead	J (Only available in Pro Tools HD)
Snap end (of selected region) to playhead	K (Only available in Pro Tools HD)
Move edit selection up	P
Move edit selection down	; (semicolon)
Tab back	L
Tab forward	' (apostrophe)
Play timeline selection	]
Play edit selection	[
Trim start to insertion	A
Trim end to insertion	S
Fade to start (available if no selection)	D
Fade (without showing Fades dialog box)	F
Fade to end (available if no selection)	G
Undo	Z
Cut	X
Copy	C

Paste	V
Separate	B
Timeline insertion follows playback (pref toggle)	N
Nudge back by next Nudge value	M
Nudge back by Nudge value	<
Nudge forward by Nudge value	>
Nudge forward by next Nudge value	/
Track view toggle	Minus key (alpha only)
Zoom toggle	E
Zoom defaults	1 through 5

Fades

Function	Key Combination
Apply crossfade to selection without accessing Fades window	⌘+Control+F (uses default fade shape)
Edit fade-in only in Fades window	Option+click+drag fade-in curve (in None Link mode only)
Edit fade-out only in Fades window	⌘+click+drag fade-out curve (in None Link mode only)
Audition start/stop in Fades window	Spacebar
Reset to default zoom in Fades window	Click on either zoom arrow
Reset standard or S-shape crossfades to default curves	Option+click in xfade window (in Equal Power/Gain modes)
Cycle up/down through Out Shape parameter options	Control+ ↑ / ↓
Cycle up/down through In Shape parameter options	Option+ ↑ / ↓
Cycle up/down through Link parameter options	↑ / ↓
Cycle up/down through preset Out Shape curves	Control+ ← / →
Cycle up/down through preset In Shape curves	Option+ ← / →

Regions List

Function	Key Combination
Select region by name	Type letter(s) A–Z. (To enable keyboard selection of regions, click box at top right of Regions list.)
Clear selected region(s) from Regions list	Shift+⌘+B
Bypass dialog boxes during deletion of audio files	Option+click Delete/Yes button in respective dialog box
Audition region in Regions list	Option+click and hold on region in Regions list
Rename region/file	Double-click region in Regions list or double-click with Grabber on region in playlist
Constrain region placement to start at play/edit cursor location or selection start	Control+click+drag region

Import Audio Dialog Box

Function	Key Combination
Remove item from list	⌘+R
Remove all items from list	Shift+⌘+R
Add all	⌘+Option+A
Random-access search through selected file	Move slider to desired location or click left/right side of slider
Import current selection	Enter
Import all	Shift+⌘+I
Convert and import current selection	⌘+C
Convert and import all	Shift+⌘+C
Add currently selected region or audio file to list	Enter or Return
Audition currently selected audio file/region	⌘+P or ⌘+spacebar
Stop audition of selected file and retain selection	⌘+P or ⌘+S
Done	⌘+W
Cancel	⌘+period key

Mixing

Function	Key Combination
Make track active/inactive	Click on track symbol in Mix window while holding ⌘ and Control keys
Set all faders to their automation null points	Option+clicking on either automatch triangle
Reset a control to default value	Option+click on Control
Headroom/Track Level/Channel Delay indicator	⌘+click on Track Level indicator
Clear peak/clip-hold from meter	Click on indicator
Peak counter reset in Headroom Indicator mode	Click on Headroom indicator
Bypass plug-in insert	⌘+click on insert name in Inserts view
Send mute	⌘+click on send name in Sends view
Toggle Send Display between All and Individual mode	⌘+click on Send diamond, then select from pop-up

Text Entry

Function	Key Combination
Move down/up rows	Tab /Shift+Tab
Move to beginning/end of word	↑ / ↓
Move single letters at a time across a name label	← / →
Select entire word	Double-click on word

Automation

Function	Key Combination
Leave absolute minimum/maximum breakpoints while trimming	Hold down Shift key while trimming
Disable auto-creation of anchor breakpoints when trimming automation of a selection	Option+Trimmer
Access Plug-In Automation dialog box	⌘+Option+Control+click on parameters (in Plug-in window) or on track display format selector (in Edit window)
Enable/disable plug-in automation	⌘+Option+Control+click on parameters (in Plug-in window) or on track display format selector (in Edit window)
Disable/enable automation playlist on selected track	⌘+click on track display format selector
Disable/enable ALL automation playlists on selected track	⌘+Shift+click on track display format selector
Vertically constrain automation movement	Shift+move automation with Grabber
Special paste of automation data between different controls	Control+⌘+V
Write automation to end of session/selection	Control+click on Transport End button
Write automation to start of session/selection	Control+click on Transport RTZ button
Write automation from start to end of session/selection	Control+Shift+click on Transport End/RTZ button
Copy to Send	⌘+Option+H
Display automation playlist of automation-enabled control	⌘+Control+click on control
Scroll to and display track in default view in Edit window	⌘+Control+click on track name in Mix or Insert window or Show/Hide Tracks list (Track defaults: disk=waveform, MIDI=regions, aux/master=volume)
Scroll to and select track in Mix/Edit windows	Control+click on track name in Mix or Edit window or Show/Hide Tracks list

When all tracks in selection are displaying automation playlists, hold down Control key during the following operations to affect all playlists on every track in selection:

Function	Key Combination
Delete	Delete
Cut	⌘+X
Duplicate	⌘+D
Copy	⌘+C
Clear	⌘+B
Insert silence	Shift+⌘+E

Numeric Entry

Function	Key Combination
Initiate time entry in Current Location and Big Counters	= or * key on numeric keypad
Initiate time entry in Edit window Start/End/Length fields	/ on numeric keypad (subsequent presses toggle through fields)
Initiate time entry in Transport window fields	Option+/ on numeric keypad (subsequent presses toggle through fields)
Capture incoming timecode in Session Setup window (with Start field selected), Spot dialog and Time Stamp Selected dialog boxes	= (hold down key for continued input)
Move sub-unit selection to the right	Period key
Move sub-unit selection to the left/right	← / →
Calculator entry mode	+ or – keys followed by offset number
Increment/decrement the current sub-unit	↑ / ↓
Clear entered numeric value and stay in Time Entry mode	Clear
Apply entered numeric value	Return or Enter
Clear entered numeric value and exit Time Entry mode	Escape

Note: When Time Code is the selected time scale, initiating time entry highlights entire field, and numeric values are entered right to left.

Peripherals Dialog Box

Function	Key Combination
Go to Synchronization window	⌘+1
Go to Machine Control window	⌘+2
Go to MIDI Controllers window	⌘+3
Go to Ethernet Controllers window	⌘+4
Go to Mic Preamps window	⌘+5

Preferences Dialog Box

Function	Key Combination
Go to Display window	⌘+1
Go to Operation window	⌘+2
Go to Editing window	⌘+3
Go to Automation window	⌘+4
Go to Processing window	⌘+5
Go to Compatibility window	⌘+6
Go to MIDI window	⌘+7

Plug-In Settings Librarian

Function	Key Combination
Save settings	⌘+Shift+S
Copy settings	⌘+Shift+C
Paste settings	⌘+Shift+V

Numeric Keypad Modes

Function	Key Combination
Transport Mode	
MIDI Metronome On/Off	7
MIDI Count On/Off	8
Merge Record On/Off	9
Loop Playback	4
Loop Record	5
QuickPunch Record	6
Rewind	1
Fast Forward	2
Record	3
Play/Stop	0
Shuttle Mode (TDM systems only)	
1 X Forward	6
1 X Rewind	4
4 X Forward	9
4 X Rewind	7
1/4 X Forward	3
1/4 X Rewind	1
1/2 X Forward	5–6
1/2 X Rewind	5–4
2 X Forward	8–9
2 X Backward	8–7
1/16 X Forward	2–3
1/16 X Backward	2–1
Loop Playback of Edit Selection	0

Note: Choose Classic, Transport, or Shuttle mode in Preferences > Operations menu.

Keyboard Input for Plug-In Parameters

Function	Key Combination
Click mouse in text field	Type desired value
Move down/up parameter fields	Tab/ Shift+Tab
Increase/decrease slider value	↑ / ↓
Input value without leaving field	Enter
Enter value and exit Keyboard Entry mode	Return
For fields that support kilohertz	Type k after number multiplies by 1000

Miscellaneous

Function	Key Combination
Display Takes pop-up list (appears only when selection start or flashing insertion point matches user time stamp of regions).	⌘+click with Selector tool at selection start or current cursor location
Set all tracks to selected record drive in Disk Allocation dialog (for Pro Tools III—on same Disk I/O only)	Option+click on record drive
Access Playback Engine dialog during Pro Tools launch	Hold down N key while launching Pro Tools
Toggle between Hide All and Show All	Option+click in Show/Hide Tracks list
Bypass repeat dialogs when multiple items will be changed by single operation (e.g., Clear, Delete, Compact)	Option+click respective Proceed button in dialog box
Wait for (MIDI note)	F11 (Preference option enabled)
Single key shortcut (with Commands Focus disabled)	Control+"single key"

MIDI Events List Entry

Function	Key Combination

(All commands below are active only when the MIDI Event List window is open.)

Function	Key Combination
Enter start time field for editing	⌘+Enter (numeric keypad)
Show Event Filter dialog box	⌘+F
Go to	⌘+G
Scroll to edit selection	⌘+H
Insert another	⌘+M
Insert note	⌘+N
Insert program change	⌘+P
Insert controller	⌘+L
Insert poly pressure	⌘+O
Delete event in MIDI Events list	Option+click

Windows Keyboard Shortcuts

Global Keyboard Commands

Function	Key Combination
Change all audio channel strips	Alt+applicable function
Change audio channel strip and all selected audio channel strips	Alt+Shift+applicable function
Toggle item and set all others to same new state	Alt+click on applicable item
Toggle item and set all others to opposite state	Ctrl+click on applicable item
Fine Tune	Ctrl+click on control slider/pot/breakpoints

Record and Playback

Function	Key Combination
Open New Track dialog box	Ctrl+Shift+N
In New Track dialog cycle through track type	Ctrl+</>
Cycle up/down through New Track Options	Ctrl+↑ / ↓
Start record	Ctrl+spacebar/F12
Stop record	Spacebar
Stop record and discard take	Esc or Ctrl+period key
Start/stop playback	Spacebar
Half-speed record	Ctrl+Shift+spacebar
Half-speed playback	Shift+spacebar
Pause (pre-prime deck for instant playback and record)	Start+spacebar or Alt+click on Transport play button
Enable/disable online record	Ctrl+Alt+spacebar
Enable/disable online playback	Ctrl+J / Alt+spacebar
Toggle record modes (normal/Destructive/Loop/QuickPunch)	Right-click on Transport record button
Loop Playback toggle	Start+click or right-click on Transport play button
Record-safe track	Ctrl+click on Record Enable button
Solo-safe track	Ctrl+click on Solo button
QuickPunch	Ctrl+Shift+P
Enter/exit record during playback in QuickPunch	Ctrl+spacebar/click on Transport Record button
Set and enable pre-/post-roll time	Alt+click with selector before/after selection
Disable pre-/post-roll time	Alt+click within selection closer to front/back
Scroll to selection start/end	← / → (when selection exceeds window view)
Toggle Transport Master (Pro Tools/Machine/MMC)	Ctrl+\

Mix and Edit Groups

Function	Key Combination
Temporarily isolate channel strip from group operation	Start+right-click any operation that affects groups
New group	Ctrl+G (with two or more tracks selected)
Suspend/resume all groups	Ctrl+Shift+G or Ctrl+click on Groups pop-up menu
Rename group	Double-click to far left of group name in the Groups list
Group enable/disable	Type ID letter on keyboard. (To enable keyboard selection of groups, click box at top right of Groups list.)
Hide all tracks	Click on track symbol in Show/Hide menu
Show group members only	Right-click on group(s) in Groups list (right-click+Shift+click for multiple groups)

Auditioning

Function	Key Combination
When Transport = Pro Tools:	
Play by pre-roll value up to selection start/end	Alt+ ← / →
Play by post-roll value after selection start/end	Ctrl+ ← / →
Play by pre- and post-roll value through selection start/end	Ctrl+Alt+ ← / →
Play by pre-roll value to current location counter time	Alt+ ← / → (when no selection)
Play by post-roll value from current location counter time	Ctrl+ ← / → (when no selection)
When Transport = Machine/MMC:	
Cue Transport to selection start/end	Ctrl + ← / →
Cue Transport with pre/post+roll to selection start/end	Alt+ ← / →

Scrub (Jog)/Shuttle

Function	Key Combination
Temporary Scrub mode when using Selector	Right-click+drag
Extend selection while scrubbing	Shift+click+drag w/ Scrubber (also in temporary Scrub mode)
Shuttle	Alt+click+drag w/ Scrubber (also in temporary Scrub mode)
Shuttle-lock	Start+number key (1–9, where 5 = real-time, 9 = max speed)
Change direction during Shuttle	+/– (e.g., shuttle backward = Start+number key+minus key)
Shuttle-lock stop	0 (press number key to resume Shuttle)
Exit Shuttle-lock mode	Spacebar or Esc

Edit Selection Definition and Navigation

Function	Key Combination
Locate play/edit cursor to next region+boundary/sync point	Tab
Locate play/edit cursor to previous region+boundary/sync point	Ctrl+Tab
Go to and select next region	Start+Tab
Go to and select previous region	Start+Ctrl+Tab
Extend selection to next region+boundary	Shift+Tab
Extend selection to previous region+boundary	Ctrl+Shift+Tab
Extend selection to include next region	Start+Shift+Tab
Extend selection to include previous region	Start+Shift+Ctrl+Tab
Return to start of session	Enter
Go to end of session	Ctrl+Enter
Extend selection to start of session	Shift+Enter
Extend selection to end of session	Ctrl+Shift+Enter
Set selection start/end during playback	↓ / ↑
Set selection start/end to incoming time code while stopped	↓ / ↑
Select entire region in Edit window	Double-click with Selector
Select entire track in Edit window	Triple-click with Selector / Ctrl+A
Extend play/edit cursor across all tracks and create selection	Alt+click in Rulers
Extend play/edit cursor or selection across all tracks	Enable All Edit group (! key) and Shift+click on any other track. (To enable keyboard selection of Groups, click box at top right of Groups List.)

Zoom

Function	Key Combination
Horizontal zoom in/out	Ctrl+] / [
Vertical zoom in/out (audio)	Ctrl+Alt+] / [
Vertical zoom in/out (MIDI)	Ctrl+Shift+] / [
Fill window with selection	Alt+click on Zoomer or Alt+F
View entire session	Double-click on Zoomer or Alt+A
Zoom vertical and horizontal axis	Hold down Ctrl key while using Zoomer
Zoom to previous orientation	Alt+click on display scale arrows
Max zoom before waveform drawn from disk	Ctrl+click on Zoomer (faster drawing from RAM)
Select five preset zoom levels	See "Commands Focus Mode" section below

Editing, Nudging, and Trimming (+/− Key Usage Is on Numeric Keypad Only)

Function	Key Combination
Change Grid value	Start+Alt++/−
Change Nudge value	Ctrl+Alt++/−
Nudge selection or region right/left by Nudge value	+/−
Nudge data within current region to right/left by Nudge value (keeps region start/end and moves underlying audio)	Start++/−
Nudge left selection boundary right/left by Nudge value	Alt+Shift++/−
Nudge right selection boundary right/left by Nudge value	Ctrl+Shift++/−
Nudge back/forward by next Nudge value	See "Commands Focus Mode" section below
Trim left edge of region to right/left by Nudge value	Alt++/−
Trim right edge of region to right/left by Nudge value	Ctrl++/−
Reverse Trimmer direction when trimming region	Alt+Trimmer
Trim up to, but not over, adjacent regions	Hold down Ctrl key while trimming
Duplicate region(s) in Edit Window	Ctrl+click selection and drag to destination
Delete selection in playlist	Backspace
Constrain audio region to vertical movement	Right-click+move audio region with Grabber
Snap region start to stationary playhead or edit selection start	Start+click new region with Grabber
Snap region to stationary playhead or edit selection sync point	Alt+Start+click new region with Grabber
Snap region end to stationary playhead or edit selection start	Ctrl+Start+click new region with Grabber

Select Edit Tools/Modes

Function	Key Combination
Shuffle	F1
Slip	F2
Spot	F3
Grid	F4
Zoomer	F5 or Ctrl+1 on alpha keyboard
Trimmer	F6 or Ctrl+2 on alpha keyboard
Selector	F7 or Ctrl+3 on alpha keyboard
Grabber	F8 or Ctrl+4 on alpha keyboard
Scrubber	F9 or Ctrl+5 on alpha keyboard
Pencil	F10 or Ctrl+6 on alpha keyboard
SmartTool	(F6 and F7) or (F7 and F8) or Ctrl+7 on alpha keyboard
Cycle through edit tools	Center mouse click
Cycle through edit modes	~ key

Memory Locations

Function	Key Combination
Create memory location	Enter (on numeric keypad)
Reset a memory location	Start+click on memory location button
Delete memory location	Alt+click on a memory location button
Recall a memory location	Period key+memory location number+period key or click on memory location button. (The first period key press is not required with Classic numeric keypad mode selected in Preferences.)

Fades

Function	Key Combination
Apply crossfade to selection without accessing Fades window	Ctrl+Start+F (uses last selected fade shape)
Edit fade-in only in Fades window	Alt+click+drag fade-in curve (in None Link mode only)
Edit fade-out only in Fades window	Ctrl+click+drag fade-out curve (in None Link mode only)
Audition start/stop in Fades window	Spacebar
Reset to default zoom in Fades window	Ctrl+click on either zoom arrow
Reset standard or S-shape crossfades to default curves	Alt+click in xfade window (in Equal Power/Gain modes)
Cycle up/down through Out Shape parameter options	Start+ ↑ / ↓
Cycle up/down through In Shape parameter options	Alt+ ↑ / ↓
Cycle up/down through Link parameter options	↑ / ↓
Cycle up/down through preset Out Shape curves	Start+ ← / →
Cycle up/down through preset In Shape curves	Alt+ ← / →

Regions List

Function	Key Combination
Select region by name	Type letter(s) A–Z. (To enable keyboard selection of Regions, click box at top right of Regions list.)
Clear selected region(s) from Regions list	Shift+Ctrl+B
Bypass dialog boxes during deletion of audio files	Alt+click Delete/Yes button in respective dialog box
Audition region in Regions list	Alt+click and hold on region in Regions list
Rename region/file	Double-click region in Regions list or double-click with Grabber on region in playlist
Constrain region placement to start at play/edit cursor location or selection start	Right-click and drag region

Commands Focus Mode

To use single keys on the commands below, click the A...Z button in the Edit window or use the Start key in combination with the single keys below.

Function	Key Combination
Zoom level 1–5	Alpha 1/2/3/4/5
Play to/from edit start by pre-/post-roll value	Alpha 6/7
Play to/from edit end by pre-/post-roll amount	Alpha 8/9
Copy edit selection to timeline selection	Alpha 0
Copy timeline selection to edit selection	0
Track view toggle	– (minus key)
Capture timecode	=
Center timeline start	Q
Center timeline end	W
Zoom toggle	E
Zoom out horizontally	R
Zoom in horizontally	T
Snap start (of selected region) to timecode	Y (Only available in Pro Tools HD)
Snap sync point (of selected region) to timecode	U (Only available in Pro Tools HD)
Snap end (of selected region) to timecode	I (Only available in Pro Tools HD)
Snap start (of selected region) to playhead	H
Snap sync point (of selected region) to playhead	J (Only available in Pro Tools HD)
Snap end (of selected region) to playhead	K (Only available in Pro Tools HD)
Move edit selection up	P (Only available in Pro Tools HD)
Move edit selection down	; (semicolon)
Tab back	L
Tab forward	' (apostrophe)
Play timeline selection	]
Play edit selection	[
Trim start to insertion	A
Trim end to insertion	S
Fade to start (available if no selection)	D
Fade (without showing Fades dialog box)	F
Fade to End (available if no selection)	G
Undo	Z
Cut	X
Copy	C

Paste	V
Separate	B
Timeline insertion follows playback (pref toggle)	N
Nudge back by next Nudge value	M
Nudge back by Nudge value	<
Nudge forward by Nudge value	>
Nudge forward by next Nudge value	/
Track view toggle	Minus key (alpha only)
Zoom toggle	E
Zoom defaults	1 through 5

Import Audio Dialog

Function	Key Combination
Add currently selected audio region/file to list	Alt+A
Convert and import currently selected audio region/file to list	Alt+O
Remove currently selected audio file/region	Alt+R
Remove all audio files/regions	Alt+M
Audition currently selected audio file/region	Spacebar
Stop audition of selected file and retain selection	Spacebar
Stop audition of selected file and go to top of scroll box	Home
Move between file windows	Tab
Done	Alt+E
Cancel	Esc or Alt+C
Random-access fwd/rew search through selected file	Drag slider to desired location or click left/right side of slider

Mixing

Function	Key Combination
Make track active/inactive	Click on track symbol in Mix window while holding Ctrl and Start keys
Set all faders to their automation null points	Alt+click on either automatch triangle
Reset a control to default value	Alt+click on control
Headroom/Track Level/Channel Level indicator	Ctrl+click on Track Level indicator
Clear peak/clip-hold from meter	Click on indicator
Peak counter reset in Headroom Indicator mode	Click on Headroom indicator
Bypass plug-in Insert	Ctrl+click on insert name in Inserts view
Send mute	Ctrl+click on send name in Sends view
Toggle Send display between All and Individual mode	Ctrl+click on Send pop-up

Automation

Function	Key Combination
Leave extremity breakpoints undisturbed while trimming	Hold down Shift key while trimming
Disable auto-creation of anchor breakpoints when trimming automation	Alt+Trimmer
Access Plug-In Automation dialog box	Ctrl+Alt+Start+click on Parameters (in Plug-In window) or on track display format selector (in Edit window)
Enable/disable plug-in automation	Ctrl+Alt+Start+click on Parameters (in Plug-In window) or on track display format selector (in Edit window)
Disable/enable automation playlist on selected track	Ctrl+click on track display format selector
Disable/enable ALL automation playlists on selected track	Ctrl+Shift+click on track display format selector
Vertically constrain automation movement	Shift+move automation with Trimmer
Special paste of automation data between different controls	Start+Ctrl+V
Write automation to end of session/selection	Start+click or right-click on Transport End button
Write automation to start of session/selection	Start+click or right-click on Transport RTZ button
Write automation from start to end of session/selection	Start+Shift+click or Shift+right-click on Transport End/RTZ button
Copy to send	Ctrl+Alt+H
Display automation playlist of automation-enabled control	Ctrl+right-click on control
Scroll to and display track in default view in Edit window	Ctrl+right-click on track name in Mix, Edit, Insert or Sends window or Show/Hide Tracks list (Track defaults: disk=waveform, MIDI=notes, aux/master=volume)
Scroll to and select track in Mix/Edit window	Right-click on track name in Mix, Edit, Insert, or Sends window or Show/Hide Tracks list

When all tracks in selection are displaying automation playlists, hold down Start key during the following operations to affect all playlists on every track in selection:

Function	Key Combination
Delete	Ctrl+Backspace
Cut	Ctrl+X
Duplicate	Ctrl+D
Copy	Ctrl+C
Clear	Ctrl+B
Insert Silence	Ctrl+Shift+E

Numeric Entry

Function	Key Combination
Initiate time entry in Current Location and Big Counters	= or * key on numeric keypad
Initiate time entry in Edit window Start/End/Length fields	/ (subsequent presses toggle through fields)
Initiate time entry in Transport window fields	Alt+/ on numeric keypad (subsequent presses toggle through fields)
Capture incoming timecode in Session Setup window (with Start field selected), Spot dialog and Time Stamp Selected dialog	= (hold down key for continued input)
Move sub-unit selection to the right	Period key
Move sub-unit selection to the left/right	← / →
Calculator Entry mode	+ or – keys followed by offset number
Increment/decrement the current sub-unit	↑ / ↓
Clear entered numeric value and stay in time entry mode	Retype value
Apply entered numeric value	Enter
Clear entered numeric value and exit time entry mode	Esc

Text Entry

Function	Key Combination
Move down/up rows	Tab /Shift-Tab
Move to beginning/end of word	↑ / ↓
Move single letters at a time across a name label	← / →
Select entire word	Double-click on word

Peripherals Dialog Box

Function	Key Combination
Go to Synchronization window	Ctrl+1
Go to Machine Control window	Ctrl+2
Go to MIDI Controllers window	Ctrl+3
Go to Ethernet Controllers window	Ctrl+4
Go to Mic Preamps window	Ctrl+5

Plug-In Setting Librarian

Function	Key Combination
Save settings	Ctrl+Shift+S
Copy settings	Ctrl+Shift+C
Paste settings	Ctrl+Shift+V

369
❄ ❄ ❄

Preferences Dialog Box

Function	Key Combination
Go to Display window	Ctrl+1
Go to Operation window	Ctrl+2
Go to Editing window	Ctrl+3
Go to Automation window	Ctrl+4
Go to Processing window	Ctrl+5
Go to Compatibility window	Ctrl+6
Go to MIDI window	Ctrl+7

Keyboard Input for Plug-In Parameters

Function	Key Combination
Click mouse in text field	Type desired value
Move down/up parameter fields	Tab/ Shift+Tab
Increase/decrease slider value	↑ / ↓
Input value without leaving field	Enter (on numeric Keypad)
Enter value and exit Keyboard Entry mode	Enter
For fields that support kilohertz	Type k after number multiplies by 1000

Numeric Keypad Modes

Transport Modes

Function	Key Combination
MIDI Metronome On/Off	7
MIDI Count On/Off	8
Merge Record On/Off	9
Loop Playback	4
Loop Record	5
QuickPunch Record	6
Rewind	1
Fast Forward	2
Record	3
Play/Stop	0

Shuttle Modes (TDM Systems Only)

Function	Key Combination
1 X Forward	6
1 X Rewind	4
4 X Forward	9
4 X Rewind	7
1/4 X Forward	3
1/4 X Rewind	1
1/2 X Forward	5–6
1/2 X Rewind	5–4
2 X Forward	8–9
2 X Backward	8–7
1/16 X Forward	2–3
1/16 X Backward	2–1
Loop Playback of Edit Selection	0

Miscellaneous

Function	Key Combination
Display Takes pop-up list (appears only when selection start or flashing insertion point matches user time stamp of regions)	Ctrl+click with Selector tool at selection start or current cursor location
Set all tracks to selected record drive in Disk Allocation dialog	Alt+click on record drive
Access Playback Engine dialog during Pro Tools launch	Hold down N key while launching Pro Tools
Toggle between Hide All and Show All	Alt+click in Show/Hide Tracks list
Bypass repeat dialogs when multiple items will be changed by single operation (e.g., Clear, Delete, Compact)	Alt+click respective Proceed button in dialog box

MIDI Events List Entry

(All commands below are active only when the MIDI Event List window is open.)

Function	Key Combination
Enter start time field for editing	Ctrl+Enter (numeric keypad)
Show Event Filter dialog box	Ctrl+F
Go to	Ctrl+G
Scroll to edit selection	Ctrl+H

} Index

B

backing up work, 28
Bars:Beats scale
 grids, working with, 156
 navigating in, 134–135
Beat Detective, 328–334
beats. *See also* Bars:Beats scale
 Beat Detective, 328–334
 Identify Beat function, 315–316
Big Counter window, 53
bit depths, 22
 for bounced files, 309
Bounce dialog box, 307–311
bouncing to disk, 306–312
 conversions on, 310–311
 saving bounced files, 311
burning CDs. *See also* bouncing to disk
 bit depth for, 309
buses
 naming, 70
 setting up, 69–70
BWF files, 21

C

capturing selections, 146–147
CDs
 backing up work on, 28
 burning CDs, bit depth for, 309
Change Continuously option, 238
Change Duration option, 237
Change Smoothly by Percentage feature, 237
Change Velocity feature, 237
channel strips, 46, 257
 fader groups on, 262
 inserts with, 258
 in Narrow Mix view, 256–257
 type of track, icon indicating, 260
Channel Strips area, Mix window, 46
click/Click tracks
 as Aux tracks, 107–108
 countoff options, 110–114

enabling click, 112–114
interoperability and, 341
latency monitoring and, 127
MIDI synthesizers, using, 111
note values, selecting, 113–114
options, setting, 110–114
plug-ins, 108–110
for recording MIDI, 224–225
setting up, 107–114
tempo options, setting, 110–114
Click/Countoff Options dialog box, 110–114
closing sessions, 29
Color Palette window, 44
 for Mix window, 49
colors
 in Edit window, 44–45
 for Mix window, 49
comments for memory locations, 166
compatible hardware list, 6
compression, 304–305
 with dither, 304
 threshold, 305
computers, 2–3. *See also* CPU (central processing unit); hard drives
Conductor ruler types, 37
consolidating in editing, 337–338
continuous files with AudioSuite, 268
control surfaces with RTAS (Real-Time AudioSuite), 274
conversions on bouncing to disk, 310–311
copying. *See also* importing audio
 automation, 296–298
 regions to tracks, 157
counter
 Big Counter window, 53
 in Transport window, 52
CPU (central processing unit), 2–3
 and host-based DAW, 2
 speed, 6
crossfades, 11
 creating, 194–196
 with Smart tool, 197–199
Custom Note Duration button, 231
customer service, 7

N

O

P

S